J027.6251
Irving, Jan, 1942-
Fanfares

2/94

Fanfares

DO NOT REMOVE
CARDS FROM POCKET

ALLEN COUNTY PUBLIC LIBRARY
FORT WAYNE, INDIANA 46802

You may return this book to any agency, branch, or bookmobile of the Allen County Public Library.

DEMCO

FANFARES
Programs for Classrooms and Libraries

Jan Irving

Illustrated by
Karen Myers

LIBRARIES UNLIMITED, INC.
Englewood, Colorado
1990

Allen County Public Library
900 Webster Street
PO Box 2270
Fort Wayne, IN 46801-2270

Copyright © 1990 Janet K. Irving
All Rights Reserved
Printed in the United States of America

No part of this publication may be reproduced, stored in a retrieval system, or transmitted, in any form or by any means, electronic, mechanical, photocopying, recording, or otherwise, without the prior written permission of the publisher.

LIBRARIES UNLIMITED, INC.
P.O. Box 3988
Englewood, CO 80155-3988

Library of Congress Cataloging-in-Publication Data

Irving, Jan, 1942-
    Fanfares : programs for classrooms and libraries / Jan Irving ; illustrated by Karen Myers.
    xvii, 194 p. 22x28 cm.
    Includes bibliographical references.
    ISBN 0-87287-655-1
    1. Storytelling--United States. 2. Children--United States--Books and reading. 3. Elementary school libraries--United States--Activity programs. 4. Activity programs in education--United States. 5. Libraries, Children's--United States--Activity programs. I. Title.
LB1042.I77   1990
027.62'51-0973--dc20   90-35913
                                                                    CIP

Fanfares to Paula Brandt and Carol Elbert, superb librarians, editors, and friends, and to Jean Jones, whose artistic projects deserve another round of applause!

Contents

Preface xi

Acknowledgments xvii

1 Chinese New Year 1
   Introduction 1
   Purpose of Program/Unit 1
   A Little Background about Chinese New Year 1
   Setting the Stage 2
   The Show Goes On 3
   The Treasure Chest 4
   In the Limelight 9
   Bibliography 10
   Encores 11

2 Mummy 12
   Introduction 12
   Purpose of Program/Unit 12
   A Little Background about Ancient Egypt 12
   Setting the Stage 13
   The Show Goes On 14
   The Treasure Chest 14
   In the Limelight 25
   Bibliography 26
   Encores 27

3 Who's Afraid of the Big Bad? 29
   Introduction 29
   Purpose of Program/Unit 29
   A Little Background about Big Bads 29
   Setting the Stage 30
   The Show Goes On 31
   The Treasure Chest 32
   In the Limelight 48
   Bibliography 49
   Encores 53

4 Cat and Mouse 54
Introduction 54
Purpose of Program/Unit 54
A Little Background about Cats and Mice 54
Setting the Stage 55
The Show Goes On 56
The Treasure Chest 56
In the Limelight 64
Bibliography 65
Encores 70

5 Whoppers 71
Introduction 71
Purpose of Program/Unit 71
A Little Background about American Tall Tales and Folklore 71
Setting the Stage 73
The Show Goes On 74
The Treasure Chest 74
In the Limelight 77
Bibliography 78
Encores 81

6 Dinosaur 82
Introduction 82
Purpose of Program/Unit 82
A Little Background about Dinosaurs 82
Setting the Stage 83
The Show Goes On 84
The Treasure Chest 84
In the Limelight 93
Bibliography 94
Encores 99

7 Pooh's Birthday Party 100
Introduction 100
Purpose of Program/Unit 100
A Little Background about Winnie-the-Pooh 100
Setting the Stage 101
The Show Goes On 102
The Treasure Chest 102
In the Limelight 110
Bibliography 111
Encores 113

8 Author! Author! 114
Introduction 114
Purpose of Program/Unit 114
A Little Background about Author Programs 114
Setting the Stage 115
The Show Goes On 116
The Treasure Chest 116
In the Limelight 121
Bibliography 122
Encores 124

9 Books: From Hornbooks to Popups	125
Introduction	125
Purpose of Program/Unit	125
A Little Background about Books	125
Setting the Stage	127
The Show Goes On	128
The Treasure Chest	128
In the Limelight	131
Bibliography	132
Encores	134
10 A Day on the Prairie with Laura Ingalls Wilder	136
Introduction	136
Purpose of Program/Unit	136
A Little Background about Laura Ingalls Wilder	136
Setting the Stage	138
The Show Goes On	138
The Treasure Chest	139
In the Limelight	144
Bibliography	145
Encores	146
11 Festival	148
Introduction	148
Purpose of Program/Unit	148
A Little Background about the Middle Ages and the Renaissance	148
Setting the Stage	150
The Show Goes On	151
The Treasure Chest	152
In the Limelight	156
Bibliography	157
Encores	160
12 Happy Holidays	161
Introduction	161
A Little Background about Winter Holidays	161
Happy Holidays Program/Unit One—A Swedish Christmas	162
Happy Holidays Program/Unit Two—The Goose Is Getting Fat	168
Happy Holidays Program/Unit Three—Boxes and Bags and Things with Tags	175
Bibliography	179
Encores	181
Resource Bibliography	183
Literature Index	187

Preface

Fanfares is the result of eight years of planning and directing children's programs in a public library. During those eight years we transformed the library meeting room into an ancient Egyptian burial chamber, held a Chinese New Year's celebration complete with Chinese lanterns and cellophane noodles, and staged readers theatre productions from Mother Goose to Dr. Seuss. We had birthday parties for Winnie-the-Pooh, made art projects inspired by Leo Lionni's mice, and explored themes ranging from our pioneer roots to prehistoric days. We even held our own Renaissance fair on the lawn during the summer months, and celebrated throughout the year with seasonal and holiday programs.

When I sat down to write about these programs, I thought of Caroline Feller Bauer's *Celebrations*, a book of holiday and theme-related programs. *Fanfares* is a book to take you through the year, one program for each month. This book begins with "Chinese New Year" and ends with a trio of happy holiday programs. In between, you will find a chapter on scary things ("Who's Afraid of the Big Bad?") that may be used in October for Halloween, a chapter on books, from hornbooks to pop-ups, that might celebrate Children's Book Week in November, and chapters on a range of topics that fit in well any time. You can use these 12 programs in any way to celebrate books with children.

These programs were planned for elementary school children, kindergarten through grade five. After the first year of the program series, I divided the group—the first program included kindergarten and grade one, the second program included grade two through grade five. Often the content of the two programs was the same, but these two age groups work at different paces, and I found that dividing them improved the results. The materials included in this book are suitable through grade six, but I used grade five as the cut-off because sixth-grade children were no longer elementary school students in my community.

A public librarian has many variables to consider: a wide age range; a throng ready to barge through the doors, or, instead, a few solitary souls who struggle in; and a mixed bag of abilities and interests. The size of your group, the ages of children you admit, and whether you use preregistration or a "come one, come all" approach are all matters you will decide based upon the community you serve, the size (and flexibility) of your staff, the restraints of your facilities, and your own philosophy of service.

Fanfares can be used for classrooms and school media center activities as well as for public library programs. The terminology "program/unit" reflects this dual purpose for each chapter. The public library may focus on the recreational and leisure-time reading interests of children more than schools do, with their need to cover topics in a curriculum sequence. This is not to say that public library programs are primarily in the entertainment business and that schools have no room for leisure-time reading. The focus may be slightly different, but the purposes are very much alike.

The scope of the programs ranges from natural science to history and from folklore to poetry. The subject areas encompass literature across the school curriculum and use books of all genres, both fiction and nonfiction, picture books as well as biographies and novels. This fairly comprehensive approach includes books on a wide range of topics that will appeal to children. Here are subjects that children are interested in and topics that books are published about. Children and books come together in *Fanfares*.

Chapters in *Fanfares* are arranged in parallel fashion. For each chapter, the introduction announces the theme, with a note concerning the chapter's scope. A brief statement of the purpose of the program/unit follows. A summary of background facts, much like a factual overview in an encyclopedia, is given; the teacher/librarian can consult the bibliography at the end of each chapter for additional information on each topic. The next section of each chapter, "Setting the Stage," explains advance preparation needed for each program/unit. "The Show Goes On," which follows, briefly outlines the steps of the program, providing an agenda. "The Treasure Chest" provides patterns for art projects, sketches and diagrams to inspire room decorations and displays, original readers theatre scripts, songs, chants, and choral readings to use in programs, as well as suggestions for creative writing. (Tips on producing readers theatre, story theatre, and other story presentations are included at the end of this preface.) "In the Limelight" suggests promotional ideas and provides a sample publicity flyer for each program. (A sample press release and public service announcement also appear at the end of this introduction.)

Fanfares focuses on books, the cornerstone for well-planned programs in public libraries. Books—beyond the textbook—are the foundation for an exciting school curriculum in which children grow up wanting to learn. The annotated bibliography for each chapter includes picture books, longer fiction, nonfiction—any genre or kind of book to interest children in the topic. For series (e.g., Graham Oakley's church mouse books), one book is annotated with other titles simply listed. Not all books in a series will necessarily be listed, however. If an author has written a number of books on the same topic (e.g., Alvin Schwartz's folklore books), separate annotations may appear.

Finally, each chapter ends with "Encores" (Other Programs and Projects), one of my favorite sections. What do you do after you've celebrated Chinese New Year with a room full of high-spirited children? You sit down and plan the next project! The last section of each chapter suggests directions to go, other related projects to plan on your own.

Readers Theatre, Story Theatre, and Other Story Presentations

Even if you've never participated in any of the dramatic presentation methods of story sharing before, I hope you'll jump right into this book and try them out with the children in your classroom or library. Don't feel as if you have to take a course in children's theatre or have a drama background to be successful. The goal is not a polished theatrical production, but rather the opportunity for you and the children you teach to make stories come alive. Here are a few thoughts on story sharing.

Storytelling is my broad term for the different methods of sharing stories orally. Reading books aloud, with expression, is one kind of storytelling, although we usually mean relating a story without the book. Storytelling may include props, costumes, flannelboards, masks, or musical instruments. I call this *media-enhanced storytelling*. Traditional storytelling usually relies only upon the voice, facial expressions, gestures, and body movements of the storyteller. Participatory storytelling involves the audience in the story, either by vocal response or by people helping the storyteller through movement and dialogue.

Story theatre combines elements of storytelling with theatre. Usually the leader or storyteller narrates a story with participants miming the actions. There are variations on this definition. In Chapter 3, "Who's Afraid of the Big Bad," there are suggested movements for children while the teacher/librarian reads. For example, for an introduction to story theatre, children could mime the wild rumpus as the storyteller reads *Where the Wild Things Are*. Puppets can act out the story as it is told by a storyteller. More advanced story theatre presentations might even have children add dialogue as the story is told by a storyteller.

Readers theatre, as the name suggests, combines reading aloud with theatre. Several readers read aloud stories, poems, or scripts with expression, some movement, and very simple costumes, if desired.

Readers theatre is a favorite method of mine for sharing stories, because it actively involves children in a whole language experience. Children often make their own scripts or become aware of how stories can be adapted for a dramatic presentation. In this way, readers theatre becomes a writing experience as well as a reading, speaking, and listening experience.

Because children read from scripts rather than memorize lines, the preparation time involved is minimal. However, I like to practice with a readers theatre group at least once before the presentation to give children an opportunity to learn to speak distinctly (slowly and with enough volume to be understood) and with expression. Some children seem to be naturals at this; others tend to be more self-conscious or less animated. I often read a part (at least in rehearsals) because I believe children will read with more expression if they can feel my enthusiasm. It's not necessary for the readers to move around a lot, but they should do something other than stand in a straight line. Having readers take a slight step forward or backward or seating some readers on stools and others crosslegged on the floor will create a more interesting "stage picture" for your audience. To exit from a scene, characters can simply turn their backs to the audience. A prop or two (not many because characters must hold their scripts) and a hat or scarf may be enough to put your audience in the mood. There are several excellent sources in the bibliography to help you further.

Choral reading is another kind of presentation suggested in this book. This ancient form of expression is currently being revived. The exercises in this book do not call for dramatic production or much reading in unison since this is difficult (children's voices tend to mush together unless you practice very precise pronunciation). Rather, choral reading here refers to group reading aloud of poems and chants—much solo work, occasional unison lines, and a number of lines that are read by individuals in a responsive way. The responsive technique involves a sort of question-answer pattern. For example:

Reader 1: Who's afraid?

Reader 2: Of what?

Reader 1: Who's afraid of the big?

Reader 3: Of the big what?

Reader 1: Who's afraid of the big bad?

Reader 4: Of the big bad what?

Reader 1: Who's afraid of the big bad WOLF!!

Some of the advantages of choral reading are group cooperation, improvement of speech—especially pronunciation—and confidence building, since children are less "exposed" than if they are reading solo parts. The overall pace is usually fairly swift so no one has time to get very "targeted." And such a group can engender the kind of enthusiasm associated with high school pep clubs. Think of all that spirit!

Sample Publicity Releases and Public Service Announcements

Use the following models to publicize your library or school programs and special events in local newspapers, newsletters, or on radio or television. In addition, the sample publicity flyers in each chapter can be printed and distributed in the school, in community centers, by the chamber of commerce, in grocery stores, or in restaurants.

SAMPLE PRESS RELEASE

From: The Public Library (or Public School)
        Address
        City

Contact: Your Name
            Telephone

For Release: Day, Month, Year

Enter the World of the Mummy at the Library

Elementary school children are invited to enter the world of the mummy at _____ Public Library on _(day) (date) (time)_. Children in kindergarten through sixth grade are eligible to attend provided they have preregistered by calling the library by _(day and date)_.

The library is planning a guided tour through the burial chamber of an ancient Egyptian tomb. Children will enjoy spell-binding stories and games related to the mummy and will make souvenirs to take home.

For further information call the library at _(phone number)_.

SAMPLE PUBLIC SERVICE ANNOUNCEMENT

_____ Public Library is celebrating Laura Ingalls Wilder Day with elementary school age children this coming week. Children in kindergarten through grade six are invited to come in costume to the library on _(day, date, time)_ and enjoy favorite stories, songs, country crafts, and cooking. Children may register by calling the library at _(phone number)_.

Acknowledgments

I would like to thank the following people for their assistance and support during the research and writing of this book: Paula Brandt and Carol Elbert gave thoughtful, well-reasoned comments on the manuscript and rekindled my spirit whenever I needed an extra boost. Jean Jones provided ideas for many of the original art projects, and Karen Myers has adapted them with flair. Many others listened, suggested new directions, answered my questions: Barbara Stein; Victoria Walton; Ann Holton; Gail Firestone; Adele Figura; Sandy Mintle; Robin Currie; my children, Kathleen and Michael; and my husband, Don. The staff at Libraries Unlimited has encouraged this project from the start. Finally, I would like to thank all the children, and the staff of Stewart Public Library, Grinnell, Iowa, for their contributions during the years these programs first took root.

1
Chinese New Year

INTRODUCTION

New Year celebrations in the United States have little to offer children except television coverage of the ball dropping in New York's Times Square at midnight or bowl games on New Year's Day. The Chinese, however, celebrate their New Year for over a month with thoughtful preparations and fine festivities. Make New Year a festive celebration this year with the activities in this chapter, and teach your students something about Chinese culture, too.

PURPOSE OF PROGRAM/UNIT

To introduce children to Chinese culture by enjoying some festivities of Chinese New Year with Chinese food, decorations, language, stories, and the creation of a paper dragon for a dragon dance.

A LITTLE BACKGROUND ABOUT CHINESE NEW YEAR (HAPPY *YUAN TAN*!)

Chinese New Year is an especially happy time for everyone because it is regarded as everyone's birthday! Unlike the brief celebration in most Western cultures, the Chinese festivities last more than a month. (Chinese New Year is celebrated by Chinese living all around the world.) Another major difference is that the holiday doesn't come at the same time each year. Chinese New Year coincides with the new moon and arrives sometime between January 21 and February 19. Here are a few facts to explore further.

- The Chinese civilization is the oldest in the world, spanning about 4,000 years. The great empire of China lasted until 1912, when the Republic of China was formed. Civil war and strife continued until the Chinese Communist Party set up China's present government. The Nationalists, who had been defeated, fled to the island of Taiwan.

- Chinese contributions to world civilization include the development of silk and inventions such as the magnetic compass, gunpowder, and movable type for printing. China is known for its artistic achievements in calligraphy, porcelain, painting, and architecture.

- The Chinese calendar is divided into twelve-year cycles. One legend says this is because Buddha invited all the animals to a meeting, but only 12 came. Thus the calendar was divided into twelve-year cycles with each year named for one of the faithful animals. Another legend says among the creatures there was a race across a river to determine whose year would come first in the cycle. Rat cleverly jumped on Ox's back, because Ox was the best swimmer, and then, at the last minute, Rat jumped ashore and won. Thus the twelve-year cycle begins with the Year of the Rat.

- Dragons are highly honored by the Chinese; the Year of the Dragon is looked forward to with great anticipation. It is considered a lucky year. Chinese dragons are beautiful, wise, and friendly, not the dreaded, venom-filled monsters that Western people have always feared. In fact, Chinese people burn incense to dragons and even ask them for advice! The dance of the dragon is a high point of Chinese New Year.

- The month before Chinese New Year many preparations are made. Houses are scrubbed and special foods are prepared. (Houses must not even be swept once the New Year begins or good fortune might be swept away!) A picture of the family's god of the kitchen is taken down and burned so he will find his way to heaven. He will return on New Year's Eve to join the real celebration.

- On New Year's Eve families stay home, burn incense, and feast. Gods bring peace and prosperity. A new picture of the kitchen god is hung on the wall.

- The Chinese New Year celebration lasts for five days. Open houses are held, presents are exchanged, and streets are filled with lively processions complete with firecrackers, a dragon dance, and a lion dance.

- Traditionally, the celebrations continued after this. The lantern festival was celebrated about ten days later. This was a three-day festival when lanterns were carried through the streets and a paper and bamboo dragon joined the fun. Today the lantern festival is not part of the Chinese New Year in the United States, where the dragon dance ends the festivities.

SETTING THE STAGE (PREPARATION)

Your classroom or library can be decorated festively and simply for this Chinese celebration with red and white paper lanterns. Directions for making these are included in this chapter. Chinese calligraphy can decorate long vertical banners. Use rice paper or a thin textured paper of any kind cut in strips approximately 9 inches by 36 inches for the banners. Mount these strips on red squares of paper for a decorative edge. Use black tempera paint and a bamboo brush (inexpensive and easy to find in most art stores) to brush calligraphic letters on the paper. Some basic Chinese characters are included in this chapter. The color scheme of red and white can be repeated with red tissue paper flowers and paper fans. These can be hung on your version of a Chinese money tree. For this traditional decoration, the Chinese hang gold coins and paper flowers on a pine or cypress branch. Simply use a small tree branch placed in a vase weighted with sand and hang gold-wrapped chocolate candy "coins" (available in candy stores and some food stores). A large needle threaded with button-twist thread can be poked through the wrapped coins to hang them on the tree.

Display as many Chinese objects as you can find. Articles of clothing, porcelain, lacquerware, elaborate chopsticks, baskets, tangrams (Chinese puzzles), and dolls might be borrowed from people in your community.

Create interest centers around the room for children to explore different parts of Chinese culture. At an arts and crafts center children can make Chinese paper cuts or a simplified Chinese lacquer plate. Books in the resource bibliography will give you other specific suggestions. If your time is limited, you may simply display Chinese arts rather than have a "hands-on" project. A paper dragon (described later) can be a group arts project in place of the individual ones.

At another interest center set up paper, bamboo brushes (purchased from an art store), and black tempera paint for children to try their hand at some simple Chinese characters. Several excellent books in the bibliography will get you started.

Chinese food is the focus for another interest center. Display Chinese cooking utensils such as a wok or a Mongolian hot pot and chopsticks. Have as many interesting Chinese ingredients on hand as you can find in your stores. Fresh vegetables might include bok choy (Chinese cabbage), bean sprouts, and Chinese pea pods. Dried foods might include Chinese black mushrooms, golden needles (dried tiger lily buds), and star anise. Ask someone who enjoys Chinese cooking to do a cooking demonstration for the children. You might even set up a large enough space for children to prepare part of a Chinese dish. Even if you don't let children do their own cooking, plan to have food for children to sample. Chinese cellophane noodles are a popular choice, especially if you practice eating with chopsticks. Rice is much too frustrating for children to pick up with chopsticks (unless it is cooked sticky "Chinese style"), but cellophane noodles mass together when fried. Children will enjoy trying to eat them with their own chopsticks. Provide each child with his or her own set of chopsticks; inexpensive sets can be purchased from Chinese restaurants or well-stocked grocery stores.

Set up another interest center on recreation. If your space is large and can accommodate active play, have a demonstration of Chinese acrobatics. A quieter alternative would be a Chinese tangram center. The Chinese tangram puzzle is a very old game invented by a man named Tan. It inspires the player to make abstract patterns or designs with the seven shapes within the puzzle. A pattern is included in the "Treasure Chest" section.

Other preparations for this program/unit include getting materials to make the paper dragon for the group arts and movement portion of the day. Children can make dragons from a large cardboard box and large streamers of crepe paper. They move their dragons to music in a simple dragon dance for the climax of the Chinese New Year party. Have enough materials so no more than eight children work on each dragon. (It will be complicated enough even for eight children to coordinate their movements.) Directions for the dragon project are included in the "Treasure Chest" section.

THE SHOW GOES ON (THE PROGRAM PLAN)

Act I—Welcome children by telling them about the celebration of Chinese New Year or by reading *The Chinese New Year* by Cheng Hou-tien or *Chinese New Year* by Tricia Brown. Play some traditional Chinese music to set the mood, then invite children to enjoy different Chinese activities at the learning centers around the room.

Act II—Children participate in the activity centers—arts, language, food, and recreation. Depending upon your schedule, you may rotate the children from one center to the next every 15 minutes. Or, you may let the children choose two of the four centers. In a classroom situation, children may have more time if you can extend this program into more than one day.

Act III—Gather the children into a group and read *Chin Chiang and the Dragon's Dance* by Ian Wallace. This beautiful picture book describes a boy's anticipation for taking part in the dance of the dragon. An alternative book choice would be *Eyes of the Dragon* by Margaret Leaf. In this story, a man is commissioned to paint a dragon on the wall of a Chinese town, but he begs the people to let him omit the eyes. When they insist that he add this feature, the dragon comes to life and terrorizes the village. Either book is an appropriate introduction to the next project.

Act IV—Divide children into groups of eight or less to make the paper dragons described in the "Treasure Chest" section.

Act V—Children crawl under the paper dragons they've made and perform a dragon dance. Keep the movements very simple, and practice first without the paper dragon because it is harder to see from underneath. Suggest that children first take a pose, bending their knees and spreading their feet about two feet apart. A suggested movement pattern is: Walk in place—right foot, left foot, right foot, left foot; walk forward—right, left, right, left; wiggle feet in place—right, left, right, left; walk in place—right, left, right, left; walk backward—right, left, right, left; wiggle feet—right, left, right, left; bow (or repeat the above dance). Play some Chinese or Javanese music while the children dance. This dance isn't intricate like the dance mentioned in the Wallace book, but it will give children a flavor of the real thing. Display the dragons in the library or in a prominent place in your school, so children can continue to enjoy them even after the event is over.

Act VI—As children leave, give them fortune cookies or a sweet dumpling. Or, give them paper fortune cookies. You can write the fortunes yourself beforehand or let the children write the fortunes. Fold the paper according to the illustration in this chapter. Then exchange fortunes. (Children will be inspired to write better fortunes if they must exchange.)

THE TREASURE CHEST

Follow the directions and illustrations to make a Chinese dragon with your students. Other games and projects shown in this section include samples of Chinese writing displayed as banners, simple paper lanterns for decorations, paper fortune cookies, and a tangram puzzle.

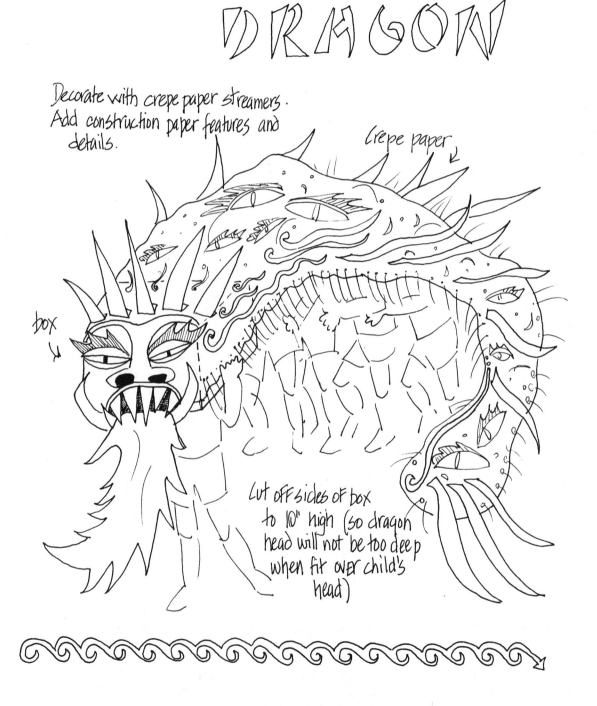

Fig. 1.1.

(Text continues on page 9.)

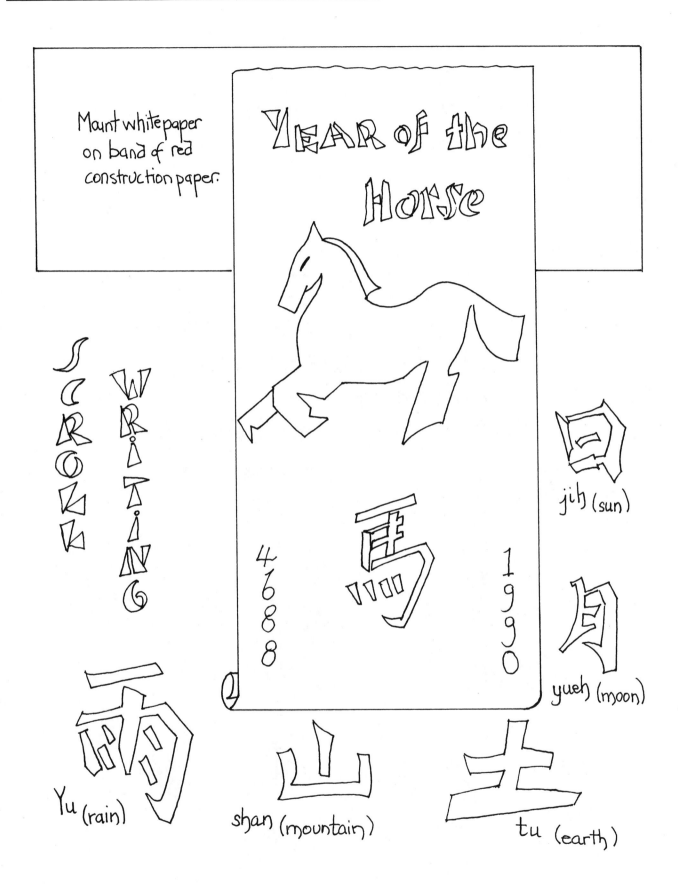

Fig. 1.2.

HANGING LANTERNS

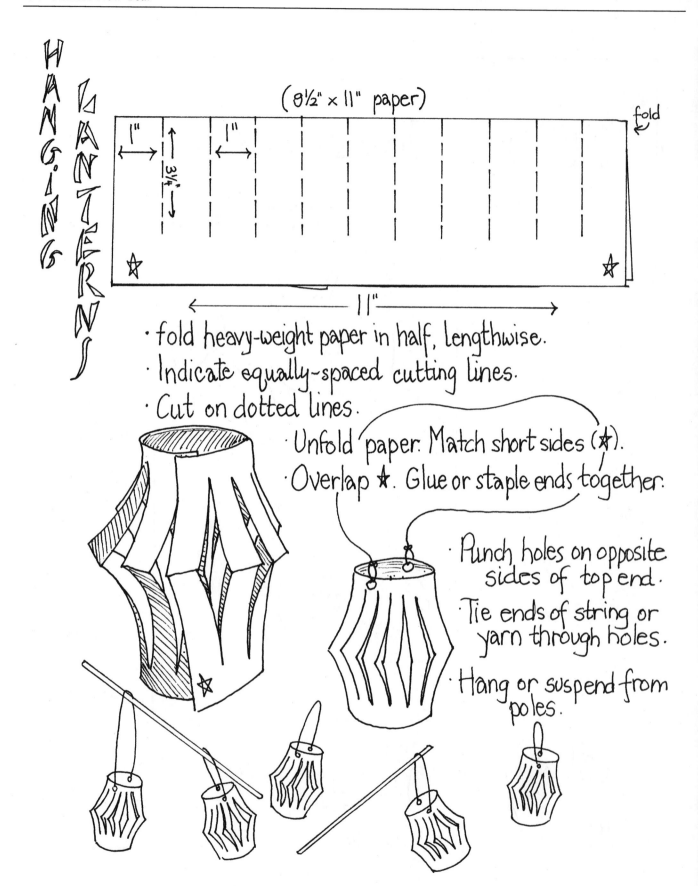

- fold heavy-weight paper in half, lengthwise.
- Indicate equally-spaced cutting lines.
- Cut on dotted lines.
- Unfold paper. Match short sides (★).
- Overlap ★. Glue or staple ends together.
- Punch holes on opposite sides of top end.
- Tie ends of string or yarn through holes.
- Hang or suspend from poles.

Fig. 1.3.

1. Write fortune on square piece of paper.

2. Fold square into triangle. (Fortune will be on inside)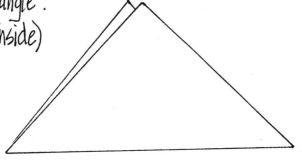

3. Fold over two sides.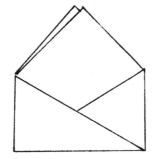

Fig. 1.4.

8 / Chinese New Year

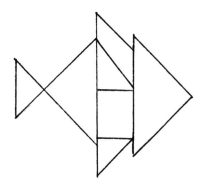
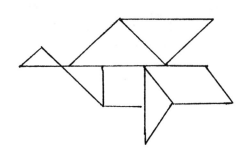

1. Enlarge and copy onto tagboard.
2. Cut out seven pieces.
3. Arrange into animal or geometric shapes.

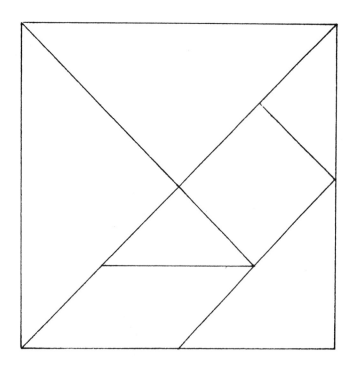
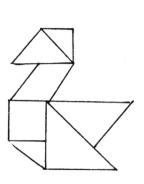

Fig. 1.5.

Chinese Dragon

Select a sturdy brown box for the head of each dragon and cut off the sides to approximately 10 inches high. Next, stretch a length of crepe paper over the box so that the paper covers the front and sides of the box and streams out to make the dragon's long body. (Standard dimensions for crepe paper are 20 inches wide by 7½ feet long.) Staple the crepe paper to the front of the box, then let children add the crepe paper streamers and construction paper features as shown in Figure 1.1.

IN THE LIMELIGHT (PUBLICITY)

Public service announcements and press releases (see the samples in the preface) may be used along with this sample publicity flyer if you are publicizing the program for a public library. Create extra interest in schools or libraries with this program/unit by making displays of Chinese writing, porcelain, books, tangrams, and the paper dragons described in the "Treasure Chest."

Fig. 1.6.

BIBLIOGRAPHY

Behrens, June. **Gung Hay Fat Choy**. Children's Press, 1982.
   Color photos show Chinese New Year celebrations with text explanations of the Chinese calendar, preparations that are made in a Chinese household, and community festivities.

Blackwood, Alan. **New Year**. Rourke, 1987.
   The origins of New Year's celebrations are traced from ancient civilizations to present-day practices in Jewish, Muslim, and Hindu cultures. It also includes a chapter titled "New Year in the Far East." The focus on Chinese celebrations includes a lively explanation of the Chinese calendar.

Brown, Tricia. **Chinese New Year**. Photographs by Fran Ortiz. Holt, 1987.
   Text and photographs describe the celebration of Chinese New Year by Chinese-Americans living in San Francisco. Various aspects of the holiday are compared to the gift-giving of Christmas and Hanukkah, the feasting of Thanksgiving, the fireworks of the Fourth of July, the costumes of Halloween, and the beginning of a new year marked by Easter. The house and food preparations will provide ideas for your own Chinese New Year celebration.

Cheng Hou-tien. **The Chinese New Year**. Holt, Rinehart and Winston, 1976.
   Details of all phases of the Chinese New Year celebration are given with accompanying scissor-cut illustrations. A valuable resource for this program/unit.

Fiarotta, Phyllis, and Noel Fiarotta. **The You and Me Heritage Tree**. Workman Publishing Company, 1976.
   Crafts from 21 U.S. traditions include brief background notes on Chinese heritage and directions for making such projects as a painted "porcelain" Mandarin egg, a decorative painting, a lacquered plate, and cut-paper creations.

Filstrup, Chris, and Janie Filstrup. **China, From Emperors to Communes**. Dillon Press, 1983.
   China, past and present, is described with special focus on holidays, the arts, recreation, and the Chinese in the United States.

Fritz, Jean. **China Homecoming**. Putnam's, 1965.
   The popular children's author returns to her hometown in China after many years, gathers many memories, and is made an honorary citizen. Sequel to *Homesick: My Own Story*.

Fyson, Nance Lui. **A Family in China**. Photographs by Richard Greenhill. Lerner Publications, 1985.
   The life of a twelve-year-old girl in rural northeast China is described as well as the changes in China since her mother was a girl.

Glubok, Shirley. **The Art of China**. Macmillan, 1973.
   Beginning with early Chinese art, this volume includes tomb statues of animals, pottery models of buildings, paintings on silk handscrolls, calligraphy, and porcelain figures—traditions that span 4,000 years.

Haskins, Jim. **Count Your Way through China**. Illustrated by Dennis Hockerman. Carolrhoda, 1987.
   Each number from 1 to 10 is presented along with a concept or story that illustrates that number. For example, the word for the number 2 is *uhr*; the People's Republic of China gave the United States two giant pandas.

Leaf, Margaret. **Eyes of the Dragon**. Illustrated by Ed Young. Lothrop, Lee, and Shepard, 1987.
   The people of a Chinese village commission Ch'en Jung, a famous dragon painter, to decorate their town wall. He sets his terms, but they insist that he paint in the eyes of the dragon, only to have the dragon come alive and destroy the wall in the end. This original story is based on Chinese legend and brilliantly brought to life with Young's pastel illustrations.

Lee, Nancy, and Linda Oldham. **Hands on Heritage**. B. L. Winch and Associates, 1978.
   This experiential approach to multicultural education explores seven cultures, including Chinese. Specific topics are art projects, such as fans and paper cuts; cooking, with recipes for almond cookies, fried wonton, and singing rice; plus games.

Tolan, Sally, and Rhoda Sherwood, eds. **China.** Photography by Yasuhiko Miyazima. Gareth Stevens, 1988.
The life of a fifth-grade girl in Beijing is described as well as a focus on Chinese New Year celebrations. Facts about China are included in the last section of the book.

Wallace, Ian. **Chin Chiang and the Dragon's Dance.** Atheneum, 1984.
As long as he can remember, Chin Chiang has dreamed of dancing the dragon's dance in the Chinese New Year procession, but when his chance comes, he is afraid he will disgrace his grandfather. The brilliantly colored illustrations will inspire dragon projects, and the story encourages children who are reluctant to try something because they are afraid they may fail.

Wiese, Kurt. **You Can Write Chinese.** Viking, 1945.
Within the framework of a story, an American boy is taught Chinese. The picture language is explained through comparing the Chinese characters with actual objects, so dozens of words are taught.

ENCORES (OTHER PROGRAMS AND PROJECTS)

Do some armchair traveling with your students to places around the world. The last chapter in this book describes a Swedish Christmas program, but instead of focusing only on holidays in other lands (which may give children the impression that people in other countries are always celebrating festivals), develop a program around an art, food, or particular feature of a country. Here are a few suggestions:

- A program entitled "Smorgasbord" might introduce a variety of Scandinavian foods and culture, from open-faced sandwiches to stories by Hans Christian Andersen. Recent picture-book versions of "The Snow Queen," "The Emperor's New Clothes," "Thumbelina," and "The Princess and the Pea," all stories by Andersen, make effective group read-alouds. (There is also a program suggestion on Andersen in Chapter 8.)

- An Australian Kangaroo Day might feature stories about the many unusual animals of this land. For example, *Wombat Stew*, by Marcia Vaughan (Silver Burdett, 1984), tells the amusing tale of a clever dingo who is tricked by a cunning group of native Australian animals as he attempts to make a "gooey brewey chewey" wombat stew.

- Punch and Judy Day could celebrate British puppetry and popular British folk tales.

- Don't overlook local resources for help in organizing your programs. High school international clubs and exchange students may be happy to share their talents and expertise.

2
Mummy

INTRODUCTION

The word *mummy* may conjure up a horror-movie image of a gauze-wrapped corpse rising from the dead. Some kids think pharaohs were the only Egyptians who were mummified. Although young people may have some misconceptions about ancient Egypt, the subject fascinates them. Capitalize on this interest (and dispel a few myths) by turning your classroom or a corner of your library into an Egyptian burial chamber. It won't cost a king's ransom (or a pharaoh's treasure trove) and you won't have to hire a consultant. In addition, everyone will have such fun that they won't even realize how much they're learning.

PURPOSE OF PROGRAM/UNIT

To introduce children to ancient Egyptian culture by recreating a burial tomb and have children create a craft project inspired by Egyptian art.

A LITTLE BACKGROUND ABOUT ANCIENT EGYPT (IN CASE YOU WERE DYING TO KNOW)

The nation of Egypt was formed around 3000 B.C. (that's almost 5,000 years ago). The ancient Egyptians were an amazing people who left us papyrus, hieroglyphics, pyramids, and mummies. This program/unit deals with ancient Egypt, not the accomplishments and daily life of modern Egypt. Here are some facts about ancient Egypt.

- The Egyptians were ruled by pharaohs who were considered gods on earth.

- The Egyptians believed in many gods including Osiris, god of the dead, Amun, god of the air, Ra, the sun god, Horus, the falcon god of light, and Anubis, the jackal-headed god who oversaw embalming. Pictures of these gods are in the wall murals of Egyptian tombs.

- The Egyptians believed in life after death and prepared the bodies of the dead with great care. It was believed that the spiritual self would live on only if the body was embalmed.

- The Egyptians were extraordinary architects. They built temples, tombs, and pyramids. The Great Pyramid is so immense that each side is longer than seven football fields! (And it is almost perfectly level.)

- Egyptian art has a distinctive style, but it doesn't look very realistic to us. Perhaps you've noticed that in Egyptian paintings a person's head and feet are always shown in profile but the shoulders are shown face forward. This didn't bother the Egyptian artist. In fact, the artists thought each part of the body was more easily recognized this way. And, after all, the paintings were meant for the eyes of the gods.

- The Egyptians were fun loving. They enjoyed feasts, hunting, and fishing. They ate all kinds of fowl, including ibises, and they hunted lions and crocodiles. Ancient Egyptians loved nature, kept house pets, and made elaborate gardens.

- Because they enjoyed life so much, Egyptians wanted to make life in the next world just as pleasant. Their tombs contained all the comforts of home. The first tombs were called *mastabas*, which means home.

- Most of our knowledge about the Egyptians comes from the tombs and their treasures. But most tombs were ransacked by grave robbers. One of the few tombs that was not is the tomb of King Tut. The story of its discovery by Howard Carter in the 1920s is almost as exciting as the treasures that were found inside the tomb.

SETTING THE STAGE (PREPARATION)

Your classroom or a corner of your library will become the burial chamber of an Egyptian tomb. Decorate the walls with murals by hanging a long strip of shelf paper or butcher paper around the room and inviting students to create scenes from Egyptian life. (Examples are illustrated in Figures 2.3 and 2.4 in the "Treasure Chest" section.) If a school class is doing this project, you will probably want to research some of the resource books in the bibliography. If you want to keep your mural simple, just brush on a row of hieroglyphics with black paint and a broad brush. See the samples in Figure 2.2.

Enlarge the Egyptian mummy pattern (Figure 2.1) to near life-size and make two paper mummy figures to flank the entrance to the tomb. If you wish to set aside a closet or a corner of the room as an inner burial chamber, make another paper mummy to mount on a refrigerator carton sarcophagus. The sarcophagus was a stone container that held the mummy case.

Inside your sarcophagus, stash a mummy. To make the mummy, you will need to borrow a mannikin. Tear an old sheet into strips about two inches wide, and start wrapping! (This operation may take more than an hour so be sure to assign the mummy wrapping to a fairly dedicated Egyptologist.) You could bury books on Egypt in the sarcophagus, too. Another kind of sarcophagus stands upright and does not contain a mummy. For this, cut a door in the front of a refrigerator carton, mount a paper mummy on the door, and leave a sign nearby that reads: "Grave robbers have visited this sarcophagus. You will find no mummy inside, but you are welcome to take a look."

Collect as much "treasure" as you can to make the burial chamber seem authentic. Remember, the Egyptians believed you *could* take it with you. Baskets of food, plumes, brass containers and lanterns, assorted crockery, and old jewelry can be arranged in prominent places. Theatre departments and second-hand stores are good sources, and kids will probably be able to find loot in their garages and basements.

To set the scene even more effectively, try to designate an area outside the burial chamber as an ante-chamber. Fill this chamber with more treasures, especially mummified animals, which is what the Egyptians did. (Stuffed animals wrapped with strips of old sheets look amazingly authentic.) I was lucky enough to have a winding stairway for my antechamber, but even a portion of a hall outside a classroom or library provides enough room to place a few "relics" that help set the mood. If a hallway is not available, create an antechamber by hanging from the ceiling a woven screen or even a plain sheet.

THE SHOW GOES ON
(THE PROGRAM PLAN)

Act I—Children are first taken on a tour of the mummy's tomb. Older children act as assistant tour guides, welcoming the "tourists" and pointing out objects in the antechamber. Guides can even warn the tourists to remain quiet so as not to disturb the spirit of the mummy. Burn some incense to help set the mood.

Act II—Children are taken into the main burial chamber and greeted by the tour director (the leader), who might wear a pith helmet. Consider darkening the room at first and using flashlights to create an eerie tomb effect. The tour director can then use the guided tour script (included in the "Treasure Chest") to tell the tourists about the tomb and Egyptian burial practices.

Act III—When the tour has ended, the tourists are invited to take home a souvenir of their trip. They will create their own miniature mummy cases (see instructions in the "Treasure Chest") and fill the cases with clothespin mummies if they wish. You can end the program here or, if time permits, proceed to acts IV and V.

Act IV—Play Mummy Wrap, or I've Got You Covered! Divide the group into teams of four or five children each. One child in each group is designated the mummy. Give all the other children rolls of toilet tissue. At the signal "ready, set, wrap!" each team begins to wrap the mummy. Encourage children to wrap individual fingers, toes, hands, feet, arms, and legs so the mummy will look more authentic. When the leader says "stop" the team with the most completely wrapped mummy wins.

Act V—The tour director takes the tourists on one last stop—to the inner burial chamber where the mummy itself is buried. If you don't have a mummy in the sarcophagus, fill the inner burial chamber with lots of books about Egypt and mummies. (See the bibliography in this chapter for suggestions.) Then all curl up in the quiet of the tomb and read. If you have played the Mummy Wrap game, you could read *M & M and the Mummy Mess* by Pat Ross. In this story, a girl wraps up her friend like a mummy in a natural history museum and is commended by the museum director for the good job.

THE TREASURE CHEST

Guided Tour Script

(Read this script or use it as a guide and retell the ideas in your own words. If older children are assistant guides you could divide the script into sections.)

Welcome to the world of the mummy! You have entered the burial chamber by way of the antechamber, or secret passageway. Imagine you have come down 30 steps, deep into the underground burial chamber. It is hot and dry here, the perfect place to preserve a mummy.

In ancient Egypt ordinary people were buried in sand pits, and when the bodies were found thousands of years later they were well preserved. But the pharaohs' bodies were given more elaborate final resting places. Above their burial chambers, some pharaohs had immense pyramids built.

Now that you have climbed down the stairs below the pyramid, tell me, what did you see in the secret passageway?

(Give tourists a chance to recall this experience. You may guide them into remembering the mummified animals and tell them that Egyptians mummified house pets, such as cats, and also more unusual animals such as gazelles and crocodiles. Ask if anyone knows what treasures were found at the entrance to King Tut's tomb. Some may know there were four golden chariots, the royal bed, and containers of food.)

Here in the burial chamber we see more treasures, things the pharaoh would need in his life after death. Here are baskets of food to enjoy in the next world. You will notice paintings on the walls that show servants and boats. *(Point to the wall murals.)* The Egyptians believed that these murals would come alive to serve the pharaoh in his next life.

Messages are written along the wall in hieroglyphics. Can anyone tell us something about hieroglyphics?

(Some children may know that hieroglyphics was a picture alphabet. There were over 700 signs, but the basic alphabet contained 24 signs. Over a period of time, the signs began to stand for sounds. Point out some of the signs for vulture, owl, foot, water, mouth. If you want to spend more time with this part of the program/unit, show children how to spell their names. Several of the books in the resource bibliography will help.)

Here is a painting of the pharaoh's procession. The pharaoh is carried in a magnificent chair called a *palanquin* by 12 men, who are his sons. Musicians and bodyguards accompany him, as well as a priest who is burning incense. *(This particular painting is available in a three-dimensional paper model from museum shops. One example can be purchased from the Museum of Fine Arts, Boston.)*

The pharaoh was more than a king to the ancient Egyptians. He was a god on earth and when he died, he joined the other gods. Egyptians believed in many gods, including Osiris, Horus, and Nut. Maybe some of you have read the Osiris myth. In this story, Osiris is killed by his evil brother, but he is restored and eventually gains immortality. The Egyptians believed everyone had a spirit or soul and they also believed in life after death. Actually, they believed in two kinds of spirits — one was called the *ba* and was shown as a winged head. The *ba* traveled from the mummy back to the world to keep contact with the living family and returned to the underworld at night. The other spirit, the *ka*, was the invisible twin of the deceased. Because it was important for the *ba* and the *ka* to recognize the person as he or she had been in life, the Egyptians took great care to preserve the mummy.

The whole process of mummification took more than two months — specifically, it took 72 days. Many religious ceremonies were performed during the process. All of the work was done under the watchful eye of the jackal-headed god Anubis, the god of the underworld. This painting shows a priest wearing the Anubis mask as he takes charge of the mummification process. *(Show a picture from a resource book.)*

During mummification, the brain and body organs were removed. This had to be done so the body would not decay, but the vital organs were considered so important that they were preserved and kept in canopic jars. These jars could be quite elaborate and on the top of each was the head of the god who protected that particular organ. The body cavity was then packed with linen bundles that had been soaked in the chemical natron, which dried out the body. After 40 days these bundles were removed and the body was rubbed with oils, and then the body was stuffed again because it had shrunk so much. The embalming cut was carefully sewn back together and sealed with a beautiful seal. Fingernails were even capped with gold. Then the body was wrapped with yards and yards of linen. Would anyone like to guess how much linen was used? Since each finger, toe, arm, and leg was wrapped individually with 20 layers of linen, it took hundreds of yards! Little charms and *shabati* figures (figures of workers who would help the pharaoh in the next world) were laid in with the linen. Then a portrait mask was placed over the head, so the *ba* and the *ka* would recognize who the mummy was. Finally, a shroud was wrapped around everything and the mummy was placed in a coffin.

Has anyone seen pictures of King Tut's coffins? King Tut was a pharaoh whose tomb was discovered not many years ago. His mummy was buried in three coffins. The outer coffin was made of wood and painted gold. The next coffin was even more beautiful, made of gold with colored glass. The last coffin was solid gold and weighed 222 pounds!

Finally, all the coffins were placed in a stone sarcophagus to protect the mummy for eternity. When everything was completed, the mummy was taken on a fancy sled to its final resting place in the burial chamber. Family members and even paid mourners led a grand procession. The burial chamber was then sealed.

This ends your tour. Thank you for entering the world of the mummy, and now your guides will show you to the rooms where you will recreate your own Egyptian treasures as a souvenir of this trip.

Egyptian Art

Figures 2.1 through 2.8 will provide plenty of ideas for turning your classroom or library into a full-scale model of an ancient Egyptian burial chamber.

Figure 2.1 is a full page mummy design to enlarge freehand or on an opaque projector. Use this for the refrigerator carton sarcophagus described in "Setting the Stage" or as life-size mummies to flank the entrance to the tomb.

The hieroglyphics (Figure 2.2) and panels for tomb paintings (Figures 2.3 and 2.4) provide examples to use when decorating the walls of your room. The diagram of the room arrangement (Figure 2.5) is a suggestion, which you may need to adapt to fit your situation.

The pattern for the mummy case (Figure 2.6; also see Figure 2.7) should be photocopied on card stock. This will give the finished project more strength than mimeograph paper or construction paper. The original mummy case was created by Jean Jones for the Egyptian mummy program I planned at Stewart Library in Grinnell, Iowa.

The sample ticket (Figure 2.8) can be photocopied on lighter weight paper. Children could color their tickets while they are waiting to be admitted to the burial chamber.

(Text continues on page 25.)

The Treasure Chest / 17

MUMMY DESIGN

Enlarge for tomb decoration.

Fig. 2.1.

18 / Mummy

Fig. 2.2.

Fig. 2.3.

Egyptian Wall Painting

Fig. 2.4.

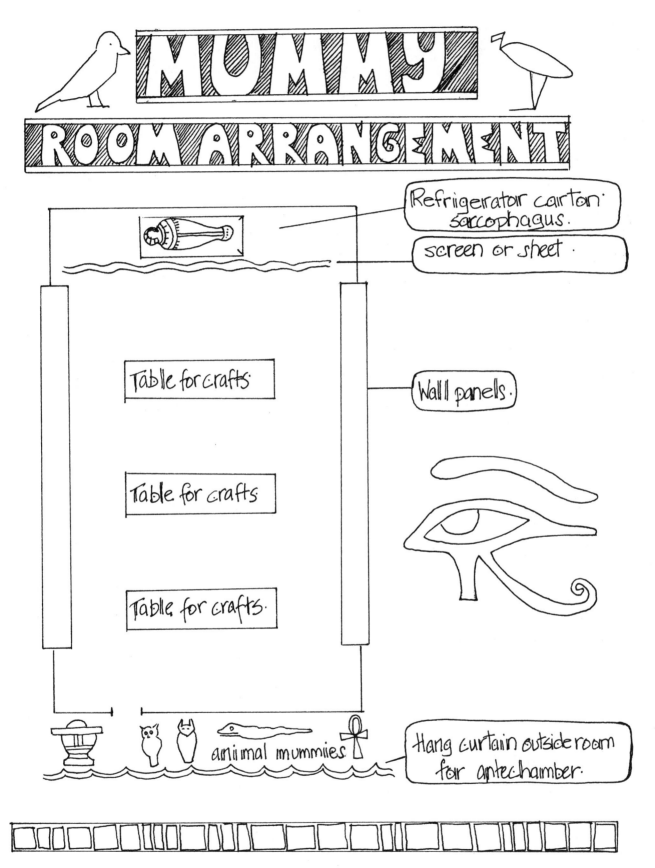

Fig. 2.5.

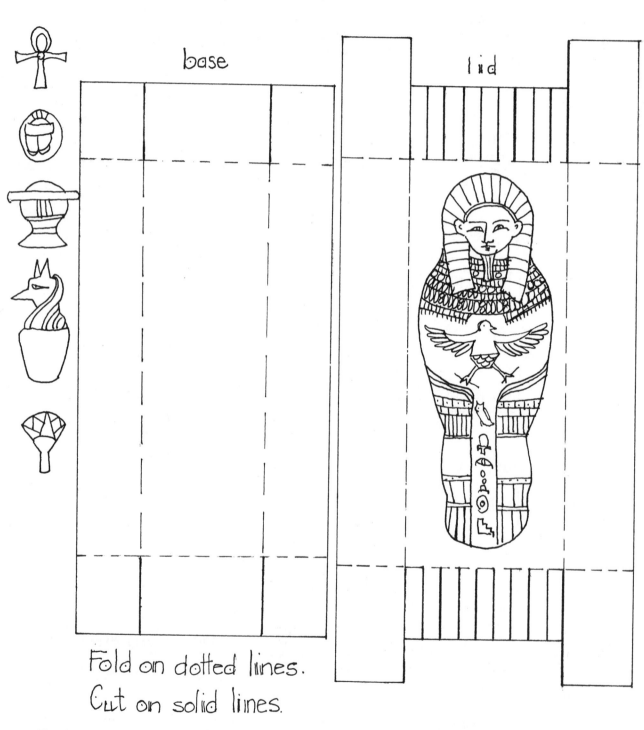

Fold on dotted lines.
Cut on solid lines.

Fig. 2.6.

Overlap strips on each end of lid to create rounded edges.

Secure ends with tape.

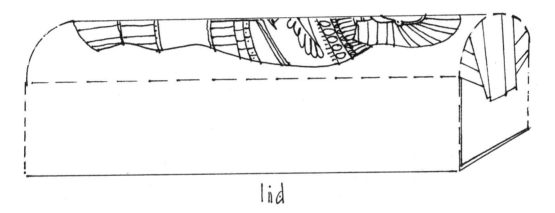

lid

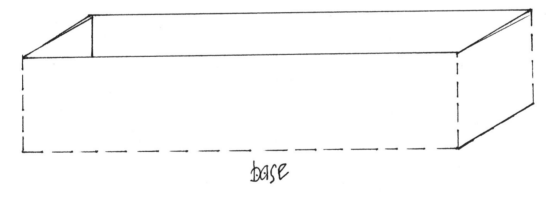

base

Fig. 2.7.

Ticket to Burial Chamber

Cut out ticket on heavy outer line.

Fig. 2.8.

IN THE LIMELIGHT (PUBLICITY)

Adapt the sample publicity releases (from the preface) for this program/unit and use the sample publicity flyer in Figure 2.9. Create additional interest by stashing mummified stuffed animals around the room and display some of the art described in this chapter.

Fig. 2.9.

BIBLIOGRAPHY

Aliki. **Mummies Made in Egypt**. Harper and Row, 1985.
   Numerous color illustrations and informative text describe the mummification process.

Boase, Wendy. **Ancient Egypt**. Gloucester Press, 1978.
   The history and way of life of ancient Egypt is told through numerous illustrations and text. The section "Preparing for the Afterlife" briefly illustrates burial practices.

Caselli, Giovanni. **An Egyptian Craftsman**. Peter Bedrick Books, 1986.
   The story of a scribe and his family who lived in Egypt around 1000 B.C. reveals everyday life, food, dress, tools, and customs.

Cohen, Daniel. **The Tomb Robbers**. McGraw-Hill, 1980.
   From its lively beginnings, this text asserts that pyramids were "a flop when it came to protecting mummies," then goes on to explore burial practices in ancient Egypt and in other cultures. Mummies shown in popular films are also described.

de Paola, Tomie. **Bill and Pete Go Down the Nile**. Putnams, 1987.
   William Everett Crocodile and Pete the Toothbrush Bird learn about ancient Egypt and then travel down the Nile with their classmates. On the trip they apprehend a jewel thief.

Ellerby, Leona. **King Tut's Game Board**. Lerner, 1980.
   Fantasy and fact combine in this story in which 16-year-old Justin Sanders and his mysterious friend Nate discover a lost treasure of ancient Egypt near the temple of Abu Simbel. A good read aloud for upper elementary students or a book gifted students would enjoy after this Egyptian unit.

Glubok, Shirley. **The Art of Ancient Egypt**. Atheneum, 1962.
   Describes the style and subjects of art in ancient Egypt from tomb paintings and mummy cases to statues of famous pharaohs, as well as everyday objects such as game boards.

Glubok, Shirley. **The Art of Egypt under the Pharaohs**. Macmillan, 1980.
   Discusses art of Egypt from a historical perspective, focusing on statues, buildings, and the wall decorations of such noteworthy pharaohs as Chephren, Hatshepsut, and Tutankhamen.

Glubok, Shirley. **Discovering Tut-ankh-Amen's Tomb**. Macmillan, 1968.
   Abridges Howard Carter's three volumes about Tutankhamen's tomb into one book for young readers. Many photographs; the text takes the reader from preliminary investigation to the discovering of the tomb and its treasures.

Glubok, Shirley. **The Mummy of Ramose**. Harper and Row, 1978.
   The last days and death of an Egyptian nobleman of the Eighteenth Dynasty are recounted along with mummification and burial rites.

How Djadja-Em-Ankh Saved the Day: A Tale from Ancient Egypt. Translated with illustrations by Lise Manniche. Crowell, 1976.
   This is a unique book. The format is a scroll, folded to fit into a slipcase and printed on paper that resembles papyrus. The tale about King Seneferu is read from right to left, the way ancient Egyptian texts would read. On the back of the scroll, you read from left to right about Egyptian beliefs and hieroglyphics.

Johnson, Paul. **The Civilization of Ancient Egypt**. Atheneum, 1978.
   This resource book for adults discusses Egyptian religious beliefs, burial practices, and the prominence and decline of the pharaohs. An enlightening discussion of pre-perspective art is included.

Knight, Joan. **Journey to Egypt**. Illustrated by Piero Ventura. Viking Kestrel, 1986.
   Part of the UNICEF series to promote understanding of the world's cultures, this book describes such sites as the pyramids, the temple of Abu Simbel, and a tomb with a mummy inside.

Lauber, Patricia. **Tales Mummies Tell**. Crowell, 1985.
   Describes all kinds of mummies, both man-made and natural. The chapter on ancient Egypt describes embalming and how it developed.

Macaulay, David. **Pyramid**. Houghton Mifflin, 1975.
   Carefully rendered drawings and brief text describe the construction of a pyramid in twenty-fifth-century B.C. Egypt.

McDermott, Gerald. **The Voyage of Osiris**. Dutton, 1977.
   Picture book version of the myth in which Osiris is killed by his evil brother but is later restored to life.

A New Look at the Treasures of Archaeology. Arco, 1980.
   Relates 11 stories of ancient world wonders and gives instructions for making projects related to these cultures.

Perl, Lila. **Mummies, Tombs and Treasure: Secrets of Ancient Egypt**. Clarion, 1987.
   Introduces the ancient Egyptian civilization and beliefs that caused them to make mummies. Preparation of the mummy, the tomb, and the ceremonies are carefully described with text, photographs, and drawings.

Reiff, Stephanie. **Secrets of Tut's Tomb and the Pyramids**. Raintree, 1977.
   Discusses the building of the great pyramids, the discovery of King Tut's tomb, and some of the strange stories associated with mummies.

Ross, Pat. **M & M and the Mummy Mess**. Illustrated by Marilyn Hafner. Viking Kestral, 1985.
   Mandy and Mimi sneak into a mummy exhibit at a natural history museum before it is scheduled to open. Their mummy wrapping gives the director a good idea after he decides the two curious girls need a creative outlet to keep them out of mischief.

Scott, Joseph, and Lenore Scott. **Hieroglyphics for Fun**. Van Nostrand Reinhold, 1974.
   Presents the 24 basic hieroglyphs, the object each represents, and the approximate sound for each sign. Also explains how to write messages using these sounds.

Stolz, Mary. **Zekmet the Stone Carver**. Illustrated by Deborah Nourse Lattimore. Harcourt Brace Jovanovich, 1988.
   A fictional account of the stone carver who created the Sphinx to please a vain Egyptian pharaoh.

Swinburne, Irene, and Laurence Swinburne. **Behind the Sealed Door**. Sniffen Court Books, 1977.
   Tells the exciting account of Howard Carter's discovery of the treasures of King Tut's tomb with text and dazzling photographs. In the back of the book, photographs of the mummy and its three cases are shown on acetate overlays so the reader can visualize how they were actually found.

Ventura, Piero, and Gian Paolo Ceserani. **In Search of Tutankhamun**. Silver Burdett, 1985.
   Numerous colored illustrations and brief text describe Howard Carter's search for Tut's tomb. Beliefs and customs of ancient Egypt are also discussed.

Weeks, John. **The Pyramids**. Cambridge University Press, 1971.
   Photographs, diagrammatic sketches, and detailed text explain how and why pyramids were constructed.

ENCORES (OTHER PROJECTS AND PROGRAMS)

Field trips to museums to discover treasures of ancient Egypt (or other cultures) would be a wonderful follow up for this program. Never discount the impact that class trips can have for children. I still remember an Egyptian statue I saw during a third- or fourth-grade class trip to the Nelson-Atkins Art Gallery in Kansas City. The figure was not even a foot high, but it was strong and brown and somehow had survived a very long time with only a small nick out of its brown paint. Our guide said the statue was over 4,000 years old and had to be kept in a climate-controlled glass case so it wouldn't disintegrate. Trying to imagine that statue as one small link to the long-ago world of ancient Egypt almost made my head spin. I never forgot that class trip, and as an adult I even went back to see that statue—just to be certain the world of Egypt and the mummy had not disintegrated.

You might encourage children and their families to plan a trip to the Field Museum of Natural History to Chicago to see its Egyptian collection. In 1988, the museum opened "Inside Ancient Egypt," a new exhibit that includes a mock-up of a two-level Old Kingdom tomb (you can actually climb down the steps), mummified animals displayed in wall niches as they would have been buried, and an ancient Egyptian marketplace with hands-on displays.

The ancient Egyptians left behind a chronicle of their lives through murals and hieroglyphics. Follow up this program/unit on ancient Egyptian artifacts with these projects:

- Students can make murals to depict scenes from their own community or country in a style reminiscent of the Egyptian murals. Focus on sports, games, or parades—activities parallel to those pictured in Egyptian murals.

- Adapt the Osiris myth using McDermott's book *The Voyage of Osiris* as a guide. Use stick puppets or retell the myth with masks and movement while a narrator tells the story.

- Use famous Egyptian monuments to inspire a creative writing project. Tell the story behind the pyramids or make up your own riddle of the Sphinx. Mary Stolz's book *Zekmet the Stone Carver* is a fictional account of the creation of the great Sphinx. Show your students pictures or slides of works of art from ancient Egypt and ask them to tell why the works were created. As an alternative project, ask students to write an interview with Howard Carter done just after he discovered King Tut's tomb.

- Discover other famous archaeological finds and make your own artifacts to take home. *A New Look at the Treasures of Archaeology* (Arco, 1980) includes the treasures of Sumeria, with a Sumerian headdress project; the excavation of Viking burial ships, with a Viking ship model project; and seven other archaeological discoveries with accompanying activities.

3
Who's Afraid of the Big Bad?

INTRODUCTION

People have always been afraid of beasts lurking in the sea, in the sky, and on land—and especially afraid of monsters in the dark corners of the night. Legends tell of beasts that no longer seem to strike fear upon the earth, but scientists still cannot fully explain all phenomena. Ghost stories may be campfire amusement, but they can also intrigue modern investigators. The term *monster* covers a wide range of beasts from werewolves to purely fictional inventions of writers and artists. Even the big bad wolf of folk tales is a kind of nursery monster. When we are young, our "big bads" may be as close to home as the monster hiding under our beds. As we grow older, we learn to laugh at some of these creatures, but find new sources of terror and amusement.

This chapter covers a wide range of big bads, from monster stories for younger children to traditional folk tales about wolves and ghosts to selected books and stories about spooky things. The chapter bibliography is certainly not comprehensive, but it provides hours of reading for monster lovers. Stories about dragons and witches have been excluded (unless they are part of a larger collection) so the bibliography would not be too "monstrous." Literature and art projects inspired by children's books are suggested as well as creative writing and creative drama activities, for a full range of spooky experiences in your classroom or library.

PURPOSE OF PROGRAM/UNIT

To explore big bads in literature and to create (or recreate) our own stories about and illustrations of scary creatures.

A LITTLE BACKGROUND ABOUT BIG BADS

So many strange and terrifying beasts have been thought to live in the world that this background can only scratch the surface. Chapter 6 will cover another kind of terrible beast, the dinosaur; the first and last chapters include something about dragons; and Chapter 2 describes mummies, another subject sometimes considered terrifying. Here is a little information about other big bads.

- The largest bird ever seen on earth was big enough to carry off an elephant! It was called the Roc and is described in *The Arabian Nights*.

- The Griffin or Gryphon was half lion, half eagle, and was so enormous that each of its claws was as large as the horn of an ox. Griffins could not be captured or killed. Their coloring was often glorious.

- Some of the terrible Greek monsters included the sphinx, part human, part lion, and part eagle; Cerberus, the three-headed dog that guarded the underworld; and the awful seven-headed hydra. Two other famous Greek monsters were Scylla and Charybdis. Scylla was a dragon-headed creature who seized sailors, and Charybdis was a whirlpool that could suck up a whole ship.

- The sea has always been full of big bads, but the most famous sea monster is the Loch Ness Monster. Tales about this Scottish beast have been around for hundreds of years, but interest has increased since the 1930s, when a road was built around the lake where the monster is said to live. Teams of scientists have used sonar and camera equipment to spot the monster, but the full story still remains a mystery.

- Werewolves, men who can change into wolves, have been described since the first century. According to legend, werewolves have long, pointed teeth, eat raw meat and any wounds they receive as wolves remain on their bodies when they change back into human form. Werewolf legends seem to be European in origin, but similar beasts (the were-tiger of India, the were-leopard of Africa, and the were-jaguar of South America) can be found in other parts of the world.

- The vampire is a fanged monster who has always been more popular in Europe than in the United States. Vampires are sometimes associated with bats. Probably the most famous vampire was Count Dracula of Transylvania, the creation of British author Bram Stoker. In the story, Dracula is a nobleman who changes into a bat at night so he can drink people's blood.

- Many monsters have been the creations of writers and motion picture producers. One of the most famous of these is the Frankenstein monster created by Mary Shelley. In the original story, Dr. Frankenstein was a brilliant but demented scientist who was expelled from the university and conducted bizarre experiments in his home laboratory. He and his assistants robbed graves for parts of human bodies, which they put together and brought to life in the form of a monster. The monster and the doctor's name are often confused: The monster is not named Frankenstein, but rather, it is Frankenstein's monster. The motion pictures with Boris Karloff as the Frankenstein monster have become as popular as the original story. Many Frankenstein-like stories have been written for children.

- Some "modern-day" accounts of monsters remain unsolved. These include stories of the Abominable Snowman, reported in the mountainous regions of Tibet, and stories of an ape-like creature called Bigfoot that has been sighted along the Pacific coasts of North America.

- Ghosts are spirits of the deceased who come back to haunt the living on earth. Ghost stories have been told all over the world but are especially popular in Scotland, England, and parts of the United States. Ghosts may take human form or appear as a skeleton or a blob wearing a sheet. Ghost stories may be humorous or they may be terrifying.

SETTING THE STAGE (PREPARATION)

Create an appropriate atmosphere for studying spooky legends and stories with the children. Books provide plenty of inspiration. You might begin by reading to children some of the stories suggested in the bibliography. But, don't show any pictures until you've given kids an opportunity to visualize on their own. Ask the children to tell you what the scary things look like. Next, look at many different kinds of illustrations as a group. Note that some monsters are funny such as Marc Brown's swamp monsters in Mary Blount Christian's books, Pat Hutchins's monsters, or the ones drawn by Mercer Mayer. Other monsters might be described as bizarre. The scraggly, slimy sorts found in William Steig's *Rotten Island* fall into this category. Still other big bads are closer to terrifying. Paul Galdone's illustrations for *The Tailypo* are one example.

After the kids have chosen the kind or kinds of big bads they want to illustrate, decorate the room with this style of monster. A few patterns have been included in the "Treasure Chest" if you need something specific to help you begin (see Figure 3.1). A simple motif might be large, yellow, spooky eyes placed all around the room, with an occasional hairy tail and monster claw sticking out of a closet, from a desk drawer, or around a corner.

Now, divide your students into interest groups—Spooky Poems and Chants to Speak Aloud (If You Dare), Readers Theatre, Spooky Writers, and two or three different Story Theatre groups that will retell stories about big bads (suggestions are given in the "Treasure Chest" for stories and methods of sharing them).

The Spooky Poems and Chants to Speak Aloud group will read poems of their choice and practice reading them aloud as a choral reading group. Jack Prelutsky and Shel Silverstein have written many poems that make excellent read-aloud selections. One of my favorites is "Enter This Haunted House" (*Where the Sidewalk Ends* by Shel Silverstein, Harper and Row, 1974). Assign each line to a different reader and practice reading the poem at a slow, steady, creepy pace. The chant "What's That?" in the "Treasure Chest" section of this chapter provides another short example.

It is best to use simple poems that read well aloud. Encourage children to read their lines with vigor and enthusiasm. Spooky poems and chants are good choices since they are best read in a slow, steady pace at an audible but restrained volume. Few lines should be read in unison, however, because this makes the reading difficult to coordinate and the lines come out garbled.

The Readers Theatre group can choose their own story to read in parts or use "Who's Afraid of the Big Bad?" from the "Treasure Chest" section. (Suggestions for doing readers theatre with children are given in the general introduction to this book.) Sometimes people like to add simple costumes when they do readers theatre. A little spooky makeup might be effective for the big bads, or you might keep the room dimly lit and let the readers use flashlights.

The Spooky Writers group can write a group story or choose individual projects from the list in the "Treasure Chest." Some of the projects are story starters, others are just little descriptions and fragments that can be part of a book called "My Book of Big Bads" or "Beast Book."

The Story Theatre groups are organized around favorite stories or picture books. The leader for each group will read the story or book at least once to group members. Children then decide what parts they would like to play. In a story theatre presentation, the leader reads or retells the basic story and participants mime the parts. If you spend more time on this activity, children can become more involved in the telling of the story. When appropriate they will have spoken lines in addition to the physical action. You can add simple costumes, masks, props, or even simple scenery, but don't let these extras overshadow the retelling of the story. Three story theatre suggestions are given in the "Treasure Chest."

THE SHOW GOES ON (THE PROGRAM PLAN)

Act I—Greet children in costume or simply darken the room a bit and read the poem "Who's Afraid?" on page 32.

Act II—Divide children into interest groups as suggested in "Setting the Stage." In a school setting you may allow time for children to participate in more than one group. In a public library setting, you will probably set a time limit for this part of the program, perhaps 20 to 30 minutes. Children may choose poetry reading, story theatre, creative writing, or readers theatre.

Act III—Each interest group shares their activity with the group as a whole. If you cannot find enough people to help you direct the children in several interest centers at once, you may decide on an alternative program. For example, choose a story that has many monsters, such as *Rotten Island*. Read this story and re-enact it with all the children taking the parts of the different rotten things. Have children create rotten things out of paper or make masks so they can re-enact the story more dramatically.

THE TREASURE CHEST

Who's Afraid?
(A Poem to Introduce the Program/Unit)

Who's afraid
of Great Big Eyes
With Bulging
Yellow
Stares?

Who's afraid
of Hairy Hands
that snatch you
From your chair?

Who's afraid of
Slimy skin
With scales
and warts
and bumps?

Who's afraid
of Beasty Things
That in the night
go THUMP?

Who's afraid of
Skeletons
Rattling
Their bones?

Who's afraid
to go to bed
in a dark room
all alone?

Who's afraid?
Why, I'm just as calm
As calm
As calm
As calm
As can be.
I don't care
what yellow-eyed
long-toothed
hairy-armed
thing is coming
down the stairs
to reach out and
grab Meeeeeee!

What's That?
(A Chant for Choral Reading)

Reader One:	What's that?	Reader Five:	two
Reader Two:	What?	Reader Six:	yellow
Reader Three:	Over there.	Reader Seven:	eyes
Reader Four:	Where?	Reader Four:	coming this way.
Reader One:	What's that	Reader Three:	I see
Reader Five:	scritching	Reader Five:	long
Reader Six:	scratching	Reader Six:	sharp
Reader Seven:	scratching?	Reader Seven:	teeth.
Reader Two:	Don't you hear a ...	Reader One:	What
Reader Five:	Mo-o-o-o-o-o-a-n	Reader Two:	do
Reader Six:	O-o-o-o-o-o-o-n	Reader Three:	you
Reader Seven:	Gr-o-o-o-o-o-a-n?	Reader Four:	want?
Reader Three:	I see	Readers Five, Six, and Seven:	Yoooooooooooooooou!

Who's Afraid of the Big Bad?
(A Script for Readers Theatre or Creative Dramatics)

Everybody knows that kids don't like to go to bed in the dark because monsters of all sizes and shapes are just lurking around in the night. In this familiar plot, three (or more) big bads threaten Alex. Alex is afraid, but he is also clever enough to talk the big bads out of getting him.

Use this script as a springboard for other stories and creative writing activities. Change the ending if you like. Does Mom find the big bads the next morning? Or does the creepy thing get Alex in the end? How do you picture the big bads?

Characters
Alex, a kid
Big Bad
Bigger Bad
Biggest Bad
Mom
Dad
Creepy Thing

Mom: Alex, turn off that TV! It's time for bed and you know you always have weird dreams when you watch television before bed!

Alex: Aw, Mom. I'm 10 years old. I'm not afraid of monsters anymore.

Dad: Alex, listen to your mother.

Alex: Aw, Dad. It's not even 10 o'clock yet.

Dad: Alex, bed!

Mom: Alex, did you clean up your room like I asked you?

Alex: Yeah, all except the closet.

Mom: Well, it's too late to finish now. Just leave the closet. I can do that part tomorrow. But turn out that light this minute!

Alex:	(*to himself*) Don't they know I hate to turn out my light? All right, I'll admit it. I hate the dark. But that doesn't mean I'm exactly afraid of anything. I mean I haven't been afraid of monsters for two years at least.
Mom:	Alex, is your light off?
Alex:	Not exactly.
Dad:	Turn that light off or I'll come up there and ...
Alex:	It's off, Dad. (*to himself*) I don't think I'll sleep all night. If I just keep the sheets pulled up high and my eyes open all night, nothing much can happen, can it?
Big Bad:	(*in a small voice*) Oooooooo
Alex:	What was that?
Big Bad:	Oooooooo
Alex:	It was probably an old hoot owl.
Big Bad:	Oooooooo
Alex:	Maybe I left the radio on.
Big Bad:	Oooooooo
Alex:	If I get out of bed to check, something might grab my leg.
Bigger Bad:	Aaaaaaaaahhhhh
Alex:	It sounds like it's getting bigger.
Bigger Bad:	Aaaaaaaaahhhhh
Alex:	If only I had my flashlight!
Bigger Bad:	Aaaaaaaaahhhhh
Alex:	I know, I'll hum and that'll drown out the noise. Hmmmmmmmmmmmmmmmmmm

Biggest Bad:	EEEEEEEEEEEEEEEEE
Alex:	(*covering his ears and shouting*) What do you want anyway?
Big Bad:	Want food!
Bigger Bad:	Want more food!
Biggest Bad:	Want you!
Alex:	Are there three of you out there?
Big Bad:	One
Bigger Bad:	Two
Biggest Bad:	Three.
Alex:	But that's not fair. Three against one.
Big Bad:	I get him first.
Bigger Bad:	How come? You got the last one. It's my turn to get one.
Biggest Bad:	But I'm the biggest. I get him in one gulp.
Alex:	(*gulp*) Hey, guys, I've got a better idea. Why don't you let me make you a bedtime snack?
Big Bad:	What's a bedtime snack?
Bigger Bad:	He's in bed and we're going to eat him up. So he's a bedtime snack! Ha! Ha!
Alex:	You've got a terrific sense of humor. But you don't even know me.
Biggest Bad:	What's your name, kid?
Alex:	Alexander. Now that you know me, you couldn't eat me.
Biggest Bad:	Why not?
Alex:	Because we're friends.

Biggest Bad:	We are?
Alex:	Sure. And because you're my friends I'll tell you what I'm going to do. I'm going to let you stay in my closet permanently. You'll never have to be left out in the cold again. I'll bet that's why you were making those awful sounds a little while ago.
Big Bad:	What awful sounds?
Alex:	(*mimicking the bads*) Oooooo! Aaaahhh! EEEEEE! You guys were probably catching cold.
Bigger Bad:	Is your closet drafty?
Alex:	Only in January.
Bigger Bad:	Would you let me have your electric blanket?
Alex:	Sure! And I'll even throw in my sleeping bag!
Biggest Bad:	But we're still hungry, kid.
Alex:	Yeah, yeah, yeah. Look, if I sneak down and make you each a peanut butter sandwich, would you promise to go to bed?
Big Bad:	Peanut butter and jelly!
Bigger Bad:	With bananas!
Biggest Bad:	And marshmallows on the side!
Alex:	OK. Just give me five minutes.
Big Bad:	This is gonna be OK.
Bigger Bad:	I like this place.
Biggest Bad:	I still say we should have eaten him.
Alex:	Here we go—three peanut butter and jelly sandwiches with bananas and marshmallows. And I even threw in a box of raisins. Now, do you all promise to go straight to bed so I can get some sleep?

All Three Big Bads:	We promise.
Alex:	It's about time. I am so sleepy. You know those big bads aren't so bad after all. Guess I'll have to get them out of my closet before Mom finds them tomorrow. But I won't worry anymore tonight.
Creepy Thing:	Oooooooo
Alex:	Aw, cut that out! Just get back in the closet and go to sleep, will you?
Creepy Thing:	Oooooo all right!
Alex:	Goodnight!
Big Bads and Creepy Thing:	Goodnight!

Spooky Writing Ideas to Scare You Out of Your Wits

Spooky Sketches

Monsters and big bads are fun to describe. Use the words in this list to write sentences describing monsters or creepy places.

scraggly
slimy
warty
stinking
clawing
snatching
hissing
scratching

Spooky Story Starters

Either as a group or individually, complete the stories that these haunting beginnings suggest. If you have time, dim the lights, switch on a flashlight, and read your story out loud to your friends in a soft and eerie voice!

Spooky Starter One: Late one night a tired traveler saw an abandoned house on a hill. Because he was so tired, he didn't think whether or not the house might be haunted. The man went inside the house, which was completely dark. Soon he was fast asleep, but less than one hour later....

Spooky Starter Two: Early one morning, even before sunrise, two boys went to a nearby lake to go fishing. By the time they arrived at their favorite spot, the sun was starting to rise over the water. The boys looked into the lake as they were casting their lines, where they were horrified to see....

Spooky Starter Three: My grandfather told me this is a true story. It happened long ago in the hills of West Virginia, where a man lived all by himself in a cabin. One night after he had bolted the door for the night, he got the uneasy feeling that someone (or some*thing*) else was in the cabin with him. The man got up from his chair and....

Story Theatre to Chill Your Bones

Group One
Rotten Island

This treasure of a book by William Steig (see annotation in this chapter's bibliography) is stocked with every abominable creature you could imagine. The illustrations will inspire children to construct their own Rotten Things that can add to a retelling of the story. Fill a box with torn paper scraps, paints, markers, glue, and any other materials you think might make monsters "huge or miserably stunted, fat or scraggly, dry or slimy, with scales, warts, pimples, tentacles, talons, fangs, extra arms, eyes, legs, tails and even heads, all in ridiculous arrangements." Mount monsters on dowels or tongue depressors so children can make them like stick puppets as you read the story.

An alternative approach to using Rotten Things puppets is to guide the children in a mime and movement retelling of this story. Select mood music to help children feel the tension in the story. Soundtracks from science fiction films often have appropriate music. Help children decide if they will be a sea monster, a land monster, or an insect. Children should then practice moving like the monster they have chosen. The leader reads the story while children pantomime the movements.

Group Two
Who's in Rabbit's House?

This picture book by Verna Aardema is stunningly illustrated by Leo Dillon and Diane Dillon. The story, a Masai tale, is told by African village actors wearing animal masks. In the story, a series of animals each tries unsuccessfully to oust the "Long One" from Rabbit's house. Finally, Frog scares the thing out and, much to the animals' delight, the Long One is only a caterpillar! One of my graduate students in a storytelling course, Joyce Denslow, used this story with her elementary students very successfully. She made masks for all the animals, distributed them to the students, and guided the kids through the actions of the story as she told it. The sixth graders became so enthusiastic they decided to learn the animals' lines, and in later retellings Joyce told the story but the students added the appropriate lines as the different animals spoke. Patterns for the animal masks are included later in this section (Figures 3.2-3.8).

Group Three
The Island of the Skog

Steven Kellogg's picture book offers many teachable possibilities. You may want to retell the story in your own words rather than read the story as it is. Select the children who will be the Rowdies, the group of mice who set sail for an island of their own only to discover that it is inhabited by a sole resident, an obviously enormous and probably terrifying Skog. The Rowdies will need to practice moving as if they are on board a boat, then creep around the island as they discover the huge footprints, and finally show how they set the trap for the monster. Children may decide to create their own dialogue or to just move and let the narrator describe what is going on. Dress your Skog in a huge sheet or bedspread to create the illusion of an enormous beast. The Skog child who is unveiled in the end, however, will want to look very vulnerable and afraid. In the

Kellogg book, a song is sung in the end by the Rowdies and the Skog, who become friends. Try setting the verse to the tune of "Twinkle, Twinkle, Little Star" (you will need to repeat the last two lines twice) and end this story theatre production on a rousing note!

Art for Big Bads

Enlarge the patterns for eyes, claws, and tails in Figure 3.1 to decorate your room in the spirit of scary things such as the Tailypo. Children will come up with additional ideas of their own, so these patterns can also serve as springboards for their imaginative creations.

Masks for *Who's in Rabbit's House?*

The patterns for these masks (Figures 3.2-3.8) are simplified from the more intricate masks by Leo Dillon and Diane Dillon in the picture book illustrations. Make the masks out of posterboard or heavy card stock and attach thin elastic bands to them so they can be held in place. Make several caterpillar masks, since each mask represents only one segment of the caterpillar.

(Text continues on page 48.)

Fig. 3.1.

Fig. 3.2.

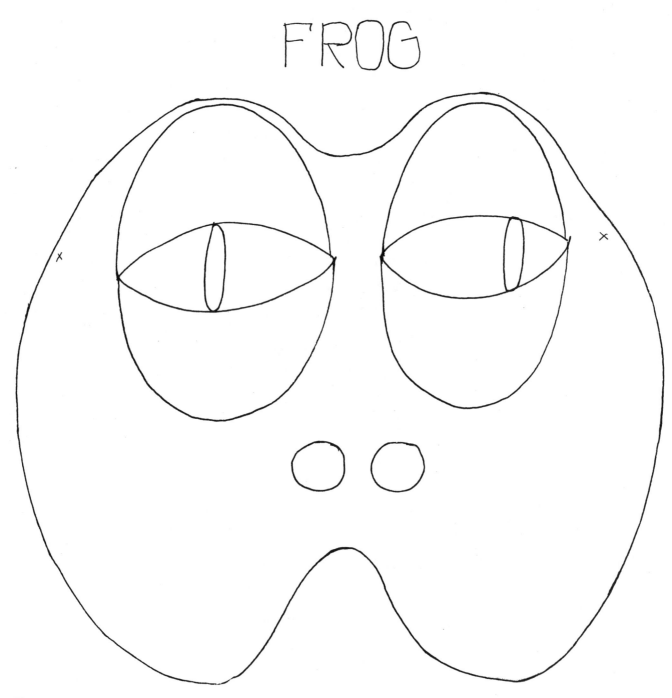

Fig. 3.3.

Fig. 3.4.

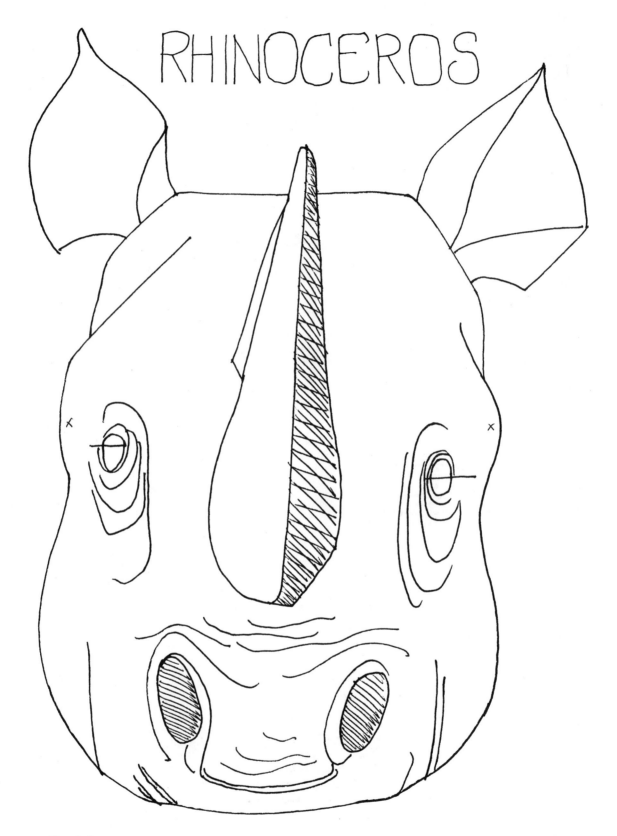

Fig. 3.5.

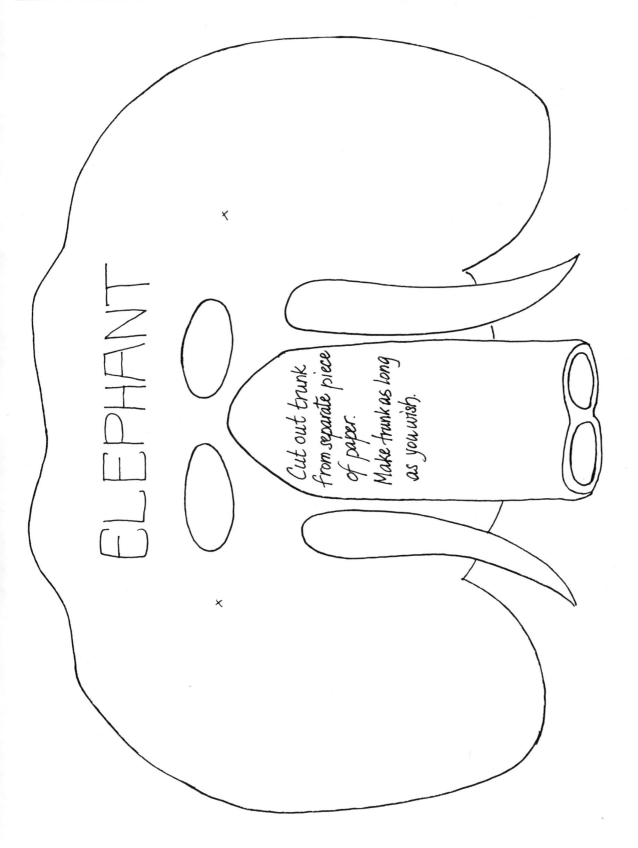

Fig. 3.6.

Fig. 3.7.

CATERPILLAR

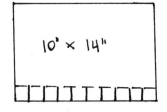

Fold 1" along long edge of 10" x 14" paper. Slash several tabs to fold line.

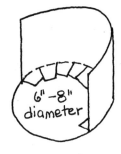

Overlap tabs. Match fold line to edge of circle. Tape tabs to circle.

Fit mask over head. Mark and cut circles for eyes.

Head segment: Add antennae.

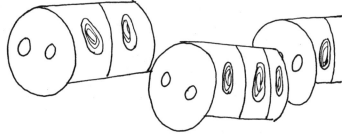

Body segments: Add vertical strips and spots.

Fig. 3.8.

IN THE LIMELIGHT (PUBLICITY)

Use the publicity ideas in the preface in addition to this sample flyer (Figure 3.9). Generate interest in this topic by reading spooky poems and chants over the radio or the public address system in your school or by having a Spooky Story Starters contest.

Fig. 3.9.

BIBLIOGRAPHY

Aardema, Verna. **Who's in Rabbit's House?** Illustrated by Leo Dillon and Diane Dillon. Dial, 1977.
   The Long One takes over Rabbit's house and threatens to trample anyone who comes near. Jackal, Leopard, Elephant, and Rhinoceros all try to get the Long One out, but Frog finally succeeds by threatening the beast, who, it turns out, is only a caterpillar. This story is told as a story within a story by Masai villagers, who don masks to tell the tale.

Christian, Mary Blount. **Swamp Monsters.** Illustrated by Marc Brown. Dial, 1983.
   Crag and Fenny, the young swamp monsters, want to eat and play like children so they go to school one day. After awhile they get homesick and return to their swamp home, where Mrs. Swamp Monster is baking mud pie for dessert.
      Also by Christian: **Go West, Swamp Monsters.** Dial, 1985.

Cohen, Daniel. **Everything You Need to Know about Monsters and Still Be Able to Get to Sleep.** Illustrated by Jack Stokes. Doubleday, 1981.
   Information about legendary monsters includes vampires, werewolves, wild men, water and land monsters, mummies, zombies, artificial men, plus assorted other monsters.

Cohen, Daniel. **Monster Hunting Today.** Dodd, Mead, 1983.
   The book recounts the popular Bigfoot and Loch Ness Monster stories plus several other lesser known tales and gives current progress in understanding these mysteries. Fascinating reading for monster lovers or to show young people that some legends of the past are still unsolved puzzles, at least to a dedicated group of scientists and adventurers.

Cohen, Daniel. **Supermonsters.** Dodd, Mead, 1977.
   Photographs and old prints illustrate this history of the popular group of monsters that includes vampires, werewolves, man-made monsters (such as Frankenstein's monster) and monster animals.

Creatures. Selected by Lee Bennett Hopkins. Illustrated by Stella Ormai. Harcourt Brace Jovanovich, 1985.
   Creepy crawly verses about witches, ghosts, and things that go bump in the night are appropriately illustrated with black and green pictures.

Daly, Nikki. **Monsters Are Like That.** Viking Kestrel, 1985.
   A boy bans his sister from his room, but when she goes in anyway and puts on his monster gloves and face paints and acts like a monster, he accepts her.

Delton, Judy. **Brimhall Turns Detective.** Illustrated by Cherie R. Wyman. Carolrhoda, 1983.
   Brimhall and his cousin Bear can't figure out what kind of monster with big feet is tramping in the snow around their house until Rabbit, wearing snowshoes, comes to visit.

Demarest, Chris L. **Morton and Sidney.** Macmillan, 1987.
   When Morton, a boy, wakes up one day, he knows something is wrong when he sees Sidney, his monster, out of the closet. The other closet monsters don't want Sidney anymore, so Morton has to come up with a plan so they will welcome Sidney back.

De Regniers, Beatrice Schenk. **Red Riding Hood.** Illustrated by Edward Gorey. Atheneum, 1972.
   In this funny verse retelling of the traditional tale, the Big Bad Wolf eats up Grandma and Red Riding Hood, who escape to complain that it was smelly inside the wolf's belly. An excellent read-aloud.

Drescher, Henrik. **Simon's Book.** Lothrop, Lee, and Shepard, 1983.
   A little boy begins drawing the story of Simon and a monster. When he leaves his desk, the drawing and his pens come alive, thus beginning a madcap chase between monster and boy.

Fagg, Christopher. **Fabulous Beasts.** Illustrated by Steve Weston. Rourke, 1981.
   This brief overview of beasts includes such legendary monsters as the sphinx family members and more recently reported ones such as the Abominable Snowman and Bigfoot. Popular reading for children but probably not a good source for reading aloud.

Flora, James. **Grandpa's Ghost Stories**. Atheneum, 1978.
  During a thunderstorm, a boy begs his grandfather to tell him ghost stories. Grandpa obliges by telling three—one about a bag of old bones that becomes a skeleton, one about a warty witch who turns a kid into a spider, and another about a ghastly ghost house inhabited by a ferocious werewolf. All tales are short and appealing to elementary school kids.

Francis, Anna B. **Pleasant Dreams**. Holt, Rinehart and Winston, 1983.
  Everything is quiet in a child's bedroom until the huge green monsters creep out of the closet. Near the end of the book, the "child" asleep is shown—a monster child who is bid goodnight by her monster parents. A funny twist at the end will be appreciated by younger children or kids who like to tell stories like this to their friends.

Gackenbach, Dick. **Harry and the Terrible Whatzit**. Seabury, 1977.
  Harry's mother goes down in the cellar to get a jar of pickles. When she doesn't come back, Harry goes down to confront the Terrible Whatzit that he believes has snatched her. As Harry becomes less and less afraid of the monster it shrinks to the size of a peanut. An excellent read-aloud for younger children and a teachable book to discuss fears.

Gackenbach, Dick. **Mag the Magnificent**. Clarion, 1985.
  Wearing his magical Indian suit, a little boy draws a magnificent monster on his wall, and then the two have magnificent adventures together when the monster comes alive. The mother makes the boy clean off his wall, but he redraws the monster small enough so he can hide it behind his mirror for safekeeping. This book can inspire children to create their own friendly and helpful monsters.

Galdone, Joanna. **The Tailypo**. Illustrated by Paul Galdone. Clarion, 1977.
  In this Appalachian ghost story, a hairy varmint haunts a woodsman who chops off its tail. The varmint keeps returning until he gets his tailypo back.

Gleiter, Jan, and Kathleen Thompson. **The Legend of Sleepy Hollow**. Illustrated by Dennis Hockerman. Raintree, 1985.
  In this retelling of the famous Washington Irving tale, Ichabod Crane, the schoolmaster, hears ghost stories one night and is later apprehended by the Headless Horseman of Sleepy Hollow.

Hawkins, Colin, and Jacqui Hawkins. **Snap! Snap!** Putnam's, 1984.
  The snap, snap that comes in the night is a big hairy monster who carries Sally off. All the other monsters fight over who will eat her until she makes them behave.

Hawkins, Colin, and Jacqui Hawkins. **Spooks**. Silver Burdett, 1983.
  Humorous illustrations and text briefly tell about famous ghosts and give pointers on hunting them.

Howe, James. **There's a Monster under My Bed**. Illustrated by David Rose. Atheneum, 1986.
  Simon is certain he has a monster under his bed because he can hear it breathing. When he explores with his flashlight, he finds his brother, Alex, who is certain there is a monster under *his* bed.

Hutchins, Pat. **The Very Worst Monster**. Greenwillow, 1985.
  The whole monster family is convinced that Billy will grow up to be the worst monster in the world so they ignore Billy's sister, Hazel. She vows to be the worst and proves it by giving Billy away. Good for role-playing activities and brainstorming what constitutes the worst behavior.

Hutchins, Pat. **Where's the Baby?** Greenwillow, 1988.
  Grandma and Mother Monster follow a trail of handprints, footprints, unraveled yarn, spilled paint, and wall drawings to Baby's room, where they find him peacefully asleep in the crib.

Hyman, Trina Schart. **Little Red Riding Hood**. Holiday House, 1983.
  This Caldecott Honor Book tells the traditional tale of the Big Bad Wolf and the little girl who ventures into the dark forest. Richly shadowed illustrations and a text framed in decorative borders make this version especially distinctive.

Johnson, Jane. **Today I Thought I'd Run Away.** Dutton, 1985.
   A boy packs his bag with things that later protect him from an ogre, a goblin, a dragon, a demon, and a monster. After he returns home and crawls into bed, he threatens to run away again tomorrow. An excellent example of a modern fantasy that borrows from folk tale motifs. Use this as a springboard for creative writing projects.

Kellogg, Steven. **The Island of the Skog.** Dial, 1973.
   The Rowdies, a group of mice, escape from a cat and set sail for their own island only to discover it is inhabited by a terrible Skog. The Skog ends up to be a small, frightened, and vulnerable creature, thus showing that fear will drive even the most meek to become monsters. The book has many teaching possibilities and is one of the focus books for the story theatre suggestions in the "Treasure Chest."

Knight, David C. **Best True Ghost Stories of the 20th Century.** Illustrated by Neil Waldman. Prentice-Hall, 1984.
   This collection by a Lay Fellow of the American Society of Psychic Research offers cases of poltergeists and phantoms reported from 1900 through 1980. Upper elementary children will enjoy reading this on their own.

Leach, Maria. **Whistle in the Graveyard: Folktales to Chill Your Bones.** Illustrated by Ken Rinciari. Viking, 1974.
   Ghost tales from all over the world begin with famous ghosts of the White House and then cover ghosts on the run, those that protect treasure, and bogeys. The tales are short, good to read aloud as a break between longer activities.

Lurie, Alison. **Fabulous Beasts.** Illustrated by Monika Beisner. Farrar Straus Giroux, 1981.
   The preface to this collection of terrifying and wonderful beasts in legends of the past draws a link between the past and present-day creatures found in out-of-the-way places.

MacDonald, Margaret Read. **When the Lights Go Out: Twenty Scary Tales to Tell.** Illustrated by Roxane Murphy. Wilson, 1988.
   This collection of folk tales to tell to children is an invaluable resource. The categories include "Not Too Scary," "Scary in the Dark," "Gross Stuff," "Jump Tales," and more. Numerous bibliographies add to the book's uses.

McEwan, Jamie. **The Story of Grump and Pout.** Illustrated by Sandra Boynton. Crown, 1988.
   A cobbler comes into the forest and makes comfortable shoes for Grump and Pout, two monsters, who change their behavior as well as their names.

McHargue, Georgess. **Meet the Werewolf.** Illustrated by Stephen Gammell. Lippincott, 1976.
   Provides both scientific information and conditions that may have been the basis for belief in werewolves, as well as stories from folklore about "shape shifting" (human beings who change into creatures). Gammell's black and gray drawings are eerie and could inspire student art projects for this program/unit.

McQueen, John Troy. **A World Full of Monsters.** Illustrated by Marc Brown. Crowell, 1986.
   This humorous approach to monster hunting points out places where monsters used to exist and even gives the telltale sounds that can tip you off to a monster. Even older kids will appreciate the funny pictures in this book.

Mayer, Mercer. **There's a Nightmare in My Closet.** Dial, 1968.
   A little boy relates how he tamed the nightmare in his closet, and in so doing gives any young child who hears the story the reassurance that he or she can gain control over nighttime fears.
      Also by Mayer: **There's an Alligator under My Bed.** Dial, 1987; **There's Something in My Attic.** Dial, 1988.

Mayne, William. **The Mouldy.** Illustrated by Nicola Bayley. Knopf, 1983.
   In this fairy tale world, Talitha, daughter of the king, agrees to marry Mouldy, the evil underground inhabitant who slightly resembles a mole. In the end, Hedgehog goes off with Mouldy and the garden of the world remains full of light and growth.

Meddaugh, Susan. **Beast**. Houghton Mifflin, 1981.
   Everyone in Anna's family has notions of how dangerous, strong, ferocious, and fearless is the beast who comes to their farm, but Anna actually meets it and finds out otherwise. Instead of being ferocious, it needs comfort and advice.

Most, Bernard. **Boo!** Prentice-Hall, 1980.
   The story of a little monster who is afraid of children ends happily when he learns to say "Boo!" and scare children.

Nic Leodhas, Sorche. **Gaelic Ghosts**. Illustrated by Nonny Hogrogian. Holt, Rinehart and Winston, 1963.
   In the introduction the author attributes the origin of the humorous ghost story to Scotland, and goes on to provide sources for the tales in this collection. Many of them are from her own background. If you plan to read these stories aloud, practice some of the Scottish words and phrases first.

Nic Leodhas, Sorche. **Ghosts Go Haunting**. Illustrated by Nonny Hogrogian. Holt, Rinehart and Winston, 1965.
   Based on ghost stories passed on to the author, this book tells about people who are held up by ghosts, doubters who become believers in ghosts, and many more tales.

Parish, Peggy. **No More Monsters for Me!** Illustrated by Marc Simont. Harper and Row, 1981.
   Minneapolis Simkin's mother won't let her get a pet so she finds a monster instead. But the monster creates too many problems so Minn gets rid of her monster and gets a kitty in the end.

Pinkwater, Daniel. **The Frankenbagel Monster**. Dutton, 1986.
   Harold Frankenbagel, in his desire to create unusual bagels, makes the Glimville Bagelunculus, a monster bagel. Harold and Professor Von Sweeney must come up with a way to stop the monster, which isn't difficult if you just wait for the bagel to grow stale. The illustrations are inspired by computer art but have that hilarious Pinkwater touch. Use this book to inspire your young writers to make up their own Frankenstein/Frankenbagel stories.
   Also by Pinkwater: **I Was a Second Grade Werewolf**. Dutton, 1983.

Ross, Dave. **How to Prevent Monster Attacks**. Morrow, 1984.
   This whimsical approach to monsters contains "useful" chapters on the topic such as "How to Spot Monsters" and "How to Monster Proof Your Bedroom." The humorous writing is aided by cartoons and little jokes throughout the book. The author has written several other books on related topics.

Ross, Tony. **I'm Coming to Get You!** Dial, 1984.
   Deep in outer space a hairy monster causes havoc, and then heads to earth where it vows to come get Tommy Brown. When the monster does come, Tommy is relieved that it is only the size of a mouse. A good story to reinforce the notion that monsters may not be as scary as we first think.

San Souci, Robert D. **Short and Shivery**. Illustrated by Katherine Coville. Doubleday, 1987.
   A wonderful collection of spooky stories from all over the world, featuring a Russian vampire, a Canadian werewolf, a hairy tailypo from the backwoods of West Virginia, plus many more. You can read these or retell them in your own words (as the author suggests).

Schwartz, Alvin. **Scary Stories to Tell in the Dark**. Illustrated by Stephen Gammell. Lippincott, 1981.
   This collection of ghost stories (jump tales to terrify or amuse) and modern scary stories that are part of American folklore begs to be read or told aloud. Illustrated with Stephen Gammell's spooky drawings.
   Also by Schwartz: **More Scary Stories to Tell in the Dark**. Lippincott, 1984.

Sendak, Maurice. **Where the Wild Things Are**. Harper and Row, 1963.
   This modern classic, about mischievous Max who sails off to the land of the wild things and in taming them, gains control over his own world is a must read for every child at some time during his or her growing up. Teachers and librarians can use it for creative dramatics and story theatre presentations.

Steig, William. **Rotten Island**. Godine, 1984.
   On Rotten Island, earthquakes, tornadoes, and lightning are frequent and only prickly plants and slimy, miserable monsters inhabit the place. The whole disgusting place gets even worse when a flower appears, setting off the violence to such an extent that everything is consumed. The island that grows up afterward is a garden paradise. This picture book has many teaching possibilities and is the focus of one of the story theatre groups described in the "Treasure Chest."

Stokes, Jack. **Monster Madness: Outrageous Jokes about Some Weird Folks**. Doubleday, 1981.
    Jokes that will have popular appeal for many children focus on monsters, ghosts, ghouls, werewolves, and related characters.

Thorne, Ian. **Frankenstein**. Crestwood House, 1977.
    One of the Movie Monster Series books, which also include *King Kong, Dracula*, and *Godzilla*. Text and photographs tell the movie story of the monster created by the mad scientist. The story of the monster's original creator, Mary Shelley, is also included along with a brief history of the story in different film versions.

Weil, Lisl. **Of Witches and Monsters and Wondrous Creatures**. Atheneum, 1985.
    Text briefly tells about fantastic beings from Egypt and Greece to the fairy tale beasts of Europe and the early days of America.

Willis, Jeanne. **The Monster Bed**. Illustrated by Susan Varley. Lothrop, Lee, and Shepard, 1986.
    Dennis, a young monster, is afraid to go to bed because humans might get him. The tale is told in verse with Sendak style monsters sprinkled throughout the story.

Winthrop, Elizabeth. **Maggie and the Monster**. Illustrated by Tomie de Paola. Holiday House, 1987.
    Every night a little monster comes shuffling about in Maggie's room. Finally Maggie confronts the monster, asks what it wants, and then helps her find it—her mother!

ENCORES (OTHER PROGRAMS AND PROJECTS)

The stories and activities in this chapter have appeal throughout the year, but Halloween is the naturally spooky season. Since I have generally excluded witches from this chapter, another program/unit can focus on Halloween, witches, and the fall season. I planned a successful library program entitled "The Great Pumpkin Meets Poltergeist" that combined pumpkin decorating, bobbing for apples (an activity that I discovered was new to many children, and telling ghost stories during the Halloween season. Junior high students were enthusiastic volunteers who came dressed in costume (the hunchback of Notre Dame, assorted witches and ghouls) and told stories to children in kindergarten through fourth grade. I found that the junior high students' inhibitions about telling stories in front of a group nearly evaporated when the room was darkened a bit so they would feel less "exposed." Most children already have their own store of ghost stories, but if they need a little direction just refer them to some of the sources in the bibliography of this chapter. The collections by Schwartz, Leach, or San Souci all are good choices since the stories are relatively short and easy to tell in your own words.

Some schools and libraries like to set up their own haunted houses at Halloween. Older children can participate in the fun of this holiday by setting up the haunted house and dressing in costume, but doing it under the guise that it is an activity they are sponsoring for younger children. Since traditional trick-or-treating has become less safe than it once was, these institutionally sponsored events—haunted houses, Halloween parties in schools and libraries, ghost story programs—are particularly important. Schools and libraries can help communities plan events that are fun for children and also safe, as well as carrying on a part of our cultural heritage.

4
Cat and Mouse

INTRODUCTION

Folklore is filled with cat and mouse tales. With few exceptions, these animals are enemies (and for good reason). Dating back to the ancient Egyptians, cats were brought into the house (and granary) for one main purpose—to get rid of mice. Throughout history, cats have been carried on ships, kept in barns, and brought into houses as pets for the same reason—to get rid of mice. While cats have generally been thought of more kindly than mice, poems, songs, and stories pay tribute to the fine if not troublesome qualities of both species. This program/unit will introduce literature and related activities about cats and mice. Since everything from picture books to longer novels has been written on this subject, this theme offers a harvest of good reading for young people.

PURPOSE OF PROGRAM/UNIT

To introduce children to literature about cats and mice and to develop related activities: creative writing, choral reading, creative dramatics, crafts, games, and food experiences.

A LITTLE BACKGROUND ABOUT CATS AND MICE

- Cats were worshipped by the ancient Egyptians (and even mummified) for their mouse-chasing abilities and for their ability to see at night. Egyptians associated the cat with the moon because a cat sleeps in a crescent shape. The Greeks even thought the cat created the moon! The Chinese also revered the cat for its night vision, while in Siam cats were given plushy cushions and gold cages.

- During the Dark Ages, cats began to be associated with witches and evil. The superstition that a black cat crossing your path brings bad luck probably dates to this time.

- Cats, according to legend, still bring good luck more often than bad luck. Two notable examples are the stories of Dick Whittington and his cat and Puss in Boots. Dick Whittington, a poor lad, buys a cat for a penny. The cat later rids a ship of its mice, is handsomely rewarded, and brings its owner such good fortune that he eventually becomes Lord Mayor of London three times. Similarly, the cat in Puss in Boots brings its master wealth and the hand of the king's daughter in marriage. Stories such as these reinforce the notion that cats are intelligent and cunning animals who bring good fortune.

- If the cat is thought to be cunning, then the mouse must be given credit for its share of craftiness. In order to survive in a world of predators, the mouse must be swift and stealthy. History and literature are not always kind to the mouse for these traits, but the famous Aesop fable of the lion and the mouse reminds us that mice can be helpful. When the mighty lion is caught in the hunter's nets, the mouse gnaws through the ropes to set the beast free.

- Famous cats and mice in legend and story include Aesop's town mouse and country mouse, Puss in Boots, Dick Whittington's cat, the three blind mice of the nursery song, the Hickory Dickory Dock mouse, and the mouse that Froggie courted. Modern stories abound from Lewis Carroll's famous Cheshire Cat and Dormouse to E. B. White's Stuart Little. The bibliography in this chapter includes numerous examples to read aloud or to suggest to children for further reading.

SETTING THE STAGE (PREPARATION)

Since there are so many cat and mouse books to inspire activities, set up learning/activity centers all over your classroom or library. You could call these centers "mouse holes" and "kitty corners." Older children can help you set up the activities. In a school setting, older children can facilitate learning in the centers during the course of this unit. In public libraries, older children and adult volunteers can assist in craft projects, games, and read-aloud groups. Adapt the following mouse holes and kitty corners to your own setting.

Pussy Cat Poems and Little Mouse Tunes, a poetry and song center, will inspire children to make up their own verses about cats and mice. Display some of the books of poetry suggested in the bibliography. Read aloud and sing along, from Mother Goose rhymes to T. S. Eliot's cat poems. Ask a musician in your school to bring in a guitar or autoharp to accompany a group sing-along of "Three Blind Mice." Play the soundtrack of the popular musical "CATS" and share the picture book of Eliot's *Growltiger's Last Stand with The Pekes and the Pollicles and The Song of the Jellicles*, with Errol Le Cain's whimsical illustrations. Prepare cat- and mouse-shaped pages using Figures 4.1 and 4.2 in the "Treasure Chest" section, for children to write their own poems. (Several starter poems are provided in the "Treasure Chest.")

The Cat Chorus, a choral reading center, will give children an opportunity for oral expression. The leader reads aloud a book with a repeated refrain, such as *My Cat Likes to Hide in Boxes*, and children chime in with the refrain. The script "Mother Goose's Cats and Mice" in the "Treasure Chest" section offers a more ambitious choral reading experience. Practice the readings aloud several times so children can read with expression and clarity. Children in this center will perform for others or record their reading to be shared later.

Mice-l-angelo's Garret, an arts and crafts center, gives children an opportunity to create mouse art. The projects include mouse finger puppets, collage pictures inspired by Leo Lionni's mice, and mouse-size creations suggested by Rodney Peppe's books. The first two projects can be made to take home. Peppe's creations—a flying basket, a ship made from a kettle, and a house made inside a shoe—can be made by the group for room display. Assemble the materials provided in the "Treasure Chest" and make several examples ahead of time.

The Cat and Mouse Playhouse, a creative dramatics center, offers a variety of play acting from mime to story theatre. The leader invites children to first warm up with "cat stretches." Children move slowly to suggestions such as "Wake up like a cat who has been sleeping in the sun," "Climb carefully up a tree to catch a bird on a top branch," and "Sneak across a wood floor to pounce on a mouse." For the story theatre portion of this activity center, children act out parts as the leader either tells or reads a story. One popular choice is Wanda Gag's *Millions of Cats*. As the old man in the story chooses the cats, children join the leader in the front of the room. They perform the various cat actions—sipping the pond water, eating the grass on the hills, scratching, and chorusing "I am!" Each child may make a cat mask to add to the drama. (A mask pattern is provided in the "Treasure Chest" in Figure 4.5.) An alternative story to share is Jack Kent's *Fat Cat*. The leader could tell the story wearing a "fat cat" costume—simply sew elastic at the top of a bedsheet and pull the costume over your head. Children become the various characters—the old woman, Skohottentot, Skolinkenlot, five birds in a flock, seven girls dancing, the lady with the pink parasol, the parson with the crooked staff, and the wood cutter—and they run underneath the sheet as the fat cat eats them. Older children might choose a more involved story such as *Puss in Boots*.

At Anatole's Tasting Party, a food center, children taste, describe, and evaluate various cheeses as if they are mice like the fictional character Anatole. The leader reads aloud the first book in the series by Eve Titus, in which a French mouse samples and rates cheeses in the Duvall Cheese Factory. As a result of Anatole's expertise, the factory becomes world famous. Prepare dozens of small signs that read "good," "extra specially good," "specially good," "not so good," and "no good." Attach the signs to toothpicks so children can place a sign in each wedge of cheese after they have sampled a bite. Choose various cheeses for this center such as Brie, bleu, and Camembert, as well as milder cheeses that many children already know.

THE SHOW GOES ON
(THE PROGRAM PLAN)

Act I—If you are introducing this program in a public library, you might begin by playing a circle game such as Mrs. Murphy's Cat. Children sit in a circle and clap a simple rhythm as they say the words "Mrs. Murphy's cat is a _____ cat," with the leader supplying an adjective that begins with the letter A. (Thus, the leader might say, "Mrs. Murphy's cat is an awful cat.") The child seated on the leader's right continues this word play game by using a descriptive word that begins with the letter B, such as "Mrs. Murphy's cat is a beautiful cat." Play continues around circle with everyone trying to keep up with the rhythm of the clap as they add to the word play.

Act II—Children choose one of the learning/activity centers, or the group could participate in the activities as a whole. Read aloud several cat poems or the "Mother Goose's Cats and Mice" script (in the "Treasure Chest") with children joining in on the refrains. Follow up by making cat masks (see Figure 4.5).

Act III—Tell or read aloud *Millions of Cats* and invite children to become the cats with their cat masks in a story theatre version of the book.

Act IV-Read one of Leo Lionni's mouse books such as *Frederick* or *Alexander and the Wind-up Mouse* and make collage mice pictures.

Act V—If you have time, read *Anatole* and have a cheese tasting party as described in "Setting the Stage."

THE TREASURE CHEST

Mother Goose's Cats and Mice
(A Script for Choral Reading)

This script is an adaptation of rhymes about cats and mice that people have enjoyed for generations. It adds lines and plays with the rhyme so children will begin to get the feeling of a chorus as they read the lines aloud together.

Reader One:	Hickory	Reader Six:	The clock
Reader Two:	Hickory	Reader Five:	Tick tock
Reader Three:	Dickory	Reader Six:	Struck one
Reader Four:	Dickory	Reader One:	One
Reader One:	Hickory	Reader Six:	And down
Reader Three:	Dickory	Reader One:	Hickory
Reader Two:	Hickory	Reader Three:	Dickory
Reader Four:	Dickory	Reader Six:	He come
Reader Five:	Dock!	Reader Two:	Hickory
Reader Six:	The mouse ran up	Reader Four:	Dickory
Reader One:	Hickory	Reader One:	Hickory
Reader Three:	Dickory	Reader Three:	Dickory
Reader Six:	the clock	All:	Hickory Dickory Dock!
Reader Five:	Dock!		

Reader One:	Here Kitty	Reader Seven:	I frightened a little mouse
Reader Two:	Kitty		Under a chair.
Reader Three:	Kitty	All:	Scat, cat!
Reader Four:	Kitty		
Reader Five:	Kitty	Reader One:	There was a crooked man
Reader Six:	Pussy cat, pussy cat	Reader Two:	And he walked a crooked mile
Reader One:	Here Kitty	Reader Three:	He found a crooked sixpence
Reader Two:	Kitty	Reader Four:	A sixpence
Reader Three:	Kitty	Reader Three:	He found a crooked sixpence
Reader Four:	Kitty	Reader Five:	Against a crooked stile
Reader Five:	Kitty	Reader Two:	And he walked a crooked mile
Reader Six:	Where have you been?	Reader Three:	To find a crooked sixpence
Reader Seven:	I've been to London	Reader Four:	A sixpence
	To see the Queen.	Reader Five:	Against a crooked stile.
Reader One:	She's seen	Reader Six:	He bought a crooked cat
Reader Two:	The Queen!	Reader Seven:	Which caught a crooked mouse
Reader Three:	The Queen?	All:	And they all lived together
Reader Four:	She's seen		
Reader Five:	The Queen!	Reader One:	The crooked man
Reader Six:	Pussy cat, pussy cat	Reader Two:	The crooked mile
Reader One:	Here Kitty	Reader Three:	The crooked sixpence
Reader Two:	Kitty	Reader Four:	The sixpence
Reader Three:	Kitty	Reader Five:	The crooked stile
Reader Four:	Kitty	Reader Six:	The crooked cat
Reader Five:	Kitty	Reader Seven:	The crooked mouse
Reader Six:	What did you there?	All:	And they all lived together
			In a crooked little house.
			The end!

Pussy Cat Poems and Little Mouse Hums

Here are a few poetry starters to get you going. Cut out the mouse and cat shapes using the patterns in Figures 4.1 and 4.2, then let children copy the following poems and supply their own descriptive words. The words do not have to rhyme since the final couplets provided will give closure to the poem.

I Like Cats

_____ cats
_____ cats
_____ cats
_____ cats

I don't care what you say.
I like cats every way!

Mice Any Way

_____ mice
_____ mice
_____ mice
_____ mice

Any size, any way
I think mice are just OK!

Pussy Cat Anywhere

Try this variation on "Pussy Cat, Pussy Cat, Where Have You Been?" Supply other places and reasons for going and complete the following questions:

Pussy cat, pussy cat
Where did you go?

_____

_____

Pussy cat, pussy cat
Where did you hide?

_____

_____

Pussy cat, pussy cat
Where are you now?

_____

_____

Projects and Patterns

Cut out cat and mouse shapes using the patterns shown in Figures 4.1 and 4.2 so that children can write their own poems. Torn paper art projects inspired by Leo Lionni's mice are shown in Figure 4.3. Children can tell mice stories with a set of mouse finger puppets (Figure 4.4) or become cats in the different cat stories with cat masks made from the pattern in Figure 4.5.

(Text continues on page 64.)

Fig. 4.1.

Fig. 4.2.

CAT and MOUSE
torn paper craft

1. tear paper into semicircle for body.

2. glue on rounded shapes for ears.

3. add stick-on dots for eyes.

4. tear tail shape or add yarn tail.

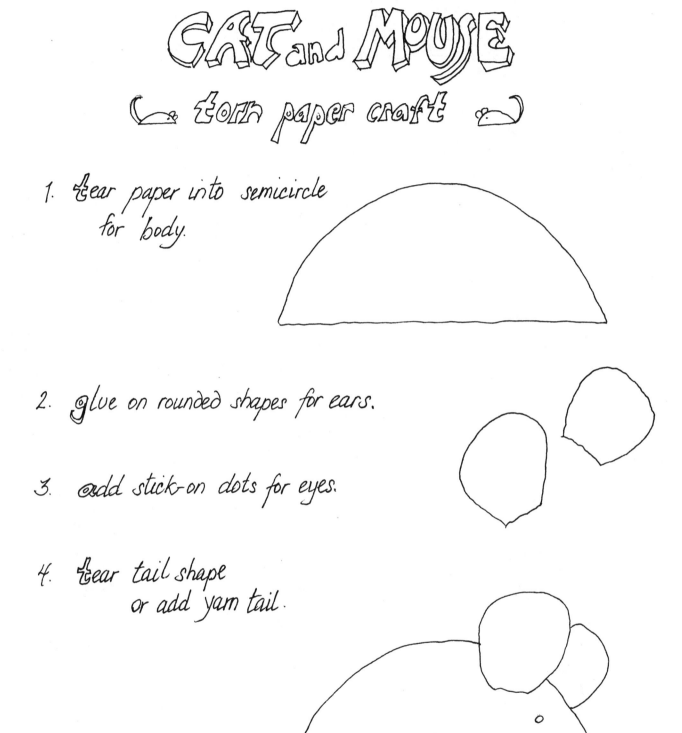

Fig. 4.3.

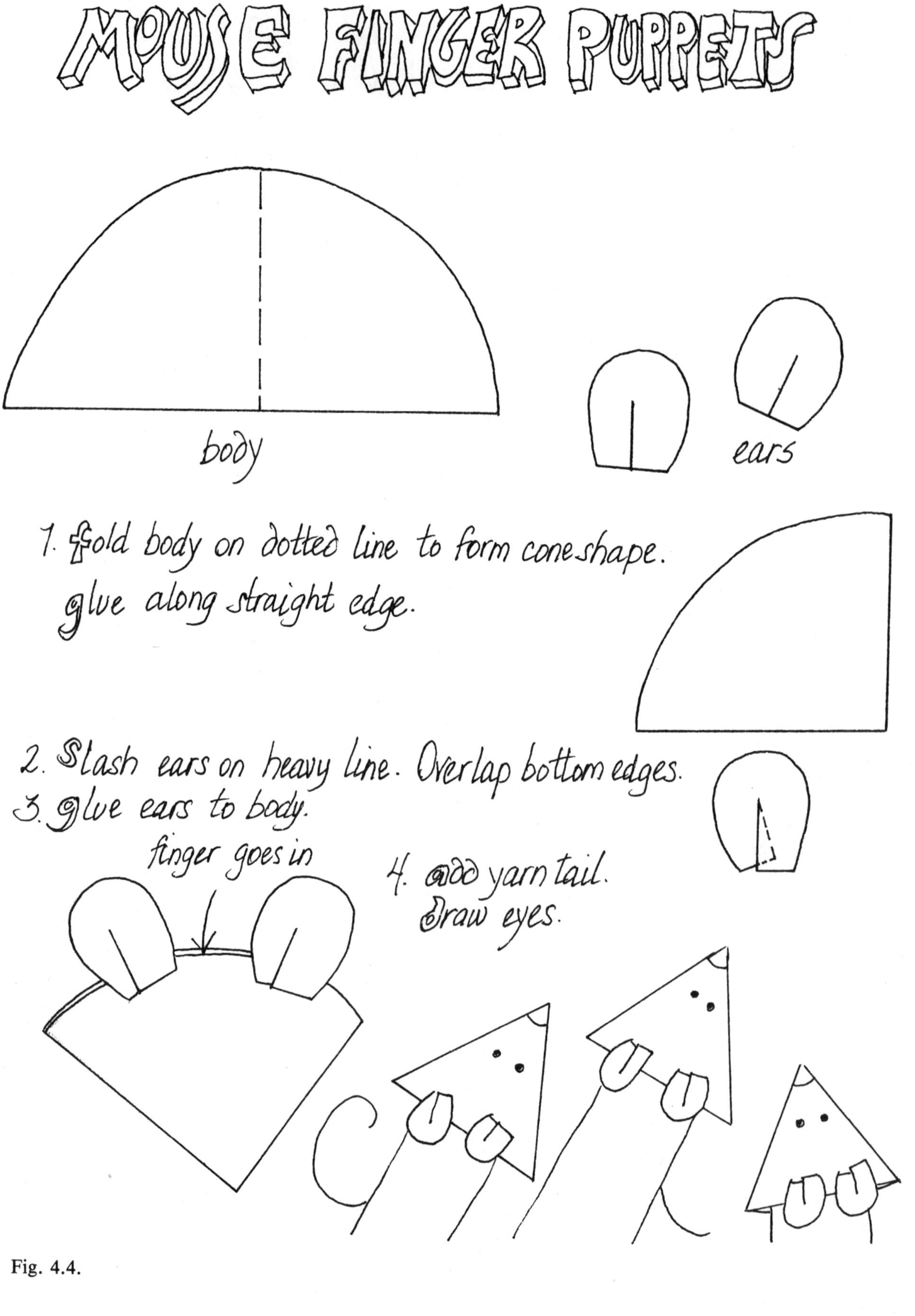

MOUSE FINGER PUPPETS

body

ears

1. Fold body on dotted line to form cone shape. Glue along straight edge.

2. Slash ears on heavy line. Overlap bottom edges.
3. Glue ears to body.
   finger goes in
4. Add yarn tail. Draw eyes.

Fig. 4.4.

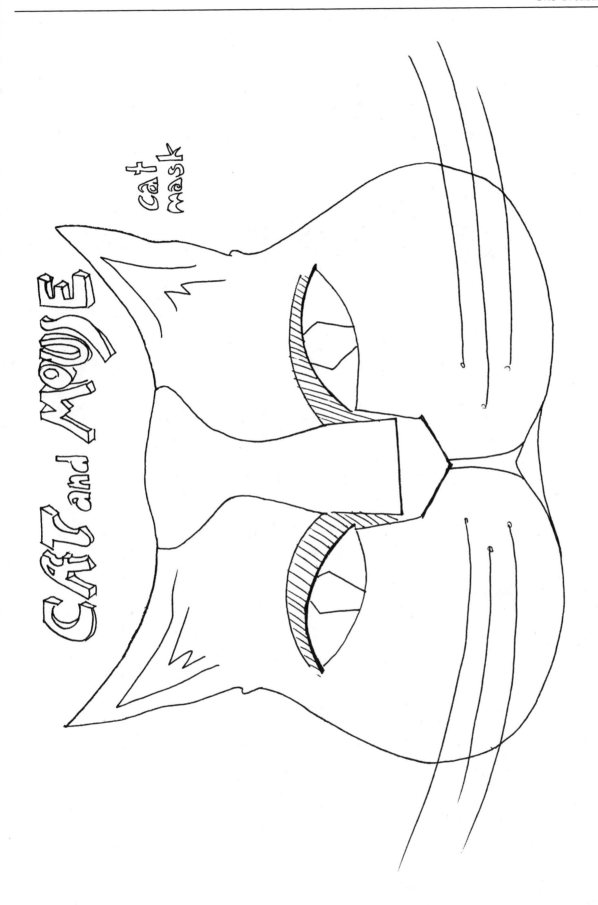

Fig. 4.5.

IN THE LIMELIGHT (PUBLICITY)

Publicize this program with publicity releases and a flyer like the example shown in Figure 4.6. Other ways to create interest include making displays in local pet stores for your library program on cats or filling a school display case with student art projects based on the ideas in this chapter.

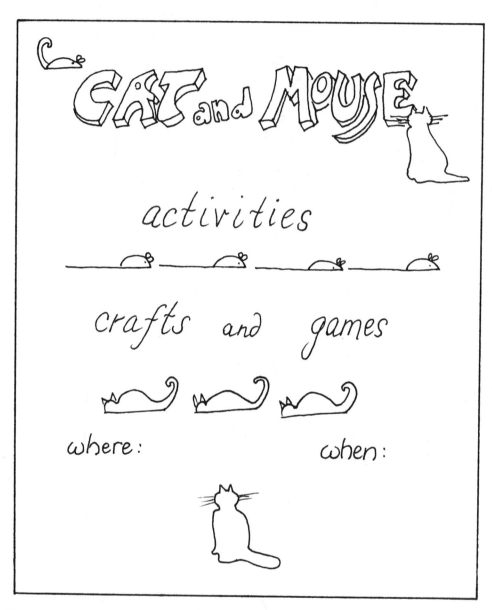

Fig. 4.6.

BIBLIOGRAPHY

The bibliography of this chapter is more extensive than in other chapters because there are so many excellent books on the subject. Nonfiction titles, other than poetry and story collections, have not been included for the most part. The books selected are good read-alouds and many call for follow-up activities; some suggestions are given along with the annotations. In most cases, one book in a series is annotated with other titles by the same author simply listed. Exceptions to this rule are the mice books by Leo Lionni that are not actually in a series. The categories for this bibliography are books about cats, books about mice, and books about cats and mice.

Books about Cats

Allen, Jonathan. **My Cat.** Dial, 1986.
 A boy describes the things his cat does such as curling up in warm places he leaves behind and playing with a feather. Children can make their own list of cat behaviors after hearing this story.

Baker, Leslie. **The Third-Story Cat.** Little, Brown, 1987.
 Alice, an apartment cat, escapes through an open window and meets a cat who takes her to the park, where she experiences new adventures. Though she is glad to return to the security of the apartment, future explorations are hinted at in the end. Children could write their own sequel.

Birnbaum, A. **Green Eyes.** Golden, 1953, 1973.
 A white cat named Green Eyes describes its first year growing up in the country. Seasonal changes as well as cat behavior are simply described and shown in big, bright pictures perfect for a young audience.

Bonsall, Crosby. **The Amazing the Incredible Super Dog.** Harper and Row, 1986.
 A little girl announces all the tricks her dog can do while her cat actually performs them. Finally, the girl praises superdog (he hasn't done anything else all along) and chides the cat.

Calhoun, Mary. **Cross Country Cat.** Illustrated by Erick Ingraham. Morrow, 1979.
 A cat, left behind in the mountains, learns how to ski until he is rescued by his family. Fantasy and reality combine so well that the reader might believe this could happen!
  Also by Calhoun: **Hot-Air Henry.** Illustrated by Erick Ingraham. Morrow, 1981.

Carle, Eric. **Have You Seen My Cat?** Watts, 1976.
 A boy asks people all over the world, "Have you seen my cat?" They respond by pointing to various cats, from lions and cheetahs to a Persian cat. He finally finds his cat, along with an assortment of kittens. Carle's bright paintings and the catalogue of cats in the end will inspire children to make cat scrapbooks.

Cat Poems. Selected by Myra Cohn Livingston. Illustrated by Trina Schart Hyman. Holiday House, 1987.
 This collection of 19 old and newer poems is illustrated with soft line drawings. Here are Eliot's jellicle cats as well as alley cats, tomcats, black cats, and white cats bright as the moon.

Cat Will Rhyme with Hat. Compiled by Jean Chapman. Illustrated by Peter Parnall. Scribners, 1986.
 Dozens of cat poems from ancient verses to contemporary ones by Ogden Nash range from praise to accounts of mischievous behavior.

Cats by Mother Goose. Selected by Barbara Lucas. Illustrated by Carol Newsom. Lothrop, Lee, and Shepard, 1986.
 Twenty Mother Goose rhymes about cats are illustrated with pictures of a kindly old woman in high top black shoes and a pointed black hat who is leading a goose. Verses include "As I Was Going to St. Ives," "Pussy Cat, Pussy Cat," and "Three Kittens Who Lost Their Mittens."

de Paola, Tomie. **The Kids' Cat Book.** Holiday House, 1979.
 Patrick learns all there is to know about cats when he goes to Granny Twinkle's for a free one.

De Regniers, Beatrice Schenk. **So Many Cats!** Illustrated by Ellen Weiss. Clarion, 1985.
   Starting out with one cat, the number grows and grows until there are 12—or is it 13? The text is rhythmical and invites reading and counting aloud.

De Regniers, Beatrice Schenk. **This Big Cat and Other Cats I've Known.** Illustrated by Alan Daniel. Crown, 1985.
   Poetry collection that pays tribute to cats and cat behavior.

Eliot, T. S. **Growltiger's Last Stand with The Pekes and the Pollicles and The Song of the Jellicles.** Illustrated by Errol Le Cain. Farrar, Straus, Giroux/Harcourt Brace Jovanovich, 1987.
   Growltiger, the pirate cat, serenades Lady Griddlebone but is unaware of the Siamese cats, who surround him and then make him walk the plank. In the second narrative poem, the incessant barking of pekes, pugs, and pollicles comes to a halt when the Great Rumpuscat appears. The third verse tells of jellicle cats wearing black ties and pearls who dance in the moonlight—a more charming cat picture. Le Cain's illustrations add another playful dimension to Eliot's much-loved verses.

Fisher, Aileen. **My Cat Has Eyes of Sapphire Blue.** Illustrated by Marie Angel. Crowell, 1973.
   Twenty-four poems about cats and their behavior from playing in boxes to stalking brooms.

Freschet, Berniece. **Furlie Cat.** Illustrated by Betsy Lewin. Lothrop, Lee, and Shepard, 1986.
   Furlie Cat is a fraidy cat until he practices being brave and scares all the neighborhood animals. When he is caught in the woods, Furlie becomes less fierce and is glad to return home.

Gag, Wanda. **Millions of Cats.** Faber and Faber, 1929.
   The classic tale of a man who goes out to get his wife a cat and ends up choosing "hundreds of cats, thousands of cats, and millions and billions and trillions of cats." Perfect for storytelling and creative dramatics.

Ginsburg, Mirra. **Three Kittens.** Translated from the Russian of V. Sutenev. Illustrated by Guilio Maestro. Crown, 1973.
   Simple text and large illustrations tell the tale of three kittens, black, white, and gray, who chase a mouse into a can of flour, crawl into a stovepipe, then go for a swim. A good pattern for children to follow in writing their own sequence stories.

Griffith, Helen V. **More Alex and the Cat.** Illustrated by Donald Carrick. Greenwillow, 1983.
   The wise old cat teaches Alex the dog lessons in three short stories. Alex, full of questions and remorse for his bad habits, has easy appeal for children.
   Also by Griffith: **Alex and the Cat.** Illustrated by Joseph Low. Greenwillow, 1982.

Hogrogian, Nonny. **The Cat Who Loved to Sing.** Knopf, 1988.
   Inspired by an Armenian cumulative tale, this story begins with a cat who loves to sing but steps on a thorn. A woman removes the thorn, takes it for a needle, and gives the cat some bread in return. Thus begins a series of trades until the cat receives a mandolin. A lilting cat song is included at the end—perfect for a sing-along!

Kahl, Virginia. **Whose Cat Is That?** Scribners, 1978.
   A small white cat that goes looking for a home is adopted by seven families who each give her a different name.

Kanao, Keiko. **Kitten Up a Tree.** Knopf, 1987.
   Minimal text and clear illustrations show a curious kitten's adventure that leaves her stuck in a tree until the mother cat comes to the rescue.

Kellogg, Steven. **A Rose for Pinkerton.** Dial, 1981.
   Pinkerton the Great Dane needs a friend so his family brings home a kitten, Rose. The cat takes over Pinkerton's place in the sun so the family seeks advice at the International Pet Show, with zany results.

Kent, Jack. **Fat Cat.** Scholastic, 1971.
   In this Danish folk tale, a cat eats a woman's gruel, the pot, the woman, and a whole host of characters before a woodcutter opens him up. This favorite book long out of print is now available in paperback.

Kits, Cats, Lions, and Tigers. Selected by Lee Bennett Hopkins. Illustrated by Vera Rosenberry. Whitman, 1979.
Cat stories, poems, and verses are divided into three sections: "Clever Cats," "Classic Cats," and "Cat Kin." Folk tales from around the world as well as noteworthies from the Cheshire Cat to the Cowardly Lion are included.

Koci, Marta. **Katie's Kitten.** Neugebauer, 1982.
Katie's kitten enjoys the comforts of home until he disobeys and tries to follow Katie to school. Koci's watercolor pictures capture the beauties of a snowy world and a cozy country home.

Larrick, Nancy, compiler. **Cats Are Cats.** Illustrated by Ed Young. Philomel, 1988.
Over 40 poems celebrate cats—lost cats, stray cats, tomcats, jellicle cats, apartment cats—and cat behavior. Young's pastel illustrations simply glow. Even if you're not a "cat person," you will be captivated!

McPhail, David. **Great Cat.** Dutton, 1982.
Great Cat arrived on Toby's doorstep one night and they become great friends. But the neighbors become afraid so Toby and Great Cat move to a small island in the ocean, where Great Cat later rescues the children who visit him often.

Mayne, William. **The Patchwork Cat.** Illustrated by Nicola Bayley. Knopf, 1981.
When Tabby rescues her patchwork quilt from the garbage, she ends up in the truck, at the dump, and on strange streets before she is returned to her home.

Nicklaus, Carol. **Harry the Hider.** Watts, 1979.
As Miranda is thinking of a trick for her cat to perform in the neighborhood circus, he is cleverly hiding himself all over the house. In the end, Harry becomes the prize. As you read the story, children can make their own predictions for places Harry will hide next.

Parish, Peggy. **The Cats' Burglar.** Illustrated by Lynn Sweat. Greenwillow, 1983.
Aunt Emma's friends think she has too many cats until a burglar breaks in.

Pinkwater, Daniel. **The Wuggie Norple Story.** Illustrated by Tomie de Paola. Four Winds, 1980.
Lunchbox Louie brings home a kitten, Wuggie Norple, who grows at such an alarming rate that Louie has to bring in a series of increasingly larger animals for comparison before his family will agree the kitten is growing.

Preston, Edna Mitchell. **Where Did My Mother Go?** Illustrated by Chris Conover. Four Winds, 1978.
Little Cat searches everywhere and asks everyone to help him find his mother, but he finds her by himself. When he does, he makes his mother promise to never go away without telling him where she is going.

Schertle, Alice. **That Olive!** Illustrated by Cindy Wheeler. Lothrop, Lee, and Shepard, 1986.
Olive the cat always hides from Andy, her owner, so the little boy leaves a tuna sandwich on the counter then waits for her return. Text and illustrations ask the reader to find the elusive cat. Good for making predictions.

Segal, Lore. **The Story of Mrs. Loveright and Purrless Her Cat.** Illustrated by Paul O. Zelinsky. Knopf, 1985.
Mrs. Loveright gets a cat to keep her cozy, but the cat is so independent there's nothing the poor woman can do to make the cat snuggle.

Stehr, Frederic. **Gulliver.** Farrar, Straus, Giroux, 1987.
Gulliver, the family cat, escapes through the car window while the family is on vacation. The frightening and lonely adventures that follow climax in a surprising reunion.

Sutton, Eve. **My Cat Likes to Hide in Boxes.** Illustrated by Lynley Dodd. Parents Magazine Press, 1973.
Many exotic cats from all over the world are compared to the narrator's cat, who hides in boxes, in this narrative poem that is excellent for choral reading.

Books about Mice

Barklem, Jill. **Autumn Story**. Philomel, 1980.
 One of four Brambly Hedge stories about a community of field mice who make amazingly intricate homes reminiscent of Beatrix Potter and a mouse version of Laura Ashley's country homes.
 Also by Barklem: **Winter Story**. Philomel, 1980; **Spring Story**. Philomel, 1980; **Summer Story**. Philomel, 1980.

Boegehold, Betty. **Pippa Mouse**. Illustrated by Cindy Szekeres. Knopf, 1973.
 Six little read-aloud/read-along stories about a gentle mouse who plays with Squirrel and Duck and hangs up a bathing cap for Christmas.
 Also by Boegehold: **Here's Pippa Again!** Knopf, 1975.

Cleary, Beverly. **The Mouse and the Motorcycle**. Illustrated by Louis Darling. Morrow, 1965.
 The much beloved tale of Ralph the mouse, who goes on many adventures on a boy's toy motorcycle, is an excellent read-aloud or can be converted into a readers theatre script. See "Encores" in Chapter 8 for some suggestions.
 Also by Cleary: **Ralph S. Mouse**. Morrow, 1982; **Runaway Ralph**. Morrow, 1970.

Fisher, Aileen. **The House of a Mouse**. Illustrated by Joan Sandin. Harper and Row, 1988.
 Mouse behavior and characteristics are explored in little poems by the famous poet. Here are poems about mouse houses, footprints, and new babies.

Holabird, Katharine. **Angelina and Alice**. Illustrated by Helen Craig. Clarkson N. Potter, 1987.
 Angelina Mouseling and her friend Alice learn that teamwork makes good acrobats.
 Also by Holabird: **Angelina at the Fair**. Potter, 1985; **Angelina Ballerina**. Potter, 1983.

Kraus, Robert. **Another Mouse to Feed**. Illustrated by Jose Aruego and Ariane Dewey. Prentice-Hall, 1980.
 Mr. and Mrs. Mouse have to work hard to make ends meet but they cannot turn away an orphaned mouse. When they are on the verge of collapse, the children get after-school jobs and do the housework so their parents can recover.
 Also by Kraus: **Pinchpenny Mouse**. Illustrated by Robert Byrd. Windmill Books, 1974; **Where Are You Going Little Mouse?** Illustrated by Jose Aruego and Ariane Dewey. Greenwillow, 1986; **Whose Mouse Are You?** Illustrated by Jose Aruego and Ariane Dewey. Collier, 1970.

Lawson, Robert. **Ben and Me**. Little, 1939.
 This diary of Amos, a poor church mouse who lives in Ben Franklin's hat, gives a mouse-size view of this famous American's life.

Lionni, Leo. **Alexander and the Wind-up Mouse**. Pantheon, 1970.
 Alexander wants to be a wind-up mouse like Willie, but when he understands that toys can break, he wishes that Willie will become a real mouse like himself.

Lionni, Leo. **Frederick**. Pantheon, 1967.
 When the other field mice gather grain for the winter, Frederick gathers sun rays and colors and words to keep them all warm when the food is gone. Frederick's signature fills the end pages that make this book a tribute to the gift of writing. Use this book as a springboard for fable writing (this is a variant of the Aesop ant and grasshopper story) or for writing mouse poems.

Lionni, Leo. **Geraldine the Music Mouse**. Pantheon, 1979.
 Geraldine nibbles an enormous cheese in the shape of a flutist who then plays music. In time, Geraldine has the gift herself.
 Also by Lionni: **The Greentail Mouse**. Pantheon, 1973; **Mouse Days**. Pantheon, 1981.

Lobel, Arnold. **Mouse Soup**. Harper and Row, 1977.
 A weasel catches a mouse to make mouse soup, but this Scheherazade convinces the weasel he needs stories in the soup and then she goes on to tell four of them. In the end, he goes out to find the actual objects in the stories. Children can concoct their own mouse soup tales. Hint: Be sure to include an object the weasel will have to find later!
 Also by Lobel: **Mouse Tales**. Harper and Row, 1972.

Mice Are Rather Nice. Selected by Vardine Moore. Illustrated by Doug Jamison. Atheneum, 1981.
Fifty poems celebrate or jeer mice, from Mother Goose rhymes to several dandies by Aileen Fisher.

O'Brien, Robert. **Mrs. Frisby and the Rats of NIMH.** Illustrated by Zena Bernstein. Atheneum, 1971.
This Newbery Award-winning novel relates the adventures of Mrs. Frisby, a widowed mouse, and her rat friends who have escaped from the National Institutes of Mental Health laboratory.

Peppe, Rodney. **The Mice Who Lived in a Shoe.** Lothrop, Lee, and Shepard, 1981.
The mice who live in a shoe decide to build a more sturdy house to protect them from the weather and from cats. Children will want to design their own mouse houses inspired by Peppe's example, photographed on the last page. His other books show vehicles constructed from common household objects.
Also by Peppe: **The Kettleship Pirates.** Lothrop, Lee, and Shepard, 1983; **The Mice and the Flying Basket.** Lothrop, Lee, and Shepard, 1985.

Sharp, Margery. **The Rescuers.** Illustrated by Garth Williams. Little, 1959.
Miss Bianca and the mice from the Prisoners' Aid Society seek to free a poet held captive in a castle in a barbaric country.
Also by Sharp: **Miss Bianca.** Little, Brown, 1962.

Titus, Eve. **Anatole.** Illustrated by Paul Galdone. McGraw-Hill, 1956.
One night as he is scavenging for food, Anatole, the French mouse, hears people complain that mice are a disgrace. Determined to elevate his reputation, the plucky mouse prepares signs to place on cheeses in the Duvall Cheese Factory so the owner will improve their quality. The factory makes suitable improvements, the cheeses become world famous, and Anatole is held in silent esteem.
Also by Titus: **Anatole in Italy.** McGraw-Hill, 1973; **Anatole and the Piano.** McGraw-Hill, 1966; **Anatole and the Toyshop.** McGraw-Hill, 1970.

Books about Cats and Mice

Freeman, Lydia, and Don Freeman. **Pet of the Met.** Viking, 1953.
Maestro Petrini the mouse is page turner for the prompter of the opera house, who keeps him hidden from Mefisto, a cat who hates mice even more than he hates music. One fateful day the mouse almost loses his life when the cat pounces on him during a performance, but in the end both cat and mouse share friendship and love of opera.

Hurlimann, Ruth. **The Cat and Mouse Who Shared a House.** Translated by Anthea Bell. Henry Z. Walck, 1973.
A cat and a mouse who share a pot of butter end up proving cats and mice can't be very trusting friends after all.

Jeschke, Susan. **Lucky's Choice.** Scholastic, 1987.
Hungry for love, Lucky the cat makes friends with Ezra the mouse. When his owner orders Lucky to kill his new friend, the two escape to the streets and are both taken in by a woman who truly appreciates animals.

Kraus, Robert. **Come Out and Play Little Mouse.** Illustrated by Jose Aruego and Ariane Dewey. Greenwillow, 1987.
Little Mouse can't come out to play during the week, but on Saturday he does. The game becomes a cat and mouse chase until dog pursues cat. The next day Little Mouse stays home to play with his family.

Low, Joseph. **Mice Twice.** Atheneum, 1980.
Cat invites Mouse to dinner so Mouse asks to bring a friend. The ravenous cat thinks "mice twice" until Mouse brings Dog. Thus begins a round of invitations and increasingly more ferocious dinner guests until Mouse brings Wasp to end Cat's attempts to bother Mouse. An excellent read-aloud for children to predict the results.

Miller, Edna. **Mousekin's Golden House.** Prentice-Hall, 1964.
Mousekin on his way home discovers a jack-o-lantern then hides inside from Owl and Cat and stays warm when winter comes.

Oakley, Graham. **The Church Mouse**. Atheneum, 1972.
>Arthur the church mouse lives peacefully with Sampson the cat, who has reformed from his former mouse-chasing days. When Sampson reverts back to his old behavior, the congregation turns on them. Only when cat and mice work together to catch a burglar is all forgiven. Sophisticated humor, in text and illustrations, will appeal to older children.
>>Also by Oakley: **The Church Cat Abroad**. Atheneum, 1973; **The Church Mice in Action**. Atheneum, 1982; **The Church Mice Adrift**. Atheneum, 1976; **The Church Mice at Bay**. Atheneum, 1979; **The Church Mice and the Moon**. Atheneum, 1974.

Roser, Wiltrud. **Lena and Leopold**. Translated from the German by Elizabeth D. Crawford. Margaret K. McElderry Books/Macmillan, 1987.
>Lena doesn't understand why her cat Leopold dislikes his toy mouse until Leopold tells her a story.

Sumiko. **Kittymouse**. Harcourt Brace Jovanovich, 1978.
>Kittymouse, an orphaned kitten, is raised by a family of mice who teach her to act like a mouse. But when the mice move into a house, the children show Kittymouse that she's a cat after all.

Titus, Eve. **Anatole and the Cat**. Illustrated by Paul Galdone. McGraw-Hill, 1957.
>Anatole and his friend Gaston begin to make mistakes in their cheese tasting at the Duvall Cheese Factory because they are threatened by Duvall's cat. In desperation, Anatole makes a cat trap so he can return to his work without distraction.

Velvet Paws and Whispers. Compiled by Jean Chapman. Illustrated by Deborah Niland. Childrens Press, 1979.
>This compendium of cat tales, legends, songs, crafts, and games also includes stories with mice in them. The cover itself will draw laughs—a cat who looks as if it has swallowed the canary is sporting a collar with four fine mice!

Waber, Bernard. **Mice on My Mind**. Houghton Mifflin, 1977.
>A sophisticated cat with a severe mouse fixation reads a newspaper want ad from a town with a mouse overpopulation. He flies off to solve their problem—and his!

White, E. B. **Stuart Little**. Harper, 1945.
>The second son born into the family is a mouse who ends up having many adventures in this classic tale.

ENCORES
(OTHER PROGRAMS AND PROJECTS)

Animal topics have unending appeal for children and the possibilities for story sharing are great. A possible topic to follow this program/unit on cats and mice is other domestic animals such as dogs. Or try a program on cats and dogs.

Many expressions in our language mention cats and mice. A few of these are: curiosity killed the cat, copy cat, looking like the cat who swallowed the canary, cat and mouse game, let the cat out of the bag, when the cat's away the mouse will play. Using these expressions, write stories with your students that suggest the possible origins of the phrases.

Other animal themes to explore include frogs and toads since there are so many stories the world over about them. Frogs are often present in fairy tales. In the world of fantasy frogs can turn into handsome princes, they can give advice, or they can frolic with witches. Modern-day stories of Frog and Toad by Arnold Lobel and the popularity of *Sesame Street*'s Kermit the frog are just a few examples you might use. Pigs are also popular subjects for books, as are spiders, and—well, the list goes on.

5
Whoppers

INTRODUCTION

In a country with such vast wonders as the Grand Canyon and Pike's Peak, tall tale characters grow up naturally. If there was wilderness to explore, forests to be cleared, and railroad to be laid, then there was need for people—real or imagined—like Daniel Boone, Paul Bunyan, and John Henry. These folk heroes and the tall tales told about them made the awesome tasks of settling the country seem less daunting. And, unlike the heroes of ancient times, the American tall tale hero performed his feats with a good dose of humor. The title of this chapter, "Whoppers," encompasses the exaggerated humor of the tall tale, but it also includes little bits of folk literature—riddles, tongue twisters, jokes, expressions that are passed down from one generation to the next. The books of Alvin Schwartz most clearly give young people an understanding of this heritage, and his collection *Whoppers* was the original inspiration for this program.

Just as a country may create the kind of heroes it needs, young people look to the tall tale characters of the past as well as the superheroes of our own day for role models. Tall tale folklore appeals most readily to young people and provides rich opportunities for the classroom teacher or librarian as well. While we can introduce the legends and heroes of the past, we can also discover the often forgotten heroines. There is the opportunity to write new tales and make up songs when only a brief reference or footnote exists about female or minority characters. This chapter provides suggestions for creative writing, food, and art activities, and many more ideas to share with children about America's unique brand of humorous folklore.

PURPOSE OF PROGRAM/UNIT

To explore American folklore—tall tales, humorous yarns, tongue twisters, jokes, and riddles—through literature and related activities.

A LITTLE BACKGROUND ABOUT AMERICAN TALL TALES AND FOLKLORE

- Legends are the stories of a people. They are similar to myth but not so apt to use the supernatural. They may have a base in fact, but generally embroider the truth. Sometimes it's hard to determine where fact stops and fiction begins. American legends that exaggerate the truth and tell about the feats of a larger-than-life hero are called tall tales.

- The yarn (tall tales are one kind) is a long rambling tale, often told in a deliberate, casual, improvisational tone. It seems to never come to the point and doesn't offer the punch lines found in witty stories. The fun is in creating a humorous, whimsical effect and providing rich details all along the way. The yarn is a bit like a babbling brook that enjoys many diversions before it finally reaches a destination. The stories of Mark Twain and Garrison Keillor are in this tradition. Yarnspinners do not really expect to be believed, but they tell their tales with utmost sincerity, a straight face, plenty of supporting detail, and even statistical evidence. (We may not actually believe that Babe the Blue Ox existed but we all know for a fact that she was 22 ax handles across the forehead.)

- Some tall tale heroes actually lived, including Johnny Appleseed, Davy Crockett, and Daniel Boone. Some historical figures such as Abraham Lincoln and George Washington are so important to our past that stories made up about them give them a legendary face in addition to the more factual accounts found in biographies.

- Many tall tale heroes are fiction or largely invention. They may represent characteristics of an occupational or ethnic group such as those embodied in the character of John Henry. Other heroes may be the invention of an author, such as Paul Bunyan, Joe Magarac, and Febold Feboldson.

- Here are some "facts" about a few tall tale characters you might wish to explore futher:

—Paul Bunyan, a logger of the North, dug the Mississippi to move his logs from Minnesota to New Orleans, cleared Iowa for corn and Kansas for wheat, and rid the country of man-eating jackrabbits. His appetite was so enormous that he kept Sourdough Slim and a whole crew of cooks busy making pancakes for himself and the other loggers. He found his famous companion, Babe the Blue Ox, one winter during the blue snow. Some sources say Paul Bunyan was the creation of a Madison Avenue advertising agency. He was a symbol of the Red River Lumber Company in Minnesota.

—Johnny Appleseed, whose real name was John Chapman, was said to have planted apple trees from Pennsylvania through the Midwest. Legends tell us he wore a cooking pot for a hat and a coffee sack for a shirt.

—Mike Fink actually was an American frontiersman and a keelboatman on the Ohio and Mississippi rivers. His great strength, boasts, and sharpshooting skills have become legendary.

—John Henry, a Black laborer, was born with a hammer in his hand, according to popular legend. The inspiration for this hero came from an actual event in the 1870s, when a man outworked a steam drill during the building of the Big Bend Tunnel on the Chesapeake and Ohio Railroad in West Virginia. John Henry was the subject of the most popular ballad about an American laborer.

—Pecos Bill, so the legend says, was born in east Texas in the 1830s but was somehow thrown from his parents' covered wagon, so he was raised by coyotes. When he drew up, he invented the lasso, the rodeo, and became the most famous cowboy of all. Legends about Pecos Bill were created from an article that first appeared in *Century* magazine in 1923.

—Febold Feboldson, the legendary farmer from Nebraska, was the invention of two newspapermen. He symbolized pioneers who made the best of a bad situation because he came up with outrageous solutions for problems on the prairie.

SETTING THE STAGE (PREPARATION)

Decorate the room with oversize objects such as giant cornstalks made of paper, gigantic soft-sculpture ears of corn, big boots, and cowboy hats. Hang butcher paper or art paper around the room for children to create their own giant murals. Make a long map of the United States and draw pictures of the folk heroes where they lived. Be sure to exaggerate a lot, since tall tale heroes were larger than life in their stature and accomplishments!

Set up a Swappin' Spot where riddles or jokes are shared. Alvin Schwartz's *Tomfoolery, Trickery and Foolery with Words* will give you examples taken from American folklore. One format for the swapping might be a display of jokes and riddles written on bright sheets of construction paper and an assortment of joke books and riddle books. Kids can write their own jokes and riddles, find some in the books, or collect them from parents and grandparents. For every joke or riddle they contribute, they can swap with one in the display. Provide kids with paper bags to collect their jokes and riddles. Suggest they decorate the outside of the bags with cartoons or jokes and call them "My Bag of Tricks."

An alternative to the above activity is the Pack of Lies. I created this "visual pun" to make a literal example of this figurative expression. I filled a laundry bag with long strips of paper, each of which had an exaggerated short tale, or a whopper, written on it. The whoppers were rolled up and secured with rubber bands so children could easily pick a lie and read it out loud to the group. This Pack of Lies gave the abstract metaphor concrete meaning and also quickly introduced the theme of the program "Whoppers." You could prepare the lies for children or have them do their own research to find tall tales in American folklore.

Another activity center or a variation on the above ideas is the Tongue Twister Tent. If you wish, make a tent from a painter's tarp or brightly colored canvas for kids to crawl under. The idea is to share tongue twisters out loud (a great way to limber up the tongue, just as singers and speech teachers suggest). Present the tongue twisters in a unique way. My visual pun for tongue twisters is pictured in the "Treasure Chest" (Figure 5.1). It's a giant tongue made from posterboard with dozens of little holes poked in the surface. Write tongue twisters (Alvin Schwartz's *A Twister of Twists, A Tangler of Tongues* supplies plenty) on small slips of paper. Roll the slips up tightly and stuff them in the holes. These will look something like giant taste buds, but are literal examples of "tongue twisters." Give children a chance to also write tongue twisters of their own.

The Yarnspinners Corner encourages children to tell or write their own tall tales. Oral storytellers might like to unwind a "story yarn" (a ball of yarn) as they tell the stories. The story could be a continuous tale or each child might tell a different story. To control the length of each segment of the tale, tie lengths of different colored yarns together. One child starts the story and unwinds the yarn, but when he or she gets to a different color the yarn is passed to the next child, who continues the story. The idea behind holding the ball of yarn corresponds to the native American "talking feather": This object is invested with meaning for Native storytellers. The person holding the talking feather is permitted to talk or to tell the story. The story yarn, then, is your totem or symbol for telling tall tales.

If you choose to have children write their own tall tales, give them plenty of examples from books or stories read aloud to them before you expect them to create their own tales. In a school setting, you will probably spend several days reading selections from the annotated bibliography in this chapter. In a public library setting, you might need to partially prepare a story ahead of time but give children the opportunity to finish the story or add details along the way. Some of the story starters given in the "Treasure Chest" section will give you ideas.

The Ballad Corner gives young musicians an opportunity to sing songs about folk heroes and to make up their own new songs to old tunes. "The Ballad of John Henry" is one song you will want to share. Since fewer tall tales and songs have been written about women, try your hand at writing ballads about both historical figures—Pocahontas or Sojourner Truth—and contemporary ones—Florence Griffith-Joyner or Sally Ride. Children can make their own songbooks to take home after the group composes the ballads.

Sourdough Slim's Kitchen is the food center, where children make whopper pancakes and top them with favorite toppings. Use the recipe for Big Batch Pancakes in the "Treasure Chest." Be sure to read or tell stories about Paul Bunyan's pancake eating as part of this learning/activity center!

THE SHOW GOES ON
(THE PROGRAM PLAN)

Act I—Greet children in costume as a popular tall tale hero or invite children to dress up themselves. As a simple alternative, simply put the name of a tall tale character on each child's back. Children then guess who they are by asking one another questions that can be answered with yes or no.

Act II—Assign children to one of the learning/activity centers—the Swappin' Spot, the Pack of Lies, the Tongue Twister Tent, the Yarnspinners Center, the Ballad Corner, or Sourdough Slim's Kitchen. In a school setting, children may participate in all of the centers during the course of this program/unit. In a public library, this may not be possible because of time restraints. If you don't use the activity center approach, share the Pack of Lies with the entire group.

Act III—Be sure to share many folk tales about tall tale heroes and heroines during this program/unit. Choose several of the picture book versions or shorter selections from the collections annotated in the bibliography. If you plan to make pancakes with the group, you will certainly want to read or tell at least one Paul Bunyan tale.

Act IV—Making whopper pancakes in small groups (part of Sourdough Slim's Kitchen) might be a fun way to end the program in a public library setting.

Act V—Save time to tell kids about other stories of the tall tale tradition. Sid Fleishman's McBroom stories and Carl Sandburg's Rootabaga stories are two examples. Check the bibliography for other suggestions.

THE TREASURE CHEST

Story Starters for Yarnspinners

These starters will generate ideas for tall tale writing activities. Before you begin this project, read a number of the starters with your students. Discuss some of the elements of the tall tale: folksy style; the admission that the storyteller doesn't always tell the truth but definitely is this time; concrete details to "prove" the truth (the squash was 102 pounds and it measured 37 and one-half inches across); and exaggerated comparisons (it was so cold our words froze in midair and we had to wait until spring to finish our conversation. The corn grew so tall it pushed right up into the clouds and caused the worst rainstorm we've had in these parts for almost a decade. That woman was so skinny she didn't even have a shadow).

Do little "warm-ups" by supplying sentences for students to finish. A few examples: "It was so cold on our street last week..." "My sister lost so much weight on her diet...." Think absurd, but begin believable.

Next are some story starters for full-fledged tall tales. Students could write the stories on long vertical scrolls—an appropriate format for a tall tale. Or they could "publish" their work on word processors or typewriters.

Story Starters

There was, in the early days of these United States, the biggest, clumsiest mountain climber and his name was....

Now I imagine you've heard tell about Paul Bunyan and his big pancakes, but wait till you hear this yarn about Big Wilma and her waffle iron.

My Great Aunt Mattie grew up on a farm a long time ago. She's told me lots of tales about life on the farm, but the one I like best is about the summer it got so hot....

I come from a long line of gardeners. I think I might have even been related to those people who gardened in the Garden of Eden. Anyway, if you don't believe that one, listen to this story about the year the corn got so tall in my dad's garden....

Big Batch Pancakes

The recipe for these pancakes first appeared in *Mudluscious: Stories and Activities Featuring Food for Preschool Children*, by Jan Irving and Robin Currie (Libraries Unlimited, 1986). Deb Lease created the recipe, but I have added a few touches of my own.

Big Batch Mix

10 cups all-purpose flour
2½ cups instant nonfat dry milk
½ cup sugar
¼ cup baking powder
2 Tb. salt

Mix above ingredients and store in large, airtight container. Put in a cool, dry place for up to eight months. This recipe will make about 13 cups of pancake mix.

Paul Bunyan's Blueberry Special Cakes

1½ cups pancake mix (recipe above)
1 egg, slightly beaten
1 cup water
3 Tb. oil

Combine ingredients and stir just until blended. Let stand 5 minutes. Pour mixture into an electric skillet. Cook 3 to 4 minutes, then turn and sprinkle a few big blueberries onto each pancake. This recipe makes 10 to 12 4-inch pancakes, but you may want to make whopper-size cakes just like Paul Bunyan would have eaten. Serve with blueberry syrup or a sprinkle of powdered sugar.

Special Project for Whoppers

Using the illustration in Figure 5.1, make a giant tongue for sharing tongue twisters with the children in your classroom or library. This makes a whopper of a display, too!

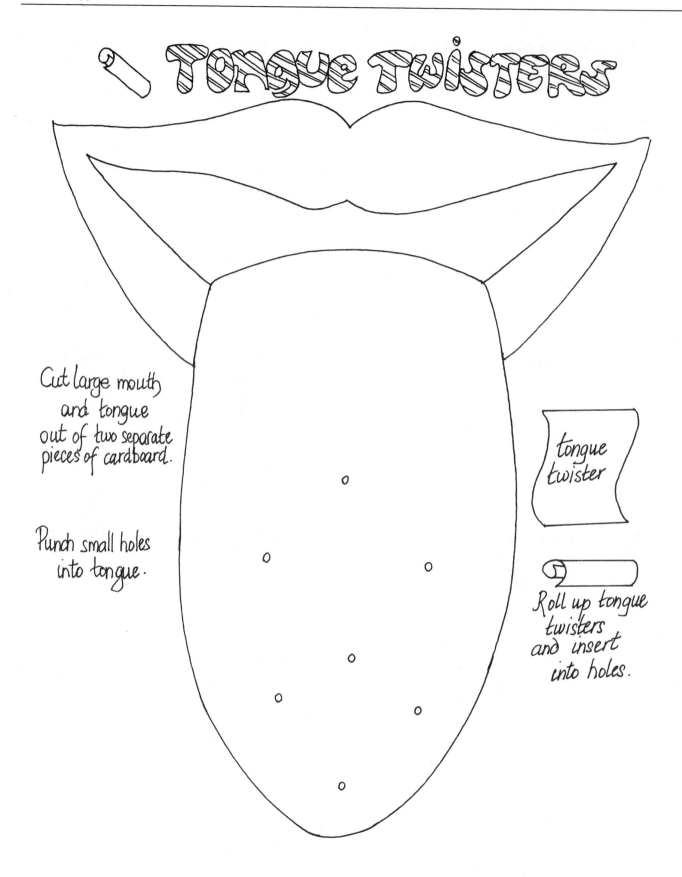

Fig. 5.1.

IN THE LIMELIGHT (PUBLICITY)

Adapt the publicity release in the preface and use the publicity flyer in Figure 5.2. The Pack of Lies, described in "Setting the Stage," makes an intriguing display/promotion idea to create interest before the program/unit begins.

Fig. 5.2.

BIBLIOGRAPHY

Aliki. **The Story of Johnny Appleseed**. Prentice-Hall, 1963.
    A gentle biography of John Chapman, the man who planted apple trees across the country, emphasizes his peace-loving nature and states repeatedly that he was friends with everyone from bears to Indians. Chapman is not the boastful figure that appears in many tall tales, but his life and legend continue to interest children.

Blair, Walter. **Tall Tale America**. Illustrated by Glen Rounds. Coward, McCann, Geoghegan, 1944.
    Relates the stories of 15 American folk heroes then proposes ways to resurrect some of them to help the United States win World War II. The last chapter draws links between American heroes in the 1940s and in the early days of our history.

Botkin, Benjamin Albert, ed. **A Treasury of American Folklore**. Crown, 1944.
    This "encyclopedia" is divided into six parts with various subsections that cover heroes, killers, miracle men, patron saints (Abraham Lincoln, Johnny Appleseed), tall talk, pranks, humorous anecdotes, yarns and tall tales, ghost stories, and ballads. An excellent teacher resource.

Cohen, Carol Lee. **Sally Ann Thunder Ann Whirlwind Crockett**. Illustrated by Ariane Dewey. Greenwillow, 1985.
    Sally Ann, wife of Davy Crockett, was "made of thunder with a little dash of whirlwind." She could do just about anything and was afraid of nothing, but she never bragged and never fought without good reason. When Mike Fink tries to scare her, she scares him until his teeth permanently rattle whenever he tries to brag again. A welcome tall tale with a heroine to include in this program/unit.

d'Aulaire, Ingri, and Edgar Parin d'Aulaire. **Buffalo Bill**. Doubleday, 1952.
    Bill Cody grew up a skilled sharpshooter and horseback rider. His accomplishments included being a Pony Express rider, a soldier in the Civil War, an Indian fighter, and star of his own Wild West Show. The bright drawings and text tell us that Buffalo Bill told his own tall tales and enjoyed the fame he won in his own lifetime.

Dewey, Ariane. **Febold Feboldson**. Greenwillow, 1984.
    Seven short chapters tell events in different years of the Nebraska farmer's life. The weather creates problems from late snow to extreme heat with grasshoppers, but Feboldson always seems to come up with solutions, even if they are outrageous.

Dewey, Ariane. **Gib Morgan, Oil Man**. Greenwillow, 1987.
    Unlike Paul Bunyan, Gib Morgan was a real oilman in Pennsylvania in the nineteenth century. He had an uncanny sense for finding oil, so he traveled from California to Mexico advising oil companies. His ideas for feeding a pipeline crew—mixing pancake batter in a storage tank then letting it flow through a pipeline to the griddle—are reminiscent of Paul Bunyan's legends.

Dewey, Ariane. **Laffite the Pirate**. Greenwillow, 1985.
    Five short tales about the daring pirate who captured ships and so much treasure that he buried it all along the coasts of Louisiana and Texas. Anyone who has ever tried to find the treasure has found only ghosts.

Dewey, Ariane. **The Tea Squall**. Greenwillow, 1988.
    When the grand women of American tall tales get together, their "tea squall" is *nothing* like a prim and proper tea party. Betsy Blizzard's pet buzzard delivers invitations to Sal Fink, Florinda Fury, Katy Goodgrit, Zipporinda, and Sally Ann Thunder Ann Whirlwind Crockett. The women ride alligators, swim, or just jump over the river to swap tales with all the trappings of tall tale humor and stuff themselves on a plentiful feast. The clothes and food described in this tale could inspire class projects. This story is a most welcome addition to American folklore, which has not produced enough good tales with female characters.

Emberley, Barbara, and Ed Emberley. **The Story of Paul Bunyan**. Prentice-Hall, 1963.
    Strong woodcut illustrations and brief text relate the gargantuan appetite and exploits of Paul Bunyan, from his clearing of the Midwest and discovery of Babe the Blue Ox to his ridding the country of man-eating jackrabbits.

Emrich, Duncan. **The Hodgepodge Book: An Almanac of American Folklore**. Illustrated by Ib Ohlsson. Four Winds, 1972.
   A grab bag about many topics: seasons, holidays, jokes, superstitions, proverbs, game rhymes, cumulative stories, and so on. Good resource for class projects.

Felton, Harold W., compiler. **Legends of Paul Bunyan**. Illustrated by Richard Bennett. Knopf, 1947.
   This compilation—almost Paul Bunyan-size—has a forword by an old logger, legends written down by Esther Shephard, Dell McCormick, Harold Felton, and others, plus poems by Carl Sandburg, and much more.

Felton, Harold W. **Mike Fink: Best of the Keelboatmen**. Dodd, Mead, 1960.
   A real person, Mike Fink was born just north of the Ohio River at Fort Pitt. He became the most famous keelboatman on the Ohio, an Indian scout, and a sharpshooter.

Felton, Harold W. **Pecos Bill and the Mustang**. Prentice-Hall, 1965.
   In this account of the legendary cowboy, Pecos Bill tames a mountain lion to ride, sleeps on a gravel bed, and eventually wins over the famous Pacing Mustang of the prairies to become his own horse.
      Also by Felton: **Pecos Bill: Texas Cowpuncher**. Knopf, 1950.

Fleishman, Sid. **McBroom's Ear**. Illustrated by Kurt Werth. W. W. Norton, 1969.
   Josh McBroom's farm grows crops quickly, but one summer the grasshoppers almost destroy the entire crop. McBroom and his children, Willjillhesterchesterpeterpollytimtommarylarryandlittleclarinda, try to beat off the grasshoppers but end up painting a giant ear of corn white to disguise it on the way to the fair. Plenty of nonsense and exaggeration in the tall tale tradition.
      Also by Fleishman: **McBroom Tells the Truth**. W. W. Norton, 1966.

Flora, James. **Grandpa's Farm**. Harcourt, Brace and World, 1965.
   These four tall tales relate stories about the big wind of '34, Grandma's miraculous cow salve, the terrible winter of '36, and the feats of Hatchy Hen.

Gleiter, Jan, and Kathleen Thompson. **Daniel Boone**. Illustrated by Leslie Tryon. Raintree, 1985.
   In this brief biography of the legendary pioneer man, Daniel Boone lives contentedly in the wilderness, using the survival skills learned from Indians when he was a boy.

Gleiter, Jan, and Kathleen Thompson. **Johnny Appleseed**. Illustrated by Harry Quinn. Raintree, 1987.
   A short biography about John Chapman, the man who planted apple trees all over the Ohio River Valley. This account acknowledges the tall tale side of the story. ("Some people claimed that his pack got so full of apple seeds that he had to wear his saucepan like a hat. Not all of the stories were true, but they showed that people thought he was something special.")

Keats, Ezra Jack. **John Henry, An American Legend**. Pantheon, 1965.
   Born with a hammer in his hand, John Henry grows up to lay railroad tracks, tunnel through mountains, and even outdistance a steam drill. Keats's bright illustrations are as full of gusto as the John Henry legend itself.

Kellogg, Steven. **Paul Bunyan**. Morrow, 1984.
   Bunyan's size and exuberance as a baby cause so many problems that his parents move to the backwoods. As years pass, he finds Babe the Blue Ox, heads west, overcomes the monstrous Gumberoos, clears the Midwest, and digs the St. Lawrence River and the Great Lakes. He also shaves the slopes of the Rockies and gouges a trench we know as the Grand Canyon. Kellogg's robust illustrations are packed with so much fun that the Bunyan legend lives all over again for another generation.

Kellogg, Steven. **Pecos Bill**. Morrow, 1986.
   As his family is crossing the Pecos River by covered wagon, young Bill is yanked overboard by a fish. Raised by coyotes, he becomes tough enough to later tackle wild critters, even the Hell's Gulch Gang. Pecos Bill invents the lasso, develops the rodeo, and becomes the best cowboy of all. Kellogg's pictures simply burst with the energy and action typified by this tall tale hero.

Leach, Maria. **The Rainbow Book of American Folk Tales and Legends**. Illustrated by Marc Simont. World, 1958.

A compendium of legends about folk heroes, state lore, local legends, bad men, tall talk, and strange tales. Amusing line drawings accompany the text. This text is an excellent resource for tales to read aloud or for a reference book on American legends not found in other sources.

Lyman, Nanci A. **Pecos Bill**. Illustrated by Bert Dodson. Troll Associates, 1980.

Raised by coyotes because he falls out of his family's covered wagon, Pecos Bill ends up being the greatest cowboy of all time. He teaches bronc-riding and hog-tying, starts the rodeo tradition, and helps increase herds.

McCormick, Dell. **Tall Timber Tales**. Illustrated by Lorna Livesley. Caxton Printers Ltd., 1972.

Paul Bunyan's adventures from Maine to California are told in a series of incidents. Bunyan digs Puget Sound, Babe the Blue Ox drinks up the river that was once in the Grand Coulee, a new cook turns Bubbling Springs Lake into pea soup, and Bunyan and his men trap giant mosquitos in their big griddle.

Pepper, Dennis. **A Book of Tall Stories**. Oxford University Press, 1987.

Several dozen tall stories appear in a tall book format. The source for the stories is the English-speaking world, not just the United States.

Rounds, Glen. **Ol' Paul, the Mighty Logger**. Holiday, 1949.

This account begins in the first person, so tales have a sense of immediacy. Bunyan tackles Skookum, a giant bullsnake, and other critters, Bedcats, and Huggags. He builds the Rockies and straightens out the Whistling River. Funny line drawings add to the humorous text.

Sandburg, Carl. **Rootabaga Stories. Part One.** Illustrated by Michael Hague. Harcourt Brace Jovanovich, 1988.

Hague's magical illustrations accompany the nonsense of Rootabaga Country peopled with the Huckabuck family, Blixie Bimber, and corn fairies.

Also by Sandburg: **Rootabaga Stories. Part Two.** Harcourt Brace Jovanovich, 1989.

Schwartz, Alvin. **Chin Talk**. Illustrated by John O'Brien. Lippincott, 1979.

Funny words and colorful phrases for talking about everyday things are arranged from A to Z. Instructions are given for making up new words.

Schwartz, Alvin. **Kickle Snifters and Other Fearsome Critters**. Illustrated by Glen Rounds. Lippincott, 1976.

Whimsical illustrations and text introduce creatures from U.S. folk literature such as the goofus bird, which flies backward, and the squonk, which cries all the time. These characters can inspire creative writing projects.

Schwartz, Alvin. **Tomfoolery, Trickery and Foolery with Words**. Illustrated by Glen Rounds. Lippincott, 1973.

Jokes and riddles taken from folklore include circular tales with no ending ("The bear went over the mountain"), hoax tales in which the ending is the trick, "catches" ("Is your refrigerator running?"), and riddles ("What's black and white and red all over?"). Includes extensive source notes and bibliography.

Schwartz, Alvin. **A Twister of Twists, A Tangler of Tongues**. Illustrated by Glen Rounds. Lippincott, 1972.

Researching his subject in the folklore collections of the Library of Congress and the University of Pennsylvania, Schwartz brings together tongue twisters that will delight young and old alike. Some are brief phrases, others are poems or stories.

Schwartz, Alvin. **Whoppers: Tall Tales and Other Lies Collected from American Folklore**. Illustrated by Glen Rounds. Lippincott, 1975.

In this collection of tall tales, the noted folklorist includes anecdotes about ordinary people, the weather, animals, and narrow escapes. The introduction and notes sections explain tall tales and give lengthy sources for the stories in the book, respectively.

Shapiro, Irwin. **Tall Tales of America**. Illustrated by Al Schmidt. Guild Press, 1958.

Colored paintings accompany nine chapters about well-known tall tale figures Pecos Bill, Paul Bunyan, and others, as well as some not so well known such as Anthony, the trumpeter of New Amsterdam.

Shepard, Esther. **Paul Bunyan.** Illustrated by Rockwell Kent. Harcourt, 1924.
  A robust account of Paul Bunyan, who digs the Columbia River for a log chute to the ocean and performs other feats that give him heroic status. Numerous sources were consulted including the advertising booklets for the Red River Lumber Company of Minneapolis, whose symbol was Paul Bunyan.

Stoutenburg, Adrien. **American Tall-Tale Animals.** Illustrated by Glen Rounds. Viking Press, 1968.
  Tales about the strange animals "lolloping around in the early days of our country, according to the stories people tell," include the squonk, a weeping creature with poor-fitting skin that makes it impossible to capture, and the whiffle-poofle Pecos Bill once met.

York, Carol. **Febold Feboldson, the Fix-It Farmer.** Illustrated by Irene Trivas. Troll Associates, 1980.
  In his desire to fix a bad situation, Febold Feboldson comes up with solutions that make fog for Nebraska, turn timber wolves into prairie dogs, and bring Death Valley sands to the western shores. Brief text can be read by children beginning to read on their own.

York, Carol Beach. **Mike Fink.** Illustrated by Ed Parker. Troll Associates, 1980.
  Mike Fink, the river boatman, tamed alligators on the Mississippi, poled keelboats on the rivers, and won almost every kind of contest people could dream up. Brief text works well as a read-aloud for a program or class period.

ENCORES
(OTHER PROGRAMS AND PROJECTS)

American tall tales are just one kind of folklore to share with children. Another focus for a program/unit might be the fable. Choose from the fables of Aesop or La Fontaine as well as Indian fables collected in The Panchatantra. Contemporary writers and illustrators often borrow from these traditions. Marcia Brown's *Once a Mouse* is one example. Other authors create their own fables. Arnold Lobel's *Fables* and Leo Lionni's many picture books including *Frederick* (a new version of Aesop's ant and grasshopper fable) are just two examples. Fables are short stories that can be retold with puppets or as story theatre, with the teacher/librarian reading or telling the story and children pantomiming the actions. Try fable writing with children. Begin with a list of maxims and then build a simple narrative around each one.

Folk tales, the largest category of folklore, offer many possibilities for programs and units. Focus on the folk tales of one country or part of the world or develop a program on one folk tale theme such as runaway food (the gingerbread boy, the pancake, the bun, johnny cake) or cooking pots (rice, porridge, pasta). Read the stories, make up your own versions, and cook the appropriate food.

Folk literature forms the basis of many of our traditions and is retold with each new generation. Programs and projects in this area will always bring forth "new clothes from old cloth," for there are as many ways to share these stories as there are people to tell them.

6
Dinosaur

INTRODUCTION

Just because dinosaurs lived more than 200 million years ago doesn't mean they have been forgotten. On the contrary, as time goes on, people seem to become even more interested in finding out all they can about these strange beasts that inhabited the earth long before the appearance of human beings. Children seem to be especially fascinated with dinosaurs, in much the same way as they are attracted to monsters and dragons. But the study of dinosaurs has an added attraction—these beasts really lived and learning about them is often a child's introduction to science. And, because we are still discovering information about these ancient beasts, the children we teach today may be the scientists of tomorrow who will answer some of the questions that still mystify us about dinosaurs.

With so many books published on the topic today, the bibliography in this chapter is lengthy, but certainly not comprehensive. (In fact, the number of books published on dinosaurs seems to increase in proportion to the length of time these prehistoric beasts have been extinct.) Fiction, nonfiction, poetry, and dinosaur art books are all included. Schools that use literature across the curriculum will find well-written books that inspire science and art projects as well as material for creative writing and dramatics. Libraries that provide programs and resources for young people will find ideas that can be adapted for their own settings. However, the dinosaur books and activities in this chapter are but a brief introduction.

PURPOSE OF PROGRAM/UNIT

To explore the world of the dinosaur through literature and art projects and to increase children's knowledge and interest in this popular topic.

A LITTLE BACKGROUND ABOUT DINOSAURS

Although dinosaurs lived more than 200 million years ago, we have only known about them for about 200 years. We are still discovering dinosaur fossils in remote parts of the world and changing our ideas about what dinosaurs looked like, how they lived, and why they became extinct. Here are a few facts to explore further.

- Dinosaurs existed for about 150 million years and lived during the Mesozoic "Middle Life" era of the world. This era is further divided into three periods: the Triassic, Jurassic, and Cretaceous.

- Dinosaurs descended from a group of reptiles known as the thecodonts, which included both lizard-like and crocodile-like animals. Their hind limbs were longer than their front limbs so many of them stood upright.

- The group of animals we call dinosaurs was so varied that over 300 kinds have been identified. Dinosaurs are roughly divided into two groups—the saurischians, or "lizard hips," and the ornithischians, or "bird hips." There are two suborders of lizard hips and five suborders of bird hips.

- Dinosaurs ranged from small bird-size beasts to the largest land creatures, the Apatosaurus (also called Brontosaurus) and Diplodocus.

- The varieties of dinosaurs included the dinosaurs with spikes and plates, such as Stegosaurus and Ankylosaurus; those with horns, such as Triceratops; the duckbills, such as Hadrosaurus; and those with claws who were carnivorous, such as Tyrannosaurus.

- The Pterosaurs, a group of flying reptiles who also lived at this time, are often confused with dinosaurs. Some Pterosaurs, such as the Quetzalcoatlus, were as large as modern-day airplanes.

- The first dinosaur fossils were found about 200 years ago. Sir Richard Owens coined the word *dinosaur* from the ancient Greek words meaning "terrible lizard," because the first dinosaurs found looked like modern-day lizards. For a long time scientists thought dinosaurs were coldblooded reptiles who laid eggs, but today, ideas are changing.

- Scientists say dinosaurs were in a class of their own and related to birds and reptiles. Some say they were coldblooded, others say maybe they were warmblooded and moved swiftly. Perhaps some dinosaurs even gave birth to their young, but we know that many dinosaurs laid eggs.

- No one knows for sure why the dinosaurs became extinct. Several theories today suggest the sun's rays were blocked from the earth by a supernova or an asteroid that collided with the earth. When the earth cooled off, the dinosaurs died. But nothing has been proved, and this is just one of the questions we still have about dinosaurs.

SETTING THE STAGE (PREPARATION)

Recreate the world of the dinosaur in your classroom or library with some large foliage decorations made out of sheets of construction paper (see the "Treasure Chest" for a few suggestions). You may want to make a few dinosaur footprints, but if you choose the footprints of a large dinosaur, you will need a large space. (The stride of the Apatosaurus was 13 feet!) In one corner of the room, make a dinosaur nest out of crumpled brown wrapping paper and fill it with footballs for the dinosaur eggs. *The Big Beast Book*, by Jerry Booth (see the bibliography), has a chart with the sizes of different dinosaur eggs.

Make a dinosaur height chart (similar to a "growth chart") with the heights of different dinosaurs marked, so children can visualize their size compared to various dinosaurs. Not all dinosaurs were huge. Children may want to compare their heights to the Compsognathus, 1 foot high, Protoceratops, 2½ feet high, and Hysilophodon, 3 feet high.

Look at the space you have available and try to creatively compare it to the world of the dinosaur. Donald Carrick's illustrations for *Patrick's Dinosaurs*, by Carol Carrick, made me consider a second-story window in the library in terms of a dinosaur's height. We placed a dinosaur eye and portion of a dinosaur head, cut out of construction paper, behind one of the window blinds so children could imagine that a dinosaur had actually joined us at the library for our dinosaur program. The illustration in the "Treasure Chest" is a pattern for a dinosaur head. This setting will also be recreated in the dinosaur dioramas that children make to take home.

Set up learning centers in your classroom or library. One group of children can write dinosaur tales. Provide children with long sheets of paper to write the story of their own imaginary dinosaur, how it lived, and why it became extinct. Carol Carrick's *What Happened to Patrick's Dinosaurs?* is a good book to read for this activity since the boy in the story comes up with his own imaginative reason that dinosaurs are no longer with us. The dinosaur tale writers could insert their own names in the titles of their stories, such as "What Happened to Debbie's Dinosaurs?" An alternative approach would be to write a group story entitled "What Happened to the Dinosaurs of Lincoln School (or Lincoln Library)?" Brainstorm ideas with the children and include several of their explanations in the story along with illustrations from every child in the group.

Several excellent collections of dinosaur poems beg to be read aloud. Pass out selections from William Cole's *Dinosaurs and Beasts of Yore*, Jack Prelutsky's *Tyrannosaurus Was a Beast*, and Lee Bennett Hopkins's *Dinosaurs* to your students so they can practice reading selections aloud.

Invite young thespians to act out their favorite dinosaur stories as members of the Dimetron Dinosaur Players. Children can adapt such books as *Danny and the Dinosaur* (Syd Hoff), *Dinosaur Bob and His Adventures with the Family Lazardo* (William Joyce), or *Tyrone the Horrible* (Hans Wilhelm). The script "Please Don't Touch the Dinosaurs" in the "Treasure Chest" provides another possibility.

Art projects may be created in another learning center. Several books in the chapter bibliography provide numerous ideas. The dinosaur diorama in the "Treasure Chest" can be made as is, or children can turn the dinosaur shapes into stick puppets as an alternative project.

Since there is an ever-growing number of exciting dinosaur books, take the opportunity to assemble a large book display in the library or classroom. Prepare bibliographies of books about related topics—archaeological digs, modern reptiles and birds, dragons—as well as bibliographies of favorite dinosaur books.

THE SHOW GOES ON
(THE PROGRAM PLAN)

Act I—Invite children to enter the world of the dinosaur by taking "dinosaur strides" into the room along the path of dinosaur footprints. Children can make guesses about what kind of dinosaur left the eggs in the dinosaur nest, then compare their own heights to the dinosaur chart.

Act II—Children may be divided into interest groups according to the ideas in "Setting the Stage" or you may read to the whole group one of the dinosaur stories listed in the bibliography. An excellent choice for a wide age group (kindergarten through the middle school grades) is Carol Carrick's *Patrick's Dinosaurs*. In this picture book, a boy tells his younger brother about dinosaurs while the younger brother imagines a variety of the huge beasts walking across their city street and peeking into the second-story bedroom window. After you read the book, ask the children if they could imagine a dinosaur visiting the classroom or library. Place a part of a dinosaur (such as the head in the "Treasure Chest" section) behind a window shade or put a clawed foot across a baseboard to help children get into the spirit of the occasion. Size relationships of people to dinosaurs are fascinating to children and this kind of exercise will encourage them to think and imagine in creative ways.

Act III—Write dinosaur tales or invite children to participate in story theatre re-enacting one of the dinosaur stories in the bibliography. Present "Please Don't Touch the Dinosaurs" (see the "Treasure Chest") as readers theatre or as a skit.

Act IV—End by making a dinosaur project children can take home. The dinosaur diorama (in the "Treasure Chest") is an excellent choice because it gives children an opportunity to make something they can use as a backdrop for their own dinosaur plays.

THE TREASURE CHEST

Please Don't Touch the Dinosaurs

Characters
Narrator
Teddy
Ms. Sawyer
Alex
Drew
Museum guide

Give children scripts so they can perform this story as a readers theatre presentation. Call the group the Dimetron Dinosaur Players.

Narrator:	Teddy Turner knew more about dinosaurs than anyone else in his class. He wasn't a showoff about this, but that didn't matter. Sometimes his classmates gave him a hard time.
Ms. Sawyer:	Class, tomorrow we will be taking a trip to the natural history museum. We will visit a special traveling exhibit of dinosaurs. This will be a wonderful opportunity to step back into time to visit the world of the dinosaur.
Teddy:	(*to himself*) If only I could really step back into the world of the dinosaur.
Alex:	Are the dinosaurs at the museum alive?
Ms. Sawyer:	No, Alex, all dinosaurs are extinct.
Alex:	What does that mean?
Ms. Sawyer:	Teddy, do you know what extinct means?
Teddy:	Yes, it means dinosaurs aren't alive. They died out more than 150 million years ago.
Ms. Sawyer:	Very good, Teddy.
Alex:	Think you're smart, don't you?
Teddy:	Not really. I just happen to like dinosaurs.
Alex:	I'll show you, you showoff!
Drew:	Aw, Alex, lay off.
Alex:	Watch your step. Nobody tells me what to do!
Narrator:	The next day at the museum Ms. Sawyer told the class....
Ms. Sawyer:	Class, the museum show will begin in 15 minutes. We have just enough time to stop at the gift shop for souvenirs. Meet back here in exactly 15 minutes.

Narrator:	Teddy bought a model of his favorite dinosaur, a muddy brown Ankylosaurus. It had armored plates across its back and was four inches high. Stamped on the bottom of its right front leg were the words "Made in Hong Kong."
Alex:	What's that thing, smart guy?
Teddy:	My name's Teddy.
Alex:	Well, Teddy bear, what's that you've got?
Teddy:	It's an Ankylosaurus.
Alex:	Bet you made that up. I've never heard of an Ankylosaurus.
Drew:	Aw, leave him alone, Alex.
Alex:	Have you ever heard of an Ankylosaurus?
Drew:	Well, no, but—
Alex:	I told you he was a showoff!
Ms. Sawyer:	Class, it's time for the dinosaur show to begin. Please take your places in line.
Alex:	I was ahead of you, Teddy bear.
Ms. Sawyer:	Class, remember, be very careful. We will enter the dinosaur exhibit in darkness. When the lights come up, the dinosaurs will seem to come alive. But these are only simulations. Nothing at all can happen to you.
Alex:	Scared, smart guy?
Teddy:	Not really—
Alex:	I would be if I were you.
Teddy:	Please, don't—
Narrator:	The next thing he knew, Teddy was shoved. The dinosaur model in his hand was thrown somewhere into the darkness.

Museum guide:	Welcome to the world of the dinosaur! When the lights come up you will see before you life-size models of five dinosaurs: the Apatosaurus, the Dimetron, the Stegosaurus, the Tyrannosaurus, and the Ankylosaurus.
Drew:	Then there *was* an Ankylosaurus!
Teddy:	I've got to find my dinosaur model!
Museum guide:	Please do not touch the dinosaurs. In a moment the spotlight will highlight the lifelike movements of each. It is very dangerous to move into the path of any of these creatures when the lights come on. Please—do not move into the spotlighted area. Stay in the dark so the dinosaurs will not see you.
Narrator:	The lights flashed on. Teddy had stepped into the spotlight to grab his dinosaur model when—
Museum guide:	Quick, turn off the lights! Who knows what might happen if the dinosaurs spot that kid!
Drew:	Alex, what did you do to Teddy?
Alex:	Me? What do you mean?
Narrator:	But it was too late. Teddy was now in the spotlight. Right there in the middle of the dinosaurs. Then there was a blinding flash of light.
Museum guide:	This is catastrophic! Nothing like this has ever happened before!
Alex:	What happened to him?
Drew:	He ... disappeared ... into thin air! Wait till Ms. Sawyer gets ahold of you, Alex.
Alex:	Me? What do you mean?
Drew:	I wouldn't be in your shoes for a million bucks!
Narrator:	Teddy did not exactly disappear into thin air. But after the blinding flash of light no one could see him, just as you can't see when a camera flashbulb blinds your eyes.
	Before Ms. Sawyer could do a thing, the muddy brown, four-inch Ankylosaurus grew to the size of an elephant. Then it came charging into the darkness and flattened Alex until he looked like a postage stamp. The words *Hong Kong* were even imprinted backwards across his nose.

Museum guide: This is unheard of! Please, clear the museum this instant!

Ms. Sawyer: Class, I have never been so humiliated in all my life. Alexander, didn't you hear what the guide said? Do not touch the dinosaurs! How will we ever explain this to your parents?

(Alex shakes his head, over which he is wearing a brown grocery bag that has Hong Kong *written backwards on it.)*

Teddy, where are you? Can you hear me?

(From offstage Teddy speaks.)

Teddy: Yes, Ms. Sawyer, I can hear you. And I want you to know that I'm really happy now. You see, I've truly entered the world of the dinosaurs. What a wonderful opportunity!

Narrator: The story you have just heard is pure fantasy. But remember, please, don't ever touch the dinosaurs if you go to a museum. And on behalf of the Dimetron Dinosaur Players, thank you!

Art Projects Featuring Dinosaurs

Use the suggestions for leaves and vines in Figure 6.1 to simulate a prehistoric world for your classroom or library. The pattern for a dinosaur eye and head (Figure 6.2) can be hidden behind a window blind for heightened interest. And the dinosaur diorama (Figures 6.3 and 6.4) makes a much appreciated project that children will take home and enjoy again and again.

(Text continues on page 93.)

Fig. 6.1.

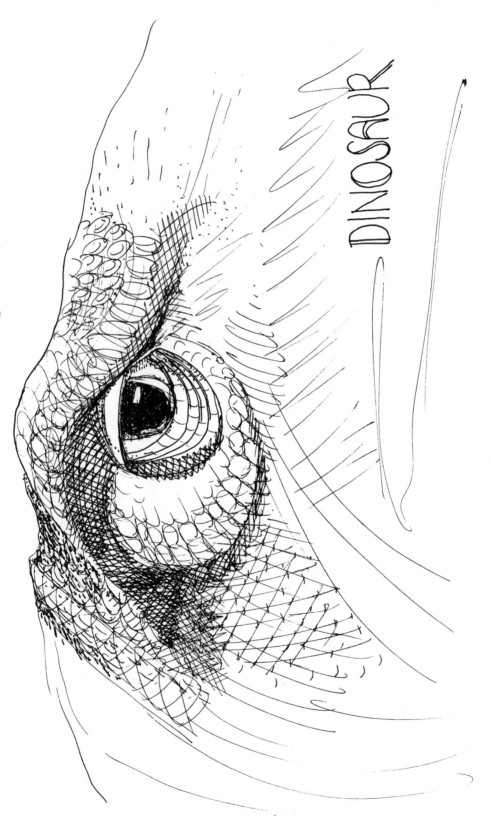

Fig. 6.2.

Fig. 6.3.

92 / Dinosaur

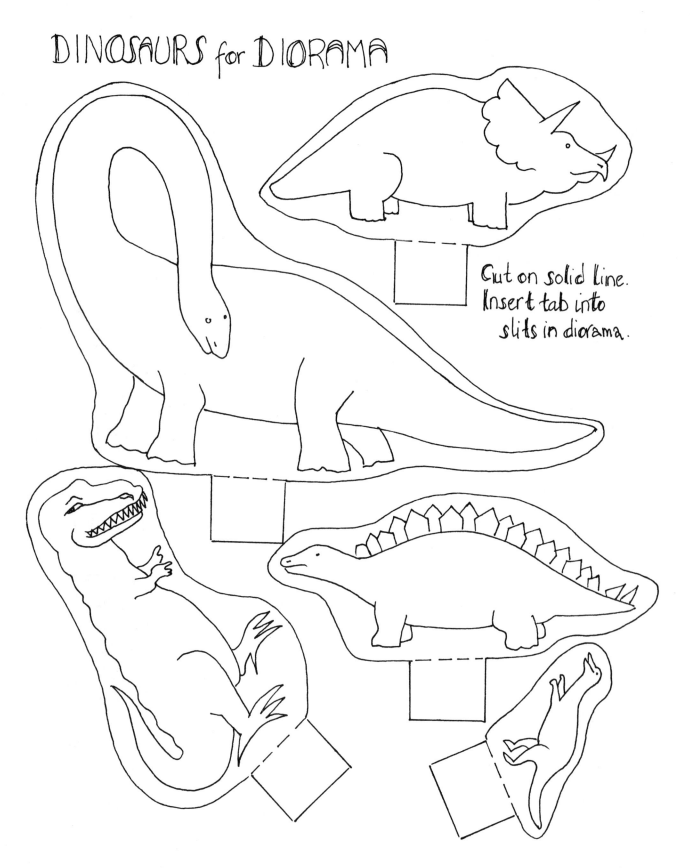

Fig. 6.4.

IN THE LIMELIGHT (PUBLICITY)

Use the flyer in Figure 6.5 to publicize this program and create dinosaur projects ahead of time to heighten interest in this program/unit.

Fig. 6.5.

BIBLIOGRAPHY

Aliki. **Digging Up Dinosaurs**. Crowell, 1981.
   Using a museum as a setting, this book shows how skeletons are used to identify various dinosaurs, how fossil hunters work, and how scientists build a complete dinosaur skeleton.

Aliki. **Dinosaur Bones**. Crowell, 1988.
   Text and illustrations briefly explain how scientists first gathered information about fossil bones found in the nineteenth century and how the fossils were formed.

Aliki. **My Visit to the Dinosaurs**. Crowell, 1985.
   A little boy visits a natural history museum and is briefly introduced to a dozen dinosaurs. The revised edition refers to the Apatosaurus rather than the Brontosaurus as in the earlier edition.

Arnold, Caroline. **Trapped in Tar: Fossils from the Ice Age**. Photographs by Richard Hewett. Clarion, 1987.
   This photo essay tells the story of the Rancho La Brea fossils—the Ice Age animals trapped in tar (*brea* is the Spanish word for tar) in the part of California that once was Mexico. The fossils found there are of animals from an age later than the dinosaurs (including mammoths and mastodons) but they range in age from 14,000 to 38,000 years old. The book shows the work of paleontologists and of the museum, built there in 1975, devoted to research and excavations.

Bates, Robin, and Cheryl Simon. **The Dinosaurs and the Dark Star**. Illustrated by Jennifer Dewey. Macmillan, 1985.
   Recent theories that an asteroid or comet struck the earth, thus bringing about the extinction of the dinosaurs, are explored.

Blumenthal, Nancy. **Count-a-saurus**. Illustrated by Robert Jay Kaufman. Four Winds, 1989.
   A jaunty counting book in rhyme spots 10 dinosaurs in silly situations; for example, "Four Iguanodon scratching itchy feet." Facts about each kind of dinosaur are given in the back.

Booth, Jerry. **The Big Beast Book: Dinosaurs and How They Got That Way**. Illustrated by Martha Weston. Little, Brown, 1988.
   This fun book is packed full of information about dinosaurs with suggestions for projects from making your own dinosaur eggs to lobbying state legislatures to name state fossils. Part of the Brown Paper School Book series.

Brandt, Keith. **Case of the Missing Dinosaur**. Illustrated by John Wallner. Troll Associates, 1982.
   The Blue Jays baseball team can't win without their dinosaur mascot, Irving, who is missing. They trace him to a circus and find out he was kidnapped to be a star of the show. This easy-to-read book combines two elements kids love—mysteries and dinosaurs.

Brasch, Kate. **Prehistoric Monsters**. Photographs by Jean-Philippe Varin. Salem House, 1985.
   This unique book makes you believe dinosaurs could still inhabit the earth because it shows photographs of realistic-looking dinosaur models in natural settings. The text provides an introduction to dinosaurs and a history of fossil excavations. Three dozen different species are described in alphabetical order.

Caket, Colin. **Model a Monster**. Blandford Press, 1986.
   Instructions are given for more than 50 dinosaur projects made from everyday materials such as pipe cleaners, corrugated cardboard, clay, sand, and even snow.

Carrick, Carol. **Big Old Bones**. Illustrated by Donald Carrick. Clarion, 1989.
   Back in the Old West, Professor Potts discovers some "big old bones" of a giant lizard. As he reassembles them, he makes a few mistakes in presenting the prehistoric "Tribrontosaurus Rex" to scientists all over the world. The author's informational note at the end explains many mistakes scientists have made in dinosaur discoveries, adding even more interest to this imaginative book.

Carrick, Carol. **Patrick's Dinosaurs**. Illustrated by Donald Carrick. Clarion, 1983.
   Patrick's older brother, Hank, tells him all about dinosaurs when they are on a trip to the zoo. Patrick imagines an apatosaurus in the zoo lake, stegosauruses walking down a city street, and a tyrannosaurus looking into their second-story bedroom window.

Carrick, Carol. **What Happened to Patrick's Dinosaurs?** Illustrated by Donald Carrick. Clarion, 1986.
Another story about Patrick, the kid who loves dinosaurs, provides an imaginary explanation of what happened to the dinosaurs. According to Patrick, dinosaurs did all the work for people but grew tired of it so they built a spaceship to leave for outer space. A good read-aloud that can be a springboard for creative writing.

Cauley, Lorinda Bryan. **The Trouble with Tyrannosaurus Rex.** Harcourt Brace Jovanovich, 1988.
This story of Ankylosaurus and Duckbill devising a plan to outwit Tyrannosaurus Rex was written for Cauley's sons, who wanted an imaginative dinosaur tale with dinosaurs that were almost human.

Cobb, Vicki. **The Monsters Who Died: A Mystery about Dinosaurs.** Illustrated by Greg Wenzel. Coward-McCann, 1983.
Paleontologists search for fossils and fit them together to form skeletons so they can understand the dinosaurs, but their ideas change as more evidence is found. Cobb shows the first reconstructions of certain dinosaurs—the Iguanodon, the Brontosaurus (now referred to as Apatosaurus)—then later reconstructions, after more fossils have been found. The ideas that scientific knowledge changes and mystery still surrounds our knowledge are clearly communicated.

Cohen, Daniel. **Dinosaurs.** Illustrated by Jean Zallinger. Doubleday, 1987.
Basic questions about dinosaurs are answered and dinosaurs are described in groups according to their physical characteristics—armored dinosaurs, horned dinosaurs, duckbills, etc.

Cole, Joanna. **Dinosaur Story.** Illustrated by Mort Kunstler. Morrow, 1974.
About one dozen well-known dinosaurs are described in a text that younger readers will be able to understand. Some recent knowledge is not included, such as the name Apatosaurus instead of Brontosaurus.

Cole, William, ed. **Dinosaurs and Beasts of Yore.** Illustrated by Susanna Natti. Collins, 1979.
Over three dozen dinosaur poems by favorite British and American children's poets, including Shel Silverstein's advice not to pinch a dinosaur because "he might get sore," Lillian Moore's conversation with a dinosaur skeleton in a museum, and William Cole's sober thought that we'll be extinct like the dinosaur in a million years.

Dinosaurs. Selected by Lee Bennett Hopkins. Illustrated by Murray Tinkelman. Harcourt Brace Jovanovich, 1987.
Building on the growing popularity of dinosaurs, the well-known poetry expert presents a collection of dinosaur poems by more than a dozen established poets. Some speculate what might happen if dinosaurs could step out of books, others admire skeletons in museums or imagine a prehistoric morning.

Dixon, Dougal. **Be a Dinosaur Detective.** Illustrated by Steve Lings. Lerner, 1988.
This book presents many dinosaur facts by asking kids to imagine they are tracking down clues from fossils. Projects such as modeling clay and clothespin dinosaurs are presented along with quizzes and a glossary.

Dixon, Dougal. **Hunting the Dinosaurs and Other Prehistoric Animals.** Illustrated by Alan Male and Steve Kirk. Photographs by Jane Burton. Gareth Stevens, 1987.
One of four titles in the New Dinosaur Library, this title examines life on Earth, focusing on dinosaur discoveries and museum restorations. Pronunciation guides and facts appear in the back.

Elting, Mary. **The Macmillan Book of Dinosaurs and Other Prehistoric Creatures.** Illustrated by John Hamberger. Macmillan, 1984.
This large book tells the story of early life on Earth with a special focus on dinosaurs and how paleontologists have learned about them through studying fossils.

Emberley, Michael. **Dinosaurs!** Little, Brown, 1980.
Emberley's step-by-step approach to drawing dinosaurs makes it possible for children to actually create pictures of their favorite creature. Instructions are given for 10 dinosaurs plus general drawing techniques, along with a little information on dinosaurs.

Freedman, Russell. **Dinosaurs and Their Young.** Illustrated by Leslie Morrill. Holiday House, 1983.
  Because of the 1978 discovery of a nest of baby duckbill dinosaurs and adult duckbill skulls nearby, scientists are now reexamining their theories about this dinosaur's behavior. Freedman gives a brief, fascinating account.

Gibbons, Gail. **Dinosaurs.** Holiday House, 1987.
  Brief text and bright pictures tell about dinosaurs who lived 70 million years ago and the fossils that were first discovered 200 years ago. About one dozen kinds of dinosaurs are described.

Gibbons, Gail. **Prehistoric Animals.** Holiday House, 1988.
  Just after the dinosaurs disappeared, other animals appeared, including the 11-foot tall Alticamelus, one of the first camels; the Platybelodon, an early elephant with a mouth something like the mouth of a hippopotamus; and the bony armored Glyptodon. Informative text and brightly colored pictures appeal to even the youngest science reader.

Glovach, Linda. **The Little Witch's Dinosaur Book.** Prentice-Hall, 1984.
  Crafts, party, and food ideas on a dinosaur theme include a dinosaur pencil case, paper-bag dinosaurs, and a dinosaur party cake with a green cream frosting.

Hoff, Syd. **Danny and the Dinosaur.** Harper and Row, 1958.
  When Danny goes to the museum, he meets a most congenial dinosaur who leaves with him, gives him a ride, plays games with Danny and a group of children, and goes on outings all over town before returning to the museum. An easy book that still delights young readers 30 years after it was originally published.

Horner, John R., and James Gorman. **MAIA: A Dinosaur Grows Up.** Illustrated by Doug Henderson. Courage Books, 1987.
  Co-authored by a paleontologist and a science writer, this fictionalized account of a Maiasaura ("Good Mother Lizard," a duckbill dinosaur) provides an exciting narrative based on scientific fact. The illustrations are big paintings by a noted dinosaur artist.

Joyce, William. **Dinosaur Bob and His Adventures with the Family Lazardo.** Harper and Row, 1988.
  The Lazardo family brings back a dinosaur from a safari in Africa. Dinosaur Bob learns to play trumpet and baseball, and becomes a treasured family member.

Kaufman, John. **Flying Reptiles in the Age of Dinosaurs.** Morrow, 1976.
  The group of flying dinosaurs known as Pterosaurs are introduced and a brief explanation tells how they evolved from wingless dinosaurs. A number of particular species are described, from those small as sparrows to others the size of airplanes.

Kellogg, Steven. **Prehistoric Pinkerton.** Dial, 1987.
  Pinkerton, a teething puppy, is taken along on a class trip to the museum. When he begins to gnaw a priceless dinosaur bone, however, trouble starts.

Klein, Norma. **Dinosaur's Housewarming Party.** Illustrated by James Marshall. Crown, 1974.
  Octopus and Green Worm decide to give Dinosaur a housewarming party when he moves into his spacious new apartment. Everyone brings housewarming presents, but the most popular gift is the purple inflatable chair from Octopus.

Knight, David C. **The Battle of the Dinosaurs.** Illustrated by Lee J. Ames. Prentice-Hall, 1982.
  Many dinosaurs—large plant-eaters, large meat-eaters, and the duckbills—are presented along with "dino-facts" such as the theories why dinosaurs became extinct.

Koontz, Robin Michal. **Dinosaur Dream.** Putnam's, 1988.
  In this wordless picture book, a boy goes to bed with an assortment of stuffed dinosaurs and travels into a dream adventure with the colossal beasts of yore.

Kroll, Steven. **The Tyrannosaurus Game.** Illustrated by Tomie de Paola. Holiday House, 1976.
  Because it's raining, a group of children make up an inside game of storytelling. Each child relates an adventure with a Tyrannosaurus and then passes the story on to the next child. The adventure include the Tyrannosaurus crashing through a window, getting stuck on the stair, and sneezing people out the door. This could inspire your students to make up their own dinosaur stories.

Lambert, David. **A Field Guide to Dinosaurs.** Avon, 1983.
   The core of this thick book is an identification of dozens of dinosaurs, divided into six subgroups. Other chapters explain the evolution of dinosaurs, fossil hunting, and museum displays, with a list of museums around the world that have special dinosaur exhibits.

Lambert, Mark. **50 Facts about Dinosaurs.** Warwick Press, 1983.
   Facts about dinosaurs are presented in a question-answer format with big, color illustrations and up-to-date text.

Langley, Andrew. **Dinosaurs.** Franklin Watts, 1987.
   This easy-to-read fact book is divided into brief sections on such topics as plant eaters, meat eaters, defense, and escape. It also includes a pronunciation key and a brief glossary.

Lauber, Patricia. **Dinosaurs Walked Here.** Bradbury Press, 1987.
   The well-known science writer explains how fossil remains tell us about prehistoric life and discusses some of the new theories about dinosaurs such as the nurturing instincts of duckbill dinosaurs.

McGowen, Tom. **Dinosaurs and Other Prehistoric Animals.** Illustrated by Rod Ruth. Rand McNally, 1978.
   Twenty-five dinosaurs are described in detail and pictured in large, color illustrations.

Mannetti, William. **Dinosaurs in Your Backyard.** Atheneum, 1982.
   Mannetti discusses new theories about whether dinosaurs were warmblooded, smart, fast moving, and the predecessors of birds.

Mash, Robert. **How to Keep Dinosaurs.** Illustrated by William Ruston, Philip Hood, and Diz Wallis. Penguin, 1983.
   This tongue-in-cheek guide to selecting and taking care of dinosaurs as pets includes such topics as "Dinosaurs for Beginners," "Dinosaurs as Lap Pets," and "Dinosaurs for Zoos."

Most, Bernard. **Dinosaur Cousins?** Harcourt Brace Jovanovich, 1987.
   The author whimsically observes similarities between various dinosaurs and modern counterparts. A few examples are the rhinoceros and the Triceratops, the Hadrosaurus (duckbill dinosaur) and the duck, the kangaroo and the Kakuru.

Most, Bernard. **If the Dinosaurs Came Back.** Harcourt Brace Jovanovich, 1978.
   A series of clever and useful statements follow the starter, "If the dinosaurs came back...." Dinosaurs are shown painting houses, plowing fields, acting as ski slopes, and in many more fun capacities.

Most, Bernard. **Whatever Happened to the Dinosaurs?** Harcourt Brace Jovanovich, 1984.
   Absurdly humorous answers to the question "Whatever happened to the dinosaurs?" suggest such possibilities as they are wearing disguises and we don't recognize them, they're lost in the middle of the jungle, they are living underground, or they are at the North Pole. The illustrations are as funny as the text.

Parish, Peggy. **Dinosaur Time.** Illustrated by Arnold Lobel. Harper and Row, 1974.
   Eleven dinosaurs are briefly described in a text appropriate for beginning readers.

Parker, Steve. **The Age of Dinosaurs!** Illustrated by John Lobben. Gareth Stevens, 1984.
   The text describes the beginnings of life and focuses on dinosaurs, grouping them according to their characteristics—"Dinosaurs with Sails," "Dinosaurs in Suits of Armor," "The Fiercest Dinosaurs."

Prelutsky, Jack. **Tyrannosaurus Was a Beast.** Illustrated by Arnold Lobel. Greenwillow, 1988.
   Fourteen dinosaurs are paid tribute with the humorous verses of this popular poet. They range from the Tyrannosaurus, who "ruled the ancient out-of-doors / and slaughtered other dinosaurs," to the plant-eating Brachiosaurus, who "nibbled leaves that were tender and green / it was a perpetual eating machine." The watercolor and pen illustrations by Lobel were among his last.

Richler, Mordecai. **Jacob Two-Two and the Dinosaur.** Illustrated by Norman Eyolfson. Knopf, 1987.
   Jacob Two-Two's father brings him a small lizard from Kenya that grows to become a dinosaur. In this deliciously humorous novel, the dinosaur creates so many problems that he and his owner run away to British Columbia. This book makes an excellent read-aloud for the middle elementary grades.

Rosenbloom, Joseph. **Dictionary of Dinosaurs.** Illustrated by Haris Petie. Julian Messner, 1980.
    The first part of this book discusses recent theories that dinosaurs may have been warmblooded. Several dozen dinosaurs are then described in an A to Z arrangement. Drawings complete the text.

Sattler, Helen Roney. **Baby Dinosaurs.** Illustrated by Jean Day Zallinger. Lothrop, Lee, and Shepard, 1984.
    Numerous baby dinosaurs are described—how they were protected, how large they were, where their skeletons have been found. A few dinosaurs whose eggs have never been found may have given birth to living young, according to this source. A time chart and pronunciations are provided for the 19 dinosaurs included in this book.

Sattler, Helen Roney. **Dinosaurs of North America.** Illustrated by Anthony Rao. Lothrop, Lee, and Shepard, 1981.
    The dinosaurs that inhabited the mass of North America during the Mesozoic era are described. Some of the latest theories about dinosaur extinction are discussed in the last chapter.

Sattler, Helen Roney. **The Illustrated Dinosaur Dictionary.** Illustrated by Pamela Carroll. Lothrop, Lee, and Shepard, 1983.
    This up-to-date reference book is so enjoyable you will want to read it from cover to cover. Special features include pronunciation and derivation for dinosaur names, numerous line drawings, and locations of dinosaurs in the United States and the rest of the world.

Sattler, Helen Roney. **Pterosaurs, the Flying Reptiles.** Illustrated by Christopher Santoro. Lothrop, Lee, and Shepard, 1985.
    This book introduces the group of flying reptiles that are often confused with dinosaurs, perhaps because they inhabited the earth at the same time. Some of the strange creatures in this group include Ctenochasma ("comb mouth"), which had hundreds of needle-like teeth in their long jaws, and Pterodaustro ("winged and hairy"), which had teeth resembling baleen.

Sattler, Helen Roney. **Tyrannosaurus Rex and Its Kin: The Mesozoic Monsters.** Lothrop, Lee, and Shepard, 1989.
    Watercolor illustrations and detailed text describe the Carnosaurs, who were swift, possibly warm-blooded, and the largest land predators.

Schwartz, Henry. **How I Captured a Dinosaur.** Illustrated by Amy Schwartz. Orchard Books, 1989.
    A little girl who is fascinated with dinosaurs finds an Albertosaurus on a camping trip.

Selsam, Millicent. **Strange Creatures That Really Lived.** Illustrated by Jennifer Dewey. Scholastic, 1987.
    Some of the strange creatures described in pictures and brief text are the 12-foot long Archelon, the largest turtle that ever lived (comparable in size to the length of a Volkswagen); the Archaeopteryx (the first bird); and the giant sloth, which was as tall as a telephone pole. The many size comparisons make the text understandable and lively to use with children.

Simon, Seymour. **The Smallest Dinosaurs.** Illustrated by Anthony Rao. Crown, 1982.
    The seven dinosaurs included in this easy text were about the size of a chicken or a dog. The topic is fascinating to children, who usually think all dinosaurs were huge.

Steiner, Barbara. **Oliver Dibbs and the Dinosaur Cause.** Illustrated by Ellen Christelow. Four Winds, 1986.
    Inspired by an incident that really happened in Colorado, this story concerns a fifth-grade boy who rallies his classmates to make the Stegosaurus the Colorado state fossil.

Sterne, Noelle. **Tyrannosaurus Wrecks, A Book of Dinosaur Riddles.** Illustrated by Victoria Chess. Crowell, 1979.
    This collection is full of whimsical riddles and illustrations, such as: "What do you get when dinosaurs crash their cars?" Answer: "Tyrannosaurus wrecks."

Wilhelm, Hans. **Tyrone the Horrible.** Scholastic, 1988.
    Tyrone the Horrible, a Tyrannosaurus Rex, bullies poor Boland dinosaur unmercifully until Boland comes up with a clever solution. This read-aloud story for children is mostly about bullies but uses dinosaur characters.

Wilson, Ron. **Pteranodon**. Illustrated by Doreen Edwards. Rourke, 1984.
  One of the more than two dozen dinosaur books of a similar format by several different authors, all published by Rourke, this volume describes the flying reptile often confused with dinosaurs. The book recounts a narrative about Pteranodon, then provides facts, and suggests simple projects at the end.

ENCORES (OTHER PROGRAMS AND PROJECTS)

The popularity of dinosaurs continues to grow, with the publication of more books each season and a flood of dinosaur-related toys and party items. The topic is good for a summer-long library program or for a school to use for a major unit or year-long theme to promote reading. Each of the learning centers suggested in "Setting the Stage" could be expanded into week-long activities. Trips to natural history museums and science centers in your community make excellent culminating events. And don't feel as if you have to be the expert on this topic. Since so many children read voraciously about dinosaurs, they will probably teach you. Ask older children in middle school to help you set up a "dinosaur dig" or a field trip for younger children to discover the natural world where you live.

7
Pooh's Birthday Party

INTRODUCTION

Winnie-the-Pooh might possibly be the "best of all possible bears." Ever since Pooh's creation in 1926, his fame has seemed to grow, and therefore he is the main subject for this chapter on book character programs. Though specific ideas are included for Pooh's Birthday Party, this chapter is intended to inspire the teacher or librarian to plan other programs and units celebrating the merits of fictional characters in children's books. Brief suggestions for other character program/units are mentioned in the "Encores" section. Also, Chapter 8 focuses on the authors of children's books, so there will be some overlap. (Some author background on A. A. Milne is given in this chapter, for example.) But this program uses the format of a party, an especially appropriate choice since parties are held in all of the Pooh books. In a school setting, the party might be the culmination of a unit on fictional book characters or on Pooh books in particular. In a public library, the party might be the program itself.

PURPOSE OF PROGRAM/UNIT

To draw children into the fantasy world of Winnie-the-Pooh through stories, songs, crafts, and foods, in a party atmosphere they will enjoy.

A LITTLE BACKGROUND ABOUT WINNIE-THE-POOH (AND HIS CREATORS)

- The author of the Winnie-the-Pooh books was A. A. Milne. Mr. Milne was born in London, England, on January 18, 1882. He was a freelance journalist in London, but he is best known for the four children's books he wrote. These books are *When We Were Young, Winnie-the-Pooh, Now We Are Six*, and *The House at Pooh Corner*. The books were written for Milne's only child, Christopher Robin, who also becomes a fictionalized character in the stories and poems. Milne died in 1956.

- The illustrator of the Winnie-the-Pooh books was Ernest H. Shepard, who was also born in London. Mr. Shepard also illustrated Kenneth Grahame's *The Wind in the Willows*, but he is especially remembered for his little pen and ink drawings in the Pooh story and poetry books. Ernest Shepard was born in 1879 and died in 1976.

- Winnie-the-Pooh is a teddy bear whose real name is Edward Bear, but he is almost always referred to as Pooh Bear or Winnie-the-Pooh, names given to him by his beloved child owner, Christopher Robin. The phrase "bear of very little brain" is also applied to him, but never maliciously. The real Pooh was a stuffed animal given to the real boy Christopher Robin when he was one year old. In the books, Pooh is sometimes shown as a toy bear, but he steps into the stories and becomes a fully animated and believable bear. Pooh gets confused about the meanings of many words, just like some children do, and gets in and out of trouble, but he is always lovable.

- Some of Pooh's companions in the stories are Piglet, a small, jumpy little pig who is ever faithful to Pooh; Eeyore, the rather gloomy gray donkey; Kanga and her baby, Roo; Rabbit; Owl; and the high-spirited Tigger. The child who interacts with all these animals is Christopher Robin.

- The setting for the Pooh stories is 100 Aker Wood, an enchanted place that children can visit only in the books by Mr. Milne, or in the program you can create for them.

- Winnie-the-Pooh was created in 1926, so he is more than 60 years old, but he seems to remain ageless and his popularity has never waned. The book publisher E. P. Dutton sold over 150,000 copies of the book *Winnie-the-Pooh* in the year it was published and sales continue to be just as high today. In addition to the original books, many other editions have been printed. (A selection of these in included in the bibliography of this chapter.)

- The actual Pooh animals have made numerous tours in the United States, but the travels took their toll on poor Pooh. He now lives in the New York Public Library.

- When Pooh turned 60 years old, in 1986, numerous activities were held in his honor in England and the United States. The International Teddy Bear Club began a 41-country tour. A Teddy Bear Picnic and Orchestral Concert were held at the Barbican Centre and a party was held at the Regents Park Zoo, both in London. Various celebrations have been held in the United States including one at the Pooh Corner Bookstore in Madison, Wisconsin.

- Walt Disney made a popular film of Winnie-the-Pooh and the Disney corporation has produced many of their own Pooh-related books. A. A. Milne's widow sold the non-book rights to Disney, who changed the style of illustration to a cartoon bear. Although Disney's Pooh has been commercially popular, educators and literary critics have criticized the Disney version of Pooh because it lacks the charm and poetic quality of the original text and illustration.

- Recurring flurries of publishing and toy-related items keep Winnie-the-Pooh ever alive to children, but nothing can quite replace the thrill of a child's adventure into the books themselves. This program will combine activities with the original stories and poems.

SETTING THE STAGE (PREPARATION)

Your classroom or library can celebrate Pooh's birthday with a party that children plan and enjoy themselves. Before the party you will want to set up different activity areas around the room.

In one corner children make their own party hats, Pooh ears on a headband, using the pattern in Figure 7.3 in the "Treasure Chest" section. In another corner, children make the party favors, Eeyore Memo Tails (samples shown in Figure 7.1), so they will be able to remember better than Eeyore. In another corner, children can write their own Pooh "hums" (their own little poems) on bear shapes (sample shown in Figure 7.2). If you have cooking facilities, another activity center could be making refreshments for the party. Many other projects might be created in activity centers as well. Children can make their own choices based on ideas in *The Pooh Party Book* or *The Pooh Get-Well Book* (both by Virginia H. Ellison).

Simple refreshments not included in these books that can be prepared just before the party might be brown bread sandwiches spread with honey and cut in the shape of a bear, fresh lemonade, and gummy bears. You could order a sheet cake decorated with Pooh Bear from your local bakery to make the party really traditional.

Decorate the room with plenty of balloons, since Pooh's parties in the Milne books always call for balloons. Order promotional items for your party from the marketing department of E. P. Dutton. They stock a Pooh poster and a brightly colored mobile of Winnie-the-Pooh hanging onto a blue balloon amid a cluster of clouds. Both items are free to teachers and librarians if you write for them. Address requests to: Children's Book Marketing, Dutton Children's Books, 2 Park Avenue, New York, New York 10016.

Children can help make invitations for the party using the sample invitation in Figure 7.4, which can also serve as a publicity announcement. Children are invited to bring along their own teddy bears or stuffed animals. Prepare bear buttons for all guest bears using the sample in Figure 7.1.

If this program is part of a longer school unit on Winnie-the-Pooh, consult *Developing Learning Skills through Children's Literature*, by Mildred Knight Laughlin and Letty S. Watt (Oryx, 1986), for further Pooh activities that are part of a full unit.

Choose a group of children to be the Pooh Corner Players, who will perform the readers theatre script provided in the "Treasure Chest." Since much of this script comes from copyrighted material, a brief outline is given. You may easily adapt the script for classroom or library purposes under the "fair use" provision of the Copyright Law of 1976.

Be sure to set aside a portion of your library or classroom for a display of Winnie-the-Pooh books and other books about bears. Make the corner as inviting as you can for browsing and reading by adding pillows, throw rugs, or a few comfortable chairs. Hang signs that read "Pooh Corner."

THE SHOW GOES ON (THE PROGRAM PLAN)

Act I—As children (and their guest teddy bears) come to the party, give the children party hats and the bear buttons that have been made ahead of time.

Act II—Sing Pooh songs from *The Pooh Song Book*. Invite a guest who plays the piano or guitar to accompany the songs, or play the records listed at the end of this chapter.

Act III—Play Pin the Tail on Eeyore or have a teddy bear parade around the room with all the guest bears.

Act IV—The Pooh Corner Players present their program.

Act V—Children sing "Happy Birthday" to Pooh (and the birthday hum that is included in the "Treasure Chest"), enjoy party treats, and make party favors to take home.

THE TREASURE CHEST

Pooh Party Hum (Tune: "On Top of Old Smokey")

We're having a birthday
Party for Pooh.
You all are invited
To celebrate Pooh. (*spoken*: Who? Pooh!)

He's stout and he's hungry
For cottleston pie
But honey's his favorite
I sure don't know why.

He likes birthday parties
So won't you all come?
And sing his fine praises
With this Pooh Bear Hum? (*spoken*: Come!)

The Pooh Corner Players Present

To complete this script you will need to go to the original sources. Commentary has been included that you might use along with the poems and stories. An alternative to this approach would be to use "In Which Tigger Comes to the Forest and Has Breakfast," a script based on the Milne story that can be found in Carolina Feller Bauer's *Presenting Reader's Theatre* (Wilson, 1987).

Pooh's Birthday Party Script

You will need at least five people, but you may want to use more than this to give more children an opportunity to read. Please note that editions referred to are those listed in the bibliography at the end of this chapter.

Choose two readers to begin with a rousing rendition of the "Anxious Pooh Song" (the song begins with the line "three cheers for Pooh"). This poem is found in Chapter 10 of the book *Winnie-the-Pooh*. The two readers alternate reading lines just as they appear in the book. After this cheery opening, the readers continue.

Reader 1: That was a little song sung by Winnie-the-Pooh, just to welcome you to Pooh's Birthday Party. Does anyone know how old Pooh is?

Reader 2: Well, he was created in 1926, so he must be more than 60 years old!

Reader 1: That's right! But you know, I don't think of Pooh as ever growing old. He seems more like Peter Pan, who never grows up.

Reader 2: I know what you mean. I don't think Pooh and his friends who live in 100 Aker Wood ever change.

Reader 1: Who is your favorite Pooh character?

Reader 2: Winnie-the-Pooh, of course.

Reader 1: Your second favorite?

Reader 2: I don't know. Piglet is such a good friend of Pooh's. But Tigger is so bouncy.

Reader 1: But so are Kanga and Roo.

Reader 2: And then there are Rabbit and Owl. And Eeyore. What a bother! He's always so gloomy!

Reader 1: Oh, Eeyore! I love him—maybe because he needs a little extra loving.

Reader 2: Remember the time he lost his tail?

Reader 1: Of course! And Pooh found it. Owl was using Eeyore's tail for a bell pull. But Pooh got the tail back, and Christopher Robin nailed it on Eeyore so everything was all right in the end.

Reader 2: I remember the time Christopher Robin said he saw a Heffalump.

For this next scene, four children take the parts of Christopher Robin, Winnie-the-Pooh, Piglet, and the narrator. The narrator reads all the description and the other three read the appropriate lines. Start at the beginning of Chapter 5, "In Which Piglet Meets a Heffalump," from the book *Winnie-the-Pooh* and continue reading for about seven pages until Pooh and Piglet say goodnight. Then continue with the following commentary:

Reader 1: And the trap is set? Do they really catch a Heffalump?

Reader 2: Don't you remember that the best part comes when Pooh goes back to the "Cunning Trap?"

Reader 1: And then he catches a Heffalump?

Reader 2: Well, not exactly. He goes back to the trap because there's a jar of honey in the bottom of the pit. Pooh sticks his head in the jar and gets stuck.

Reader 1: Oh, no!

Reader 2: Oh, yes! In the meantime, Piglet goes to the trap to see if they caught a Heffalump.

Reader 1: And did they?

Reader 2: Let's just finish the scene.

The readers continue with the story in Chapter 5 of *Winnie-the-Pooh*, as the narrator says, "So he crept to the side of the Trap and looked in...." Continue reading the last two and a half pages of the chapter in character.

The next portion of this script continues the theme of Pooh getting stuck in tight places. The commentary continues.

Reader 1: Pooh always seems to get stuck in tight places.

Reader 2: Remember the time he went to visit Rabbit and got stuck in Rabbit's hole? Everybody tried to pull him out, but the only thing that worked for Pooh was to go on a diet so he would get thin enough to pop out of Rabbit's hole.

Reader 1: Teddy bears seem to have a problem with being chubby. There's a popular A. A. Milne poem about that. Here's a bit of it.

(*Reader 2 reads the last eight lines of "Teddy Bear" from* When We Were Very Young.)

Reader 1: I can think of one time that I would like to be a bear.

Reader 2: When?

Reader 1: In wintertime! Here's a poem about that.

(*Reader 1 reads "Furry Bear" from* Now We Are Six.)

Reader 2: In the wintertime I'm always reminded of the Pooh hum "tiddely pom." Let's have everyone here help me read this poem. When I say the words "tiddely pom," I will point to you and you say them along with me.

(*Reader 2 reads the "tiddely pom" poem from Chapter 1, "In Which a House Is Built at Pooh Corner for Eeyore," from* The House at Pooh Corner.)

Reader 1: That poem makes me feel cold, just like the song Christopher Robin sings when he leads the expotition to the North Pole.

(*Reader 1 reads the song "Sing Ho! for the Life of a Bear!" from Chapter 8, "In Which Christopher Robin Leads an Expotition to the North Pole," from* Winnie-the-Pooh.)

Reader 2: Because we are celebrating Pooh's birthday at a party we would like to read about another birthday party, for Eeyore.

Choose five children to read the following parts through this scene: Narrator, Eeyore, Pooh, Piglet, Owl. Begin reading Chapter 6, "In Which Eeyore Has a Birthday and Gets Two Presents," from *Winnie-the-Pooh*.

Narrator: One day Eeyore the donkey was looking especially sad so Pooh asked him why he seemed so sad.

The reading begins with Eeyore's line, "Sad? Why should I be sad?" and continues with the dialogue between Pooh and Eeyore. The scene ends with Eeyore's line, "...if everybody else is going to be miserable too—"

Reader 1: Well, Pooh, of course, knows what to do. He goes home to find a present for Eeyore.

Reader 2: What does he find?

Reader 1: A jar of honey, but—

Reader 2: But what?

Reader 1: He remembers that he ate the honey. So Pooh goes to Owl to ask advice.

The two children reading Owl and Pooh parts begin when Pooh greets Owl, "Good morning," and continue reading for two and a half pages until Pooh says, "Oh, I see."

Reader 2: In the meantime, Piglet trots off to his house to get a balloon for Eeyore. But, on the way, he falls down and—

Readers continue with the bang of the balloon line and continue reading their parts until Eeyore is "as happy as could be."

Reader 1: And now we will leave 100 Aker Wood so we can all sing our own birthday song for Pooh. Will you all join me in singing "Happy Birthday" to Pooh?

Art Projects for Pooh's Party

Make bear buttons (Figure 7.1) for the children to pin on their favorite stuffed animals, and use the patterns for bear shapes, bear party hats, and Eeyore's tail (Figures 7.1-7.3) to complete the festivities.

(Text continues on page 110.)

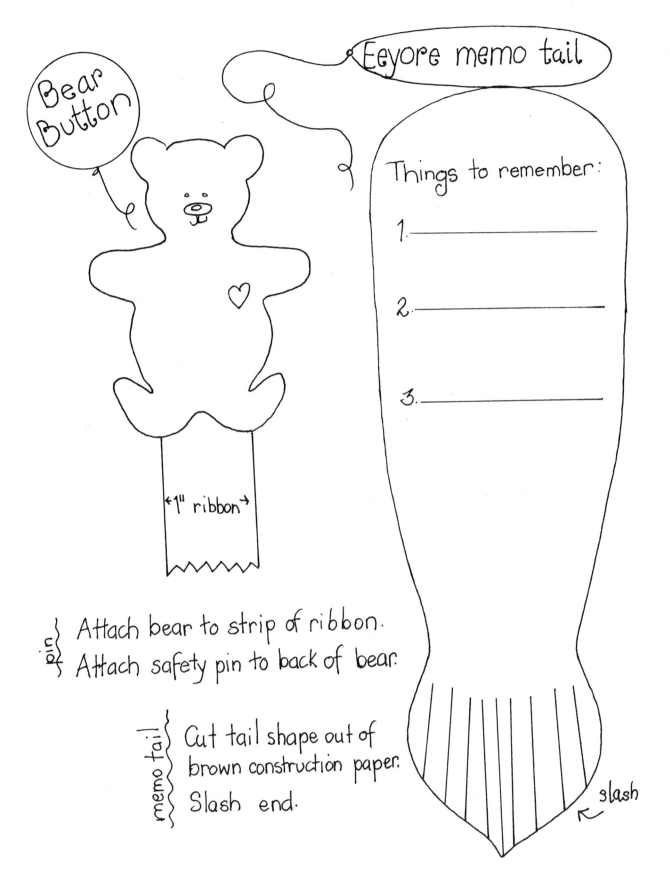

Fig. 7.1.

Fig. 7.2.

Bear Party Hat

1. Cut headband out of 1½" wide strip of brown construction paper. Adjust to head size. Overlap ends and staple.

2. Cut crosspiece out of 1½" wide strip of brown construction paper (approx. 10" long - fit to size)

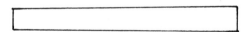

3. Cut two brown ears construction paper ear shapes.

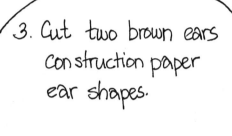

4. Staple ears to crosspiece.

fold ears up on fold line.

5. Staple crosspiece to headband.

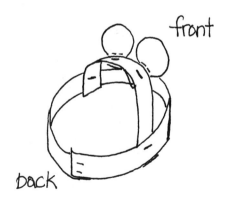

Fig. 7.3.

IN THE LIMELIGHT (PUBLICITY)

The publicity flyer for this program takes the form of a party invitation. Use the sample provided in Figure 7.4 and fill in your own details.

Fig. 7.4.

BIBLIOGRAPHY

The Pooh Books and Related Titles

Ellison, Virginia H. **The Pooh Cook Book**. Illustrated by Ernest H. Shepard. Dell, 1969.
　Inspired by the Pooh storybooks, this popular cookbook (now, unfortunately, out of print, but check your library) presents appealing recipes in such chapters as "Smackerels, Elevenses, and Teas" and "Provisions for Picnics and Expotitions." Many recipes include honey (of course); others are for typical Pooh foods such as "Cottleston Pie" and "Cucumber or Mastershalum Leaf Sandwiches." A particularly intriguing recipe for "Hip Papy Bthuthdth Thuthda Bthuthdy Cake I" (yes, that's the correct spelling!) calls for 1-2-3-4 ingredients. The method is as fun as the cake. Shepard's illustrations and quotes from Milne's books will encourage children to read the original books.

Ellison, Virginia H. **The Pooh Get-Well Book**. Illustrations by Ernest H. Shepard. Dell, 1973.
　This addition to the popular Pooh activity book series includes recipes and activities "to help you recover from Wheezles and Sneezles." The recipe for "Honey and Lemon Juice for a Squeaky Voice" sounds so comforting that children should call for more home remedies. Tigger's recipe for "Honey-Peach Extract of Malt" might be served after you read Chapter 2 of *The House at Pooh Corner*. There are dozens of good ideas, including large pictures of the main characters for children to trace on their own.

Ellison, Virginia H. **The Pooh Party Book**. Illustrated by Ernest H. Shepard. E. P. Dutton, 1971.
　This companion to *The Pooh Cook Book* is just as appealing, although it is also out of print. Check your library for a copy. Decorations, food, games, and favors are suggested for parties including: An Eeyore Birthday Party; A Picnic, Swimming, and Expotition Party; A Honey-Tasting Party for Pooh; and A Woozle-Wizzle Snow Party.

Milne, A. A. **The Christopher Robin Story Book**. Illustrated by Ernest E. Shepard. E. P. Dutton, 1966.
　Published in this format for the first time in 1966, this volume contains 19 poems selected by the author from his two books of poetry and six stories from the two storybooks.

Milne, A. A. **The House at Pooh Corner**. Illustrated by Ernest H. Shepard. E. P. Dutton, 1928.
　In this second collection of Pooh Bear stories, we meet a bouncy new friend, Tigger, and find Pooh and Piglet trying to help their friend Eeyore by building him a house.

Milne, A. A. **Now We Are Six**. Illustrated by Ernest H. Shepard. E. P. Dutton, 1927.
　Christopher Robin shares center stage of this second volume of poetry with his friend Pooh Bear in the poems "Us Two" and "The Friend." There are also poems about "sneezles" and raindrops and solitude.

Milne, A. A. **Pooh Goes Visiting**. With decorations after the style of Ernest H. Shepard. Adapted by Robert Cremins. Intervisual Communications, 1987.
　This "carousel" book, in which the reader ties back the cover to form five three-dimensional scenes, shows Pooh gulping down honey and later shows him stuck in Rabbit's hole. This is a fascinating addition to the Pooh library that will make an excellent display item.

Milne, A. A. **Pooh and Some Bees**. With decorations after the style of Ernest H. Shepard. Adapted by Robert Cremins. Intervisual Communications, 1987.
　A companion volume to *Pooh Goes Visiting*, this carousel book displays five scenes with Pooh climbing the honey tree, floating into the air with a blue balloon in hand, and then being shot down.

Milne, A. A. **Pooh's Alphabet Book**. Illustrated by Ernest H. Shepard. E. P. Dutton, 1975.
　This small book explores the alphabet with words and brief excerpts from Milne's books. Some entries are characters, such as Christopher Robin and Eeyore, and others are concepts or objects, such as mistake and honey.

Milne, A. A. **Pooh's Counting Book**. Illustrated by Ernest H. Shepard. E. P. Dutton, 1982.
　The numbers one to ten are introduced with excerpts from Milne's books of prose and poetry. The number two, for example, is illustrated with part of the poem "Us Two." Small book format is good for small group sharing but not for a large storytime group.

Milne, A. A. **When We Were Very Young.** Illustrated by Ernest H. Shepard. E. P. Dutton, 1924.

Christopher Robin is the central character of this first volume of poems though several bears appear in the verses. Some favorite poems include "Buckingham Palace," "Four Friends," and "Disobedience," with the memorable and repeated line "James James Morrison Morrison Weatherby George Dupree."

Milne, A. A. **Winnie-the-Pooh.** Illustrated by Ernest H. Shepard. E. P. Dutton, 1926.

In this collection of stories we are introduced to Edward Bear, better known as Winnie-the-Pooh, and his friend Christopher Robin. Pooh often gets into tight spots, but his loyal friends Piglet, Kanga, Rabbit, and Owl generally help him out. Together they go on an "expotition" to the North Pole, nearly catch a Woozle, and give the melancholy donkey Eeyore a cheery birthday party.

Milne, A. A. **The World of Pooh.** Illustrated by Ernest H. Shepard. E. P. Dutton, 1957.

The two classic storybooks *Winnie-the-Pooh* and *The House at Pooh Corner* are presented in one volume, with full-color illustrations in addition to the already familiar black-and-white sketches.

The Pooh Song Book. Words by A. A. Milne. Music by H. Frazer-Simson. Illustrated by Ernest H. Shepard. E. P. Dutton, 1961.

This volume contains 17 hums, 14 songs, and a musical accompaniment to "The King's Breakfast." Context from the books is provided for each hum.

Resources for Other Book Character Programs

Anderson, Gretchen, ed. **The Louisa May Alcott Cookbook.** Illustrated by Karen Milone. Little, Brown, 1985.

The author researched nineteenth-century cookbooks and combined these with excerpts from *Little Women* and *Little Men* in which the foods are mentioned.

Boxer, Arabella. **The Wind in the Willows Country Cookbook.** Illustrated by Ernest H. Shepard. Scribners, 1983.

Five categories of recipes, "Food for Staying at Home," "Food for Staying in Bed," "Food for the Storage Cupboard," "Food for Excursions," and "Food for Celebrations," are inspired by the memorable characters in Kenneth Grahame's classic. Children will especially love "Toad-in-a-Bad-Hole" (the egg and sausage dish) in tribute of Toad.

Macdonald, Kate. **The Anne of Green Gables Cookbook.** Illustrated by Barbara Di Lella. Oxford University Press, 1988.

Little quotes from the Anne of Green Gables books introduce such delectable treats as "Miss Ellen's Pound Cake." Some are perfect for an Anne of Green Gables picnic program—"Poetical Egg Salad Sandwiches" and "Old-Fashioned Lemonade."

MacGregor, Carol. **The Fairy Tale Cookbook.** Illustrated by Debby L. Carter. Macmillan, 1982.

This appealing cookbook invites children to reread the fairy tales as the recipes are prepared. The perfect book character party might include "The Wicked Queen's Poison Baked Apples" from *Snow White*, "Strega Nona's Magic Pasta," and "The Witch's Gingerbread House Cookies."

Travers, P. L., and Maurice Moore-Betty. **Mary Poppins in the Kitchen.** Illustrated by Mary Shepard. Harcourt Brace Jovanovich, 1975.

When Mrs. Brill, the Banks family cook, has to take an emergency leave, Mary Poppins steps into the kitchen. Little stories about the beloved English nanny combine with menus and recipes from an Edwardian kitchen. Prepare some of the dishes ahead of time or ask children to make them for this program. Try some of the "very" British ones such as Dundee Cake or shepherd's pie.

Sound Recordings

Milne, A. A. **The Poems of A. A. Milne.** Read by Judith Anderson. Caedmon.

Twenty-two poems from the two poetry books by Milne are read by the famous British actress.

Milne, A. A. **Winnie-the-Pooh.** Starring Jack Gilford. Golden Records.
Music and a jolly reading by the Broadway comic actor combine to give a variety of Pooh and Christopher Robin hums.

Milne, A. A. **Winnie-the-Pooh and Eeyore.** Told and sung by Carol Channing. Caedmon.
This spirited recording presents four chapters from Milne's books including the Heffalump and the Woozle episodes.

Milne, A. A. **Winnie-the-Pooh and Kanga and Roo.** Told and sung by Carol Channing. Caedmon.
Among the episodes on this record is the hilarious one when Baby Roo is captured and Piglet slips into Kanga's pouch.

ENCORES (OTHER PROGRAMS AND PROJECTS)

Book parties and programs can be planned around other favorite fictional characters. Here is a starter list to get you going.

- Monkey around with everyone's favorite, Curious George. Serve banana milkshakes and make monkey-face masks. Houghton Mifflin will send you a poster of George and Book Mates sells the stuffed toy to brighten up your room. Book Mates, a division of Listening Library, sells books and cassettes along with related puppets and stuffed animals. For information, write Listening Library, Park Avenue, Old Greenwich, Conn., 06870-9990.

- Throw a Wild Things Party with children making paper bag versions of Maurice Sendak's popular characters so everyone can join in the rumpus when you read the story aloud.

- Invite your students to come as favorite book characters at a Mad Tea Party. Selected characters can read the tea party scene from *Alice in Wonderland*. Share riddles and serve tea sandwiches.

- Another favorite party I've planned uses a Peter Rabbit theme. Since Beatrix Potter's books are too small to read in a large group, divide children into small, Peter Rabbit-size groups and select an older child or parent to share favorite Potter stories. Serve carrot sticks, cucumber sandwiches, and camomile tea.

- Plan your own book party using suggestions from the chapter "Book Parties" in Caroline Feller Bauer's *Handbook for Storytellers* (ALA, 1977), or use the book character cookbooks listed in the bibliography for this chapter.

8
Author! Author!

INTRODUCTION

While authors of books for young people may never hear the resounding chant "Author! Author!" upon the final curtain of a children's play or the reading of a children's book during library storytime, they are becoming celebrities nonetheless. Some educators and consultants decry this trend because they feel the emphasis should be upon the literature itself and not upon the authors. The class assignment that requires each student to write a letter to a "real live author" has been soundly criticized as a tiresome exercise at the very best, and certainly one that keeps authors from writing their books. In spite of this criticism, children are fascinated with meeting and knowing more about the authors and artists of the books they have come to love. This chapter suggests ways to bring authors into your classroom or library.

The structure of this chapter differs somewhat from the other chapters in this book. It is less "fact packed" in terms of specific information about specific authors. Several books in the chapter bibliography will give you that kind of information. Rather, this chapter provides models for developing author-related programs of your own.

PURPOSE OF PROGRAM/UNIT

To introduce children, teachers, librarians, and interested adults to the authors/illustrators of books through a variety of author-related program ideas.

A LITTLE BACKGROUND ABOUT AUTHOR PROGRAMS

Author-related programs include the author focus program, in which the author does not make a personal appearance. These may range from birthday parties for the author to full-scale units in which children study an author's life and works in depth. Several sources listed in the bibliography will aid the teacher or librarian in developing programs of this kind.

One particularly good source for author-related programs is Sharron L. McElmeel's *An Author a Month (for Pennies)*. In the introduction to her book, McElmeel points to one advantage of studying literature by focusing on an author: The student gains an understanding of the whole body of work of that author and can see relationships between the works. Often, books are influenced by incidents in the author's life as well.

Author visits range from an appearance in a school or library for a day or several days to a longer author-in-residence arrangement in which the author works with children over a period of time. Most of the information given in this chapter refers to a brief author visit, but the full range of possibilities is examined in David Melton's excellent book *How to Capture Live Authors and Bring Them to Your Schools*. (Full bibliographic and ordering information is given in the bibliography for this chapter.)

Another kind of author visit that has not been as fully explored in the literature is the visit by telephone, or the author conference call. More information is provided in the next section about this activity.

SETTING THE STAGE (PREPARATION)

First, decide what kind of author program/unit you want to plan. Is it an author-related program, an author visit by phone, or a personal appearance by an author? The following steps briefly describe each.

The author-related program might take the form of an author birthday party or an event that celebrates the works of a single author. The planning and format for this kind of program would be similar to the Pooh's Birthday Party program/unit described in Chapter 7. A list of suggested author programs and activities for an author-related program appear in the "Encores" section of this chapter. As well, sources in the bibliography will provide author-related program ideas.

The author visit by telephone can be an alternative to the more expensive and complicated personal appearance. The Iowa City public school system has been using conference calls to introduce elementary school children to authors for several years. Victoria Walton and Barbara Stein, elementary media specialists in Iowa City, are enthusiastic about the benefits. The expense, for example, is minimal. If you are interested in exploring this, first talk with your local telephone company about renting or purchasing a speaker phone, so the author's voice can be heard by the entire class of students.

Select the author to call in much the same way as you would choose an author for any program. Begin with authors who write books your students are especially interested in. Contact the author's publisher to see if the author would be receptive to a phone call. Perhaps the publisher can suggest other names if your first choice doesn't work out.

Contact the author by letter or phone to arrange a time for the conference call. Some authors will only agree to do a few calls a year. Others feel this is a reasonable alternative to traditional methods of keeping in touch with kids that still leaves them enough time to write their books.

Before you place the conference call, have your students do biographical research in standard reference sources, just as they would if the author were making a personal appearance at your school or library. Some standard reference sources are listed in the bibliography. My favorite is *Something About the Author*, but smaller school systems and libraries may not be able to afford this source. In any case, children should be familiar with the basic facts of the author's life so their questions go beyond the information found in standard sources. In addition to biographical background, students should be familiar with the books the author has written. Students should read one or two of the author's books on their own, but the classroom teacher or librarian can read one book aloud to the class as well. Finally, make a list of questions to ask during the call. Students can work in groups to write questions and then one person from each group can be the designated communicator when the call is placed.

Make the call at the appointed time with the communicators asking questions for the entire class. A 15- to 20-minute long distance telephone call will be the cost for your students to get acquainted with an author. If you have selected an author who is interested in talking with children and have made an effort to prepare your students, the experience should be worthwhile. As a follow up, have students write thank-you notes to the author.

With this much advanced preparation involved in a brief telephone visit with an author, you're probably wondering if you can handle the work (not to mention the expense) of bringing a real live author to your school or library. Look over "Planning an Author's Visit" in the "Treasure Chest" section to see briefly what an author visit entails. Also read "School Visits: The Author's Viewpoint," by Betty Miles and Avi (listed in the bibliography). Both sources, in addition to David Melton's book mentioned above, emphasize the necessity for good advance planning.

Perhaps you already know some authors in your geographical area who might come to your school. Librarians often know their state's or region's writers. Don't overlook local talent.

If you want to look beyond your own locality, you can turn to major publishers for ideas. Houghton Mifflin, for example, will provide a list of their authors, grouped by geographical area of the United States, who are interested in doing appearances. They have an outline of procedures for the author event with a discount available to the school or organization for any of the author's books that are sold. (This is one way to defray your expenses in paying the author's honorarium.) To receive this information, write: Houghton Mifflin Company, Children's Books Promotions, Two Park Street, Boston, Massachusetts 02108. For those authors who do not make personal appearances, Houghton Mifflin offers a series of author videotapes for purchase or rental. Dell also provides a geographical listing of their authors with guidelines and assistance in scheduling author visits. For more information, write: Dell Publishing Company, Publicity, Books for Young Readers, 1 Dag Hammarskjold Plaza, 245 East 47th Street, New York, New York 10017.

As one who has both planned author visits and been a visiting author/storyteller, I reiterate what others have said: Not all authors are effective with young audiences, so it's best to invite someone that you (or a trusted colleague) have heard. Schools and libraries need to make their expectations and arrangements quite clear with the author ahead of time so the resulting visit will be successful for everyone. Some authors will do large assemblies, other will not. Some prefer smaller groups to lumping the entire student body into the gym for a mass reading or question-and-answer period. If you do choose the large assembly approach, try not to make the age range so broad (kindergarten through eighth grade, for example) that the author has to be all things to all people. All of these are matters that should be discussed with the author.

An important decision will be what classes or children will be involved. If the author visit will include several schools in a district, you will have to decide how students are selected to attend. I do not advocate choosing only the students who are the best readers or the best writers. Learning disabled children, slow readers, and underachievers often can benefit more than we know. Perhaps all the students in the third or fourth grade in the school district, for example, might attend the author visit one year. Plan an annual event so that all children will have this opportunity sometime during their elementary years.

Of course, this will all take effort. Consider cooperating with several groups or organizations. This is an excellent opportunity for schools and public libraries to share resources. A planning committee of teachers and public children's librarians can generate more ideas and enthusiasm than single sponsorship. Some cities even have networks for sharing visiting authors. The Phoenix, Arizona, area, for example, has a children's literature network of teachers, librarians, bookstore owners, and anyone else interested in children's literature. They inform one another about authors, storytellers, and educators who are coming to their area so everyone can benefit. Perhaps the author will agree to meet with classes at the school and then end the day with an informal chat at the public library. Be considerate of the author, and don't make the schedule too long.

You will probably want to have copies of the author's books for sale at the event. Consult the sources in the bibliography for details about this. In any case, you will have to decide how to handle autographing. Generally authors agree to autograph their books, but you will need to set aside uninterrupted time for them to do this. You definitely want to avoid having the author besieged by crowds of eager children thrusting slips of paper for autographing. One answer is to ask the author to autograph bookplates (for those children purchasing books) and/or bookmarks (that you photocopy for all children) ahead of time. Sample bookmarks and bookplates have been provided for this purpose in Figures 8.1 and 8.2 in the "Treasure Chest."

THE SHOW GOES ON (THE PROGRAM PLAN)

This plan is up to you. Since the programs described in this chapter are general guidelines, the assumption is that you've already decided what goals you wish to accomplish, how many appearances the author will make, and where and when you'll schedule lunch, autograph sessions, small group meetings with the author, and so on. If the program is author related, use the activities and ideas in the "Treasure Chest" and look for a balance between story sharing and other activities.

THE TREASURE CHEST

Planning an Author Visit
by Ann Holton, Mick Moore, and Martha Melton

I am greatly indebted to these women for an outstanding planning document. Ann Holton is a media specialist at Penn Elementary School, Iowa City, Iowa; Martha Melton is a language arts resource specialist for the Iowa City Community School District; and Mick Moore was a fifth- and sixth-grade teacher at Penn Elementary until her death in October 1988. Ann graciously gave me permission to use this document in its entirety as a tribute to Mick.

I. Choosing the Right Author

   A. Consider the age level with whom the author will work.

   B. Decide what the visit should accomplish (set criteria). Example: Do you want the author to interact with the students in specific ways or on specific topics?

   C. Begin an investigation for an author.

      1. Talk with media specialists.

      2. Attend authors' presentations at educational conferences (NCTE, IRA, etc.).

      3. Contact publishers and ask for recommendations of authors who meet the criteria you have established and are within your budget.

II. Advance Planning for Visit

   A. Contact the publisher to invite the author and establish the fee.

   B. Determine how the visit will be financed. Possible sources:

      1. Parent organizations

      2. Professional organizations

      3. Community organizations

      4. Sale of author's books

      5. Fund raising activities such as book fair sales, carnival revenue, candy sales, etc.

   C. Verify the commitment with the author.

      1. Define parameters. Discuss scheduling, format of sessions, group size, etc.

      2. Find out whether he or she is interested in additional engagements while in the area (lunch/dinner presentations, another school or organization, etc.).

      3. If autographing sessions are part of the plan, discuss procedures, times, and so on with the author.

   D. If books are to be sold and autographed, consult with the publisher(s) about discounts, policies on returns, postage, etc. Order both hardback and paperback copies, but more paperback copies.

   E. Make arrangements for lodging and meals. Establish procedures for charging with the hotel prior to the visit.

   F. Arrange for transportation both to your city and around the city during the author's stay.

   G. Arrange for publicity.

      1. Newspapers (local, school, educational)

      2. Promotional materials (posters, brochures, etc.)

      3. Media (local TV and radio stations)

III. Curriculum Planning (Pre-Activities)
   A. Oral literature focusing on author's visit
      1. Choose at least one book by the author and have all classroom teachers involved in the project read it aloud to their students to develop a common basis for discussion.
      2. Read other books by the author to students in small groups and have them compare and contrast the author's works.
   B. Develop novel units that include comprehension activities such as building background, predicting, summarizing, and comparing as well as art activities, writing activities, and other appropriate extension activities.
   C. Select a literary element (e.g., characterization) and develop a format for studying and comparing this element in several of the author's books.
   D. Have students give book talks on books by the author.
   E. Use art as a medium for discussing and comparing books.
   F. Incorporate literature into other appropriate curricular areas.

IV. Day of the Visit
   A. The success of the visit depends upon pre-planning, the preparation of students, and communication between the staff and the author.
   B. Provide a warm, inviting atmosphere for students, staff, and the author.
   C. Have students' relevant art work displayed for the visit.
   D. Schedule the day according to what you want to accomplish.
   E. Plan the day carefully down to the minute, remembering to include breaks.
   F. If an autographing session is part of the day, provide a table and comfortable chair. Have someone available to assist and to keep the author from being detained by "talkers."
   G. Lunch is a good time for the author to interact with staff, administrators, and board members. Make it special!
   H. Consider videotaping the day's events. (Be sure to clear this with the author *prior* to the visit.)

V. Curriculum Planning (Post-Activities)
   A. Have small group discussions about students' impressions of the author's visit.
   B. Read similar novels by other authors and compare and contrast with the works of the visiting author.
   C. Using the following authoring cycle, have each student publish a piece of writing.
      1. Engage in pre-writing activities such as brainstorming, gathering information, reflection, and discussion
      2. Draft piece
      3. Revise piece with help of peer(s)
      4. Conference with teacher
      5. Edit piece with peers and teacher
      6. Publish piece
      7. Discuss this authoring process in view of the author's presentations and the information he or she gave about the process he or she uses

Enjoy yourself! You will be spending the day with someone special; make it profitable and fun for students, staff, and the author.

Projects for Author Visits

Photocopy the examples given in Figures 8.1 and 8.2 for bookplates and bookmarks so children will have souvenirs from the visiting author program.

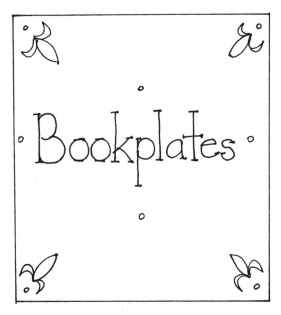

Fig. 8.1.

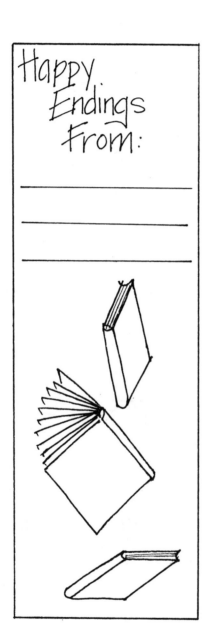

Fig. 8.2.

IN THE LIMELIGHT (PUBLICITY)

If you are publicizing the author visit, you will receive promotional material from the publisher. The publicity flyer shown in Figure 8.3 can be sent home from school with children or distributed at the library for additional interest.

Set up displays of the author's books using eye-catching, story-related items in your classroom or library. A display of dance shoes, canes, and straw hats, for example, might accompany Stephen Gammel's Caldecott Award-winning book *Song and Dance Man*. Toy motorcycles and a mouse-size helmet made out of half of a pingpong ball might accompany Beverly Cleary's book *The Mouse and the Motorcycle*.

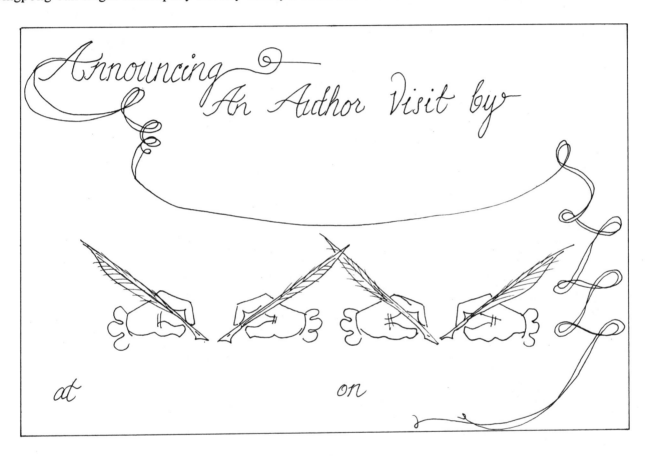

Fig. 8.3.

BIBLIOGRAPHY

Because of the multifaceted nature of this chapter, the bibliography is divided into the following subdivisions: Basic Biographical Sources about Authors, Selected Biographies about Authors, and Author Visits and Programs.

Basic Biographical Sources about Authors

Contemporary Authors. Edited by Susan M. Trotsky. Gale Research Series.
   This bio-bibliographical guide to current writers in nearly every field includes children's authors. Generally, living authors and those deceased 1960 or later are included, although some deceased since 1900 whose works are still of interest can be found here. Entries include personal information, home address, agent's address, career, writings, works in progress, sidelights, and biographical sources. Latest volume serves as index to the full series. Smaller public libraries might invest in this set for the entire library if *Something About the Author* is not obtained for the children's department.

Fifth Book of Junior Authors and Illustrators. Edited by Sally Holmes Holtze. Wilson, 1983.
   The first volume of this series was produced in 1935 because of the growth in the field of children's literature, and the series has continued to grow in popularity. Each volume contains about 250 names. A typical entry includes a photograph, a signature, a biographical sketch, and a list of selected writings. The index in the latest volume is cumulative for the whole series.

Hopkins, Lee Bennett. **Books Are By People.** Citation Press, 1969.
   Each volume includes interviews (104 in the first book, 65 in the second) with well-known authors and illustrators of books for young people. Photographs and pronunciations of names are provided. Entries vary from two to four pages. This is not the most up-to-date source, but the idea behind the volumes, that books are by people, is an important idea for children to understand.
   Also by Bennett: **More Books by More People.** Citation Press, 1974.

Something About the Author. Edited by Anne Commire. Gale Research Series.
   This continually updated series (begun in 1971) provides extensive biographical information and photographs about both well-known and lesser known authors and illustrators of books for young people. Personal information, career highlights, writings, and commentaries are included. This is the most comprehensive source for the study of contemporary children's authors. The latest volume has a cumulative index to the entire series. Each volume is arranged alphabetically.

Something About the Author: Autobiography Series. Edited by Adele Sarkissian. Gale Research Series.
   This new series, begun in 1986, invites prominent authors and illustrators of books for children and young adults to write extended essays about themselves. Each "mini autobiography" is approximately 10,000 words.

Yesterday's Authors of Books for Children. Edited by Anne Commire. Gale Research Series.
   This two-volume series serves as a companion to the *Something About the Author* series, which now covers live authors or those who have died since 1961. YABC brings together authors who died before 1961, including personal information, career and writings, adaptations, and sidelights. Numerous photographs and illustrations from authors' books are included.

Selected Biographies about Authors

Bassett, Lisa. **Very Truly Yours, Charles L. Dodgson, Alias Lewis Carroll.** Lothrop, Lee, and Shepard, 1987.
   In this playful biography of the creator of the most famous children's literature classic, the reader discovers an unusual assortment of facts, letters, photographs, riddles, and puzzles. This creatively presented biography might inspire student-written author biographies.

Cleary, Beverly. **A Girl from Yamhill: A Memoir**. Morrow, 1988.
    In this autobiography, Beverly Cleary writes about growing up in Yamhill and Portland, Oregon. She combines her experiences of living on the farm and in the city during the 1920s with numerous anecdotes that bring her childhood alive for the reader. The book is written for older children, but makes a good teacher resource to use with younger children who are discovering this popular author.

Collins, David. **The Country Artist: A Story about Beatrix Potter**. Illustrated by Karen Ritz. Carolrhoda, 1989.
    Despite her distant parents, Beatrix Potter grew up with a devoted governess, nurse, and butler who brought her animals and encouraged her early artistic talents. The life of the creator of Peter Rabbit and friends is told in five fascinating chapters for middle elementary children and is an excellent resource for programs/units on Potter.

Hyman, Trina Schart. **Self-Portrait: Trina Schart Hyman**. Addison-Wesley, 1981.
    Sprinkled throughout with color paintings by the artist herself, this chatty story of the life of the Caldecott winner is one of the Self-Portrait Collection. Other titles focus on Margot Zemach and Erik Blegvad.

MacDonald, Ruth K. **Dr. Seuss**. Twayne Publishers, 1988.
    In this first full-length critical study of the popular picture book artist-author, MacDonald explores the author's place in children's literature as much as she recounts his life. This source, one of the Twayne Children's Literature Author Series, is intended for an older audience (grades nine and up) and is a useful teacher resource.

Nixon, Joan. **If You Were a Writer**. Illustrated by Bruce Degen. Four Winds Press, 1988.
    This is not a biography like the other titles listed here. Rather, it tells the story of Melia's mother, who is a writer, and how she gets her ideas. Nixon is telling both her own story and that of all writers for children who ask such questions as, "How do you start a story?"

Stevenson, James. **Higher On the Door**. Greenwillow, 1987.
    Stevenson's familiar watercolor illustrations accompany a vividly detailed and sometimes humorous text about his growing up in a small town in the 1930s. Pictures (and comments about his neighborhood), his fears, accomplishments, and a sneak at his brother's diary should give children ideas for telling their own lives.

Author Visits and Programs

Dow, Marilyn Schoeman. **Young Authors Conference: Kids Writing for Kids**. The Write Stuff, 1985.
    Step by step plans to implement a young authors conference include pointers on author visits as part of the conference. This paperback resource guide is available from The Write Stuff, 2515 39th Avenue, S.W., Seattle, WA 98116.

Laughlin, Mildred, and Letty S. Watt. **Developing Learning Skills through Children's Literature**. Oryx, 1986.
    Many author programs can be developed from the literature programs in this source for kindergarten through grade six.

McElmeel, Sharron L. **An Author a Month (for Pennies)**. Libraries Unlimited, 1988.
    Complete program activities for programs/units on nine picture book authors and illustrators, to feature one author a month during the school year, forms the basis of this resource book. Capsule author units with brief ideas to develop more fully on your own are provided for three more authors to round out the year. Photographs of authors and biographical information are included along with an idea cupboard for each featured author.

Melton, David. **How to Capture Live Authors and Bring Them to Your Schools**. Landmark Editions, 1986.
    This is a chatty, practical, and essential source for planning author visits that every school system and public library interested at all in the topic should own. A question-and-answer format informally gives the bulk of the information but there are many quotes from noted authors and illustrators as well as Melton's illustrations. Available from the publisher: Landmark Editions, Inc., 1420 Kansas Avenue, Kansas City, MO 64127.

Miles, Betty, and Avi. "School Visits: The Author's Viewpoint." **School Library Journal** (January 1987): 21-26.

This must-read article complements Melton's book and the author visit plan in this chapter very well. It presents many of the points already discussed from the viewpoints of two authors.

ENCORES (OTHER PROGRAMS AND PROJECTS)

Here are some of my favorite author focus programs, which you might plan in your school or library. The list includes both contemporary and past authors of books for young people.

- Beverly Cleary Day—Make motorcycle helmets for Ralph out of halves of pingpong balls and rubber bands, read readers theatre scripts from favorite Cleary stories, and make Dear Ramona or Dear Mr. Henshaw diaries.

- Judy Blume Day—Select favorite Blume stories to read aloud, especially passages from *Tales of a Fourth Grade Nothing* and *Superfudge*, and serve a chocolate fudge cake with a turtle decoration to remember Fudge's infamous act of eating Dribble, his brother's pet turtle. If you plan this program for Blume's birthday (February 12), you can also make birthday valentines to send to the author.

- Dr. Seuss Day—Seuss's books make terrific readers theatre scripts, especially *Horton Hatches a Who* and *Green Eggs and Ham*. Even middle school kids enjoy taking part! Serve deviled green eggs and make puppets or draw pictures of your favorite character à la Seuss.

- Chris Van Allsburg's Fantasy World—Make up a game à la *Jumanji*, try your hand at creative writing after reading *The Mysteries of Harris Burdick*, and read *The Wreck of the Zephyr* just up to the climax, letting kids finish reading the story themselves or encourage them to create their own endings.

- Hans Christian Andersen Day—Acquaint children with this creator of the modern fairy tale through a story of his life. Favorite stories to read and then turn into skits or creative dramatics scenes are "The Princess and the Pea" and "The Emperor's New Clothes." Make shoebox scenes depicting favorite Andersen tales. A bed from a doll house piled with many mattresses and a single split pea recalls "The Princess and the Pea." Miniature objects such as acorn cups could accompany "Thumbelina."

- Shel Silverstein Day—Pass the poetry around and let children choose their favorite Silverstein poems to read aloud. Record your favorites for class use. Silverstein writes about the everyday scene or experience but causes us to look humorously or more carefully than we did before. Some typical topics are messy rooms, nail biters, and thumb suckers. Other topics are unpredictable combinations—hippopotamus sandwiches or hats made from toilet plungers. Give your students similar subjects for poems and let them create their own offbeat verses. For even more fun, write the students' work on a place where the sidewalk ends outside the school or library.

- A Rudyard Kipling "Just So" Day—Turn Kipling stories into puppet plays or simply read them aloud. Make elephant crafts to remember "The Elephant's Child." Make a list of your favorite Kipling phrases and coined words.

9
Books
From Hornbooks to Popups

INTRODUCTION

With thousands of books surrounding us, from telephone books to encyclopedias to paperback books sold in the grocery store to fine leather volumes in rare book libraries, we might assume that books are as old as the history of people. We forget that printed books as we know them today are only about 500 years old. Before that, books were much different. This program will briefly look at different kinds of book formats past and present and introduce the world of book publishing today. Two unusual formats—the colonial hornbook and the modern pop-up book—will be introduced through projects your students can make. This program/unit can be used any time during the year, but it makes a fascinating beginning to the school year during September or an appropriate addition to Children's Book Week in November. Of course, you can use it any time to promote books, reading, or literacy. Suggestions for other programs and projects appear in the "Encores" section of this chapter.

PURPOSE OF PROGRAM/UNIT

To introduce the history of books and printing, to look at book publishing today, and to create two examples of unusual book formats: the colonial hornbook and the modern pop-up book.

A LITTLE BACKGROUND ABOUT BOOKS

The earliest "books" were not books as we know them at all. They were clay tablets with curious wedge-shaped marks called cuneiforms. These tablets were created about 3000 B.C. by the ancient Babylonians. Other early books include the papyrus scrolls made by the ancient Egyptians, medieval parchment manuscripts from Europe, and the "rag-paper" books that were printed in China. (For information about the ancient Egyptians see Chapter 2, "Mummy," and for a program on the Chinese see Chapter 1, "Chinese New Year.") Here are some facts about early books and some information about book publishing today to explore further.

- The ancient Egyptians produced papyrus, an early kind of paper, from the papyrus plant. They cut the stems of the plant into thin strips, pressed the strips together in layers, and pounded the layers flat. The surface was polished with ivory until it was soft. Individual strips were pasted end to end to make a long strip, which was rolled around a painted stick to make a scroll. The Egyptians wrote their hieroglyphics (literally, "priest writing") on the papyrus scrolls with pens made of sharpened reeds and ink made from soot and water. The papyrus scroll was used for thousands of years, even by the Greeks and Romans.

- By the Middle Ages, the form of manuscripts was beginning to resemble the books of today. A sheet of parchment was folded over and tied together to create a volume known as the codex. Parchment, made from calf or sheep skin, began to replace papyrus at this time. The animal skins were washed, scraped, and rubbed until smooth.

- For hundreds of years, the only books were made by monks in the early Christian church, who sat in monasteries painstakingly writing each book by hand. These beautiful volumes were called manuscripts, which means "to write by hand." The pictures added to the writing were called illuminations.

- The Chinese first developed movable type. Some sources date this invention around the year 1045, but explain that the use of movable type was too cumbersome for the Chinese because their language is made up of thousands of characters. Still, the Chinese made use of wood-block printing and made paper from old rags, fishing nets, and bark. Rag paper eventually replaced the parchment used in Europe.

- The invention of the printing press in the West is generally attributed to Johannes Gutenberg in Germany around 1440. Gutenberg adapted the wine press to make the first printing press. Gutenberg's printing press could make 300 copies a day, and quickly became so popular that over 1,000 print shops were set up in Europe by the year 1500 and over a million books had already been produced. The early printed books are called incunabula, from the Latin word for cradle.

    Some of the first printers were Aldus Manutius in Venice, Italy, Christopher Plantin in Antwerp, Belgium, and John Newbery in London. John Newbery was the first man to make his living printing and selling children's books. The John Newbery Medal is given in his honor by the American Library Association each year for the best children's book published in the United States.

- In the early days in the United States books were expensive and so was the paper they were printed on. In fact, paper was so expensive that a special book called the hornbook was created. A single sheet of printed paper was glued to a wooden paddle. Then a horn from an animal was melted down to become a transparent cover that protected the printed page. The printed matter usually contained the alphabet, prayers, and vowel sounds to teach children how to read. The hornbook often had a hole in the handle so children could fasten it to their belts. In the 1700s, hornbooks were even made out of crisp gingerbread; children were allowed to eat the part of the hornbook that they had learned. Another type of book popular in the past was the chapbook. These little books were pamphlets of stories sold for a penny by peddlars or chapmen from the 1500s through the 1700s.

- Printing developments in the past 100 years have made books (as well as magazines, newspapers, and other printed matter) readily available. One of these developments was the invention of the linotype machine in the 1880s, which could set an entire line of type in one operation. Developments in photography later led to offset printing, and today computer typesetting and electrostatic printing help the publishing industry produce books to answer our growing information and recreation needs.

- About 30,000 new books are published each year in the United States by approximately 3,000 publishing companies. Some of these books are paperbacks; some are textbooks; some are subscription books, such as encyclopedias; but a large portion of the books are trade books. Trade books are sold in bookstores and are of a general nature. They may be cookbooks, biographies, books for children, or books for adults.

- Many unusual kinds of books are produced today including the toy or novelty book. The first pop-up book, a version of *Little Red Riding Hood*, was published in 1855 by Dean of London. Soon after, German publishers got into the novelty book field and produced books with dissolving pictures. (Dissolving pictures operate something like the iris of a camera. The viewer rotates a wheel to change one scene to another one positioned underneath it.) Currently, an exciting variety of novelty books is available. Some books have flaps to lift, others have moving parts, some have figures that pop up, and some open out into houses or scenery. Some books have sounds and smells and fuzzy surfaces. Book formats are becoming so varied and unusual that credit is sometimes given to design and paper engineering as well as to the illustration.

- You may wish to identify some of the following book terms with the children: book spine, title page, colophon, copyright notice, publishing house, and editor. Consult some of the books in the resource bibliography at the end of this chapter to help children become familiar with the fascinating world of publishing. Most children are quite interested in book publishing and will enjoy the many new books on this topic.

SETTING THE STAGE (PREPARATION)

Since this program/unit focuses on the history of books, especially book formats, set up book displays. One display might focus on early book formats. You can purchase pictures on papyrus from the museum shop in the Field Museum of Natural History in Chicago, so your students can visualize this kind of paper. Make your own scrolls simply by gluing a length of art paper to wooden dowels. Scrolls were used by the ancient Egyptians, Greeks, and Romans.

The colonial hornbook that inspired the student project in this chapter is available from The Horn Book, Inc. It is a 3" x 5" facsimile of the kind of paddle-shaped book children used in the seventeenth century. Tiny brass tacks and brass strips hold the text page to the wooden paddle. A heavy plastic sheet covers the text rather than the actual animal horn that would have been used in the seventeenth century. This hornbook will make a handsome addition to your display. Send $5.95 to Horn Book, Inc., 14 Beacon Street, Boston, MA 02108. Facsimiles of old books are often available in bookstores, so you should be able to make an attractive display that will create interest in older books.

The second kind of book children will create during this program/unit is the pop-up book. Facsimile editions of old toy books are available in many bookstores. Try to include some of these along with a variety of modern pop-up books for a display. Suggestions for a few of these books are included in the bibliography.

If you wish to purchase a few of the novelty books for your classroom or library, here are a few criteria to keep in mind:

1. Is the book printed on heavy enough stock to withstand repeated manipulation of its parts?

2. Is the kind of manipulation appropriate to the book? (Is it an intricate part of the story line or the purpose or is it just a gimmick?)

3. Is it clear how to manipulate the book? (If you are supposed to lift flaps or turn dials, are arrows or instructions included?)

You may also wish to create related book displays on the bookmaking process. Printers are reluctant to provide press sheets or book signatures because industry standard requires that anything not made into a book be destroyed. If you can secure these examples of stages of a book from a local printer, your students will be able to visualize how a book is made. Field trips to local printers and binders are good culminating experiences for this unit. See the "Encores" section for suggestions for related programs.

Finally, assemble materials for the two projects described in the "Treasure Chest" section.

THE SHOW GOES ON
(THE PROGRAM PLAN)

Act I—Tell the "story of the book" in your own words based on information in this chapter and in the resource books in the bibliography.

Act II—Children make their own colonial hornbooks (see Figure 9.2).

Act III—Show the many unusual formats of books published today. Find as many pop-up and novelty books as you can. Libraries do not usually collect many books of this kind. Ask children why this is the case. Ask children what kinds of books they particularly enjoy and why.

Act IV—Children create their own pop-up books based on the example in Figure 9.1 or on ideas listed in the resource bibliography.

Act V—Children eat or make their own gingerbread hornbooks (or decorate gingerbread hornbooks that you already have made).

THE TREASURE CHEST

Art Projects Related to Book Formats

Follow the illustrations to make a simple pop-up book (Figure 9.1) and a colonial hornbook (Figure 9.2) with your students. Other pop-up books are described in various books listed in the bibliography.

Colonial Hornbook

Cut out paddle shapes from plywood using the pattern shown in Figure 9.2. Give each child a copy of the text shown. (This should be copied on cardstock, not on thin paper.) Children can color in the decorations and write their names in the empty space. Because the scale of this project is small, children usually can't write small enough to copy as much text as I have included. Glue the text to the paddle and apply a coat of varnish used in decoupage. This kind of varnish dries quickly and makes a hard finish.

(Text continues on page 131.)

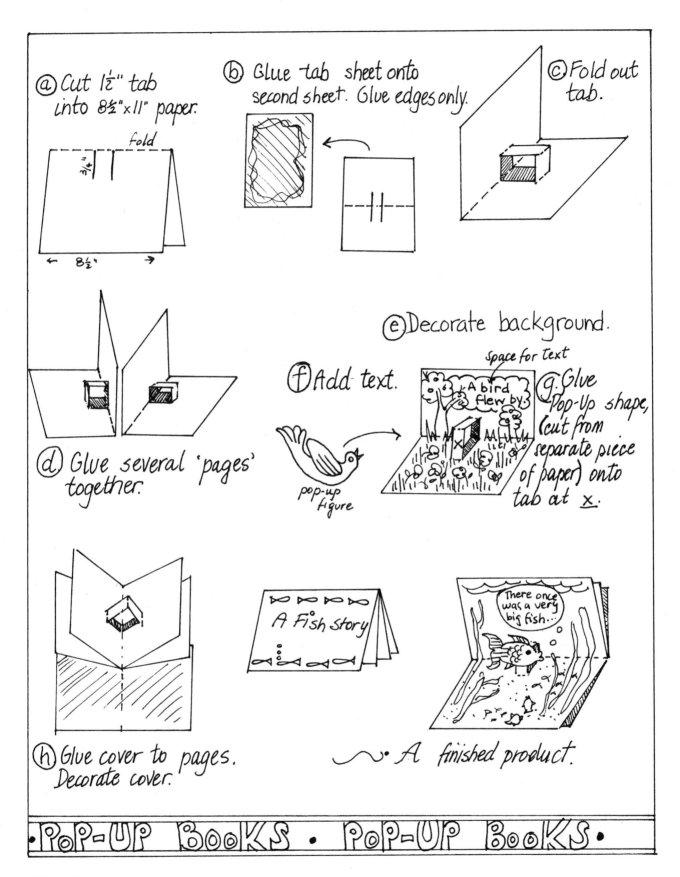

Fig. 9.1.

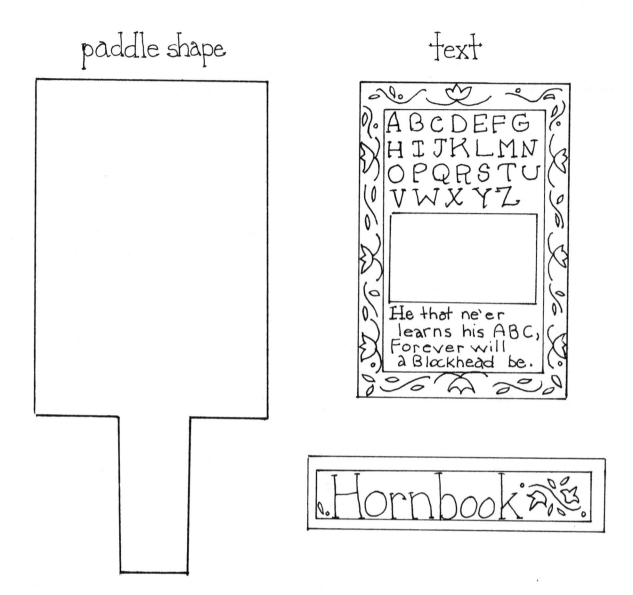

Fig. 9.2.

IN THE LIMELIGHT (PUBLICITY)

Publicize this program with the flyer shown in Figure 9.3. You can advertise Children's Book Week with the children's hornbooks and pop-up books made in this program/unit. This is a way to promote your classroom's or library's activities even after the event.

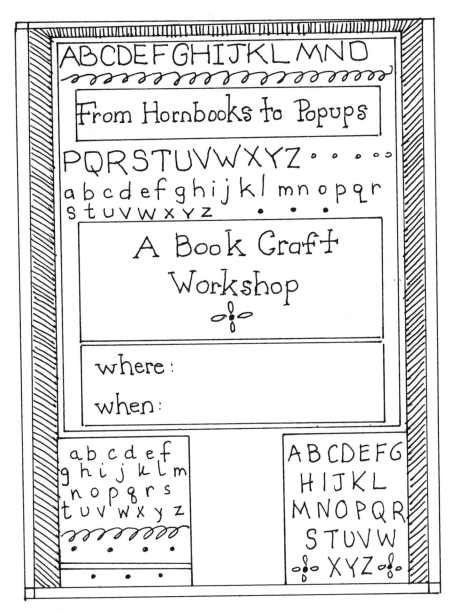

Fig. 9.3.

BIBLIOGRAPHY

List of Pop-Up or Novelty Books for a Display

These books are a sample of the many fascinating novelty books available today—accordian, three-dimensional pictures, lift the flap, popup, and revolving pictures. Each book has been selected as an excellent example of its category. (Criteria for evaluating novelty books are included in "Setting the Stage.")

A. Apple Pie. Pictures by Tracey Campbell Pearson. Dial, 1986.
This accordian book is a modern variant of the popular Kate Greenaway book that begins, "A, Apple Pie. B, Bit it. C, Cut it," and so on through a series of mishaps and adventures.

Ahlberg, Janet, and Allen Ahlberg. **The Jolly Postman**. Little, Brown, 1986.
The jolly postman delivers letters to all our favorite nursery time characters including the Three Bears, Cinderella, Goldilocks, and the Big Bad Wolf. The letters all can be pulled from envelopes that are bound in the book.

Alexander, Martha. **Three Magic Flip Books**. Dial, 1984.
Held in a small box, three sprightly, wordless books flip to tell the stories of a magic box, a magic picture, and a magic hat.

Bemelmans, Ludwig. **Madeline**. Viking Kestrel, 1987.
Three-dimensional pictures show the old house in Paris, a pop-up Miss Clavel whisks down the stairs with Madeline in her arms, and all the little girls pop up in Madeline's hospital room. A come-to-life version of the favorite book originally published in 1939.

Crowther, Robert. **The Most Amazing Hide-and-Seek Alphabet Book**. Viking Kestrel, 1977.
Each letter of the alphabet pulls down or turns over to reveal a surprising series of animals, such as a giraffe whose neck elongates from the letter G, a koala bear sliding down the letter K, and an owl opening his eyes behind an O.

de Paola, Tomie. **Giorgio's Village**. Putnam's, 1982.
Six three-dimensional scenes stand up as the pages are turned, revealing events in an Italian village from morning till night. Other manipulatives include a pull tab that moves little puppets of Punchinello and his fair lady and another tab that sets in motion the bell ringers in a clock tower.

The Genius of Lothar Meggendorfer. Designed by David Pelham. Illustrated by Jim Deesing after Lothar Meggendorfer. Paper engineering by Tor Lokvig. Random House, 1985.
The nineteenth-century German innovator in the art of moving picture books is honored with this reproduction of some of his finest animated pictures. A "front" and "back" view of one of his mechanisms is shown so the reader can visualize the engineering genius behind the toy book.

Hansel and Gretel. Design and paper engineering by James Roger Dias and Sandra Tiller. Lothrop, Lee, and Shepard, 1982.
One of four titles in a series of accordian books that fold out from a three-dimensional, house-shaped book. This concept combines the format of an accordian book with the idea of a doll house and will charm children and adults alike.

Knight, Joan. **Journey to Egypt**. Illustrated by Piero Ventura. Design and paper engineering by Dick Dudley and David A. Carter. Viking Kestrel, 1986.
One of the UNICEF books of three-dimensional and movable scenes. This one shows engineers reconstructing the temple of Abu Simbel, a burial tomb with a mummy case that opens, and a giant pyramid that pops up from the desert.

Littlejohn, Claire. **Aesop's Fables**. Dial, 1988.
Nine fables spring to life. Pull the tabs and the greedy fox springs for grapes, the hare leaps into the race with the tortoise, and meat falls out of a dog's mouth.

Miller, Jonathan. **The Human Body.** Designed by David Pelham. Viking, 1983.
   Three-dimensional, movable models show such fascinating parts of the anatomy as the walls of arteries dilating, movement of bones in the inner ear, and the movement of the tongue and jaw.

Miller, Jonathan, and David Pelham. **The Facts of Life.** Viking, 1984.
   Three-dimensional moving illustrations show the anatomy of the uterus, penetration of the ovum by sperm, development of the fetus, and the birth of a baby through a bony pelvis. An invaluable teaching tool.

Miranda, Anne. **Baby Walk.** Illustrated by Dorothy Stott. E. P. Dutton, 1988.
   This lift-and-look flap book continues an action, thus showing sequencing and cause and effect. For example, the phrase "Go bump" is illustrated with a picture of a teddy bear in a stroller going over a curb. Lift the flap and the bear bounces out of the stroller.

Nister, Ernest. **Revolving Pictures.** Intervisual Communications, 1979.
   Reproduced from the 1892 book, each picture revolves—something like a camera shutter—to reveal another picture. The victorian scenes illustrate little poems on the facing pages.

Provenson, Alice, and Martin Provenson. **Leonardo Da Vinci.** Paper engineering by John Strejan. Viking, 1984.
   Three-dimensional and movable pictures show this multitalented Renaissance man studying the heavens, painting a mural that changes before our eyes, and painting the Mona Lisa on an easel that stands up from the book in a three-dimensional courtyard.

Scarry, Huck. **Looking into the Middle Ages.** Intervisual Communications, 1985.
   Castles, medieval towns, and a Gothic cathedral rise before your eyes in stand-up illustrations.

The Three Pigs. Illustrated by John Wallner. Intervisual Communications, 1987.
   In this lift-the-flap book, pictures on the flap fold back to reveal the words. Young children will enjoy following the familiar story and learning the words as they read. A rotating wheel mechanism shows the wolf chasing two little pigs as they make a hasty retreat to the third little pig's house.

Wylie, Stephen. **There Was an Old Woman.** Illustrated by Maureen Roffey. Harper and Row, 1985.
   A noisy bunch of animals keeps an old woman awake in this cumulative story that is told with words printed on flaps that lift to reveal a picture. Good for teaching word recognition.

Resource Books for This Chapter

Aliki. **How a Book Is Made.** Crowell, 1986.
   The many steps in the creation, publication, and acquisition of a book are described in detailed, cartoon-style illustrations with accompanying text.

Bartlett, Susan. **Books, a Book to Begin On.** Illustrated by Ellen Raskin. Holt, Rinehart, and Winston, 1968.
   Traces the history of books from storytelling and early record-keeping on clay tablets and papyrus to medieval scrolls, the invention of printing, and hornbooks.

Gibbons, Gail. **Paper Paper Everywhere.** Harcourt Brace Jovanovich, 1983.
   Brief text and illustrations show how paper is made from logs and processed at a paper mill. The illustrations also show another story: the many fun uses children find for paper, from making paper dolls and paper airplanes to party decorations. The paper making process is, of course, an important part of the bookmaking process.

Greene, Carol. **How a Book Is Made.** Children's Press, 1988.
   A "new true" book, part of an easy reading series that describes the evolution of a book from the author's idea through the editorial process, design, production, advertising, and sales. Photographs accompany the text.

Greenfield, Howard. **Books, from Writer to Reader.** Crown, 1976.
   A chapter is devoted to every party responsible for the creation and publication of books including the copy editor and the production supervisor. Advances in computer typesetting are not addressed, but the information given is both detailed and well written.

Hiner, Mark. **Paper Engineering for Pop-Up Books and Cards.** Tarquin Publications, 1985.
   With 10 working models, a whole range of exciting possibilities opens up for making your own elaborate pop-up books. Some models include the moving arm technique and the rotating disc.

Irvine, Joan. **How to Make Pop-Ups.** Illustrated by Barbara Reid. Morrow Junior Books, 1987.
   Detailed, step-by-step instructions for making pop-up books contain such projects as window cards, a pop-up valentine, and devices that push and pull and turn that can be used in student bookmaking projects.

Kehoe, Michael. **The Puzzle of Books.** Carolrhoda, 1982.
   The role of each person involved in the creation and publication of a book is described as the book moves from the writer to the reader. Included are the editor, the typesetter, the keyliner, the camera person, and the binder. Focus is placed on the production of the book that includes using computers in the process. No mention is made of advertising and marketing.

Nixon, Joan Lowery. **If You Were a Writer.** Four Winds, 1988.
   Melia spends the day with her mother and discovers how a writer gets ideas for books.

Simon, Irving. **The Story of Printing from Wood Blocks to Electronics.** Illustrated by Charles E. Pont. Harvey House, 1965.
   This story of the birth of printing, from Chinese wood-block printing to the codex and Gutenberg's modified wine press, also includes Renaissance improvements to type design and more modern linotype methods. Computerized technologies developed after publication of the book, so these are not mentioned.

Weiss, Harvey. **How to Make Your Own Books.** Crowell, 1974.
   Step-by-step instructions are given for making one-of-a-kind books of your own such as diaries and photo albums. Details are given for sewing the book and making covers.

ENCORES (OTHER PROGRAMS AND PROJECTS)

Chapter 8, "Author! Author!" encourages children to become authors of their own books. After children have followed the steps in the authoring cycle (described on page 118), have them publish their works and possibly bind them in attractive covers.

Students particularly interested in writing might consider entering their books in contests. For complete information, write to the National Written and Illustrated By ... Awards Contest for Students, Landmark Editions, Inc., P.O. Box 4469, Kansas City, Missouri 64127.

Related topics you could cover include calligraphy, printing processes, parts of a book, and paper making. Several sources in the resource bibliography will help. Other topics might be book care and book preservation. Children's librarians often have standard presentations on these topics; children could produce their own skits and puppet shows to teach book care to their classmates.

A study of book prizes might begin yet another related program/unit. Many children are familiar with the Newbery and Caldecott prizes, given each year by the American Library Association, for the best written children's book and the best illustrated children's book published in the United States. Displays of Newbery and Caldecott award winners create interest in books children might not discover on their own. Encourage children to find out about the many other book awards given, both for children's books and for books in general. A few awards to explore include the Pulitzer Prize, the Nobel Prize, the National Book Awards, the Hans Christian Andersen Medal, the Laura Ingalls Wilder Award (see Chapter 10, "A Day on the Prairie with Laura Ingalls Wilder"), the Coretta Scott King Award, and the Regina Medal. More than half the states in the United States have awards that are selected by children. Does your state give such an award? Write to other states and find out what kids there like. Are their ideas different from yours? If there is no state or local award in your area for children's books, consider having a contest in your classroom or library. Book awards guarantee interest in the books and promote reading. This is an outstanding way to develop early reading habits in children.

10
A Day on the Prairie with Laura Ingalls Wilder

INTRODUCTION

We have all grown up on the prairie ever since Laura Ingalls Wilder recreated her pioneer world, as snug as a log cabin in Wisconsin or a dugout in Plum Creek but also as chilling as the blizzards and as devastating as a plague of grasshoppers across the grasslands. Few authors are as widely read and continue to be loved by children as much as the author of the *Little House* books. Teachers and librarians know that the only regret children have about Wilder's books is that once they've read them all, they will search for a long time to find something else just as satisfying. This program/unit, "A Day on the Prairie with Laura Ingalls Wilder," is a separate chapter from "Author! Author!" because it treats the pioneer life and places that Laura describes as well as the biographical events in her life and episodes in the books.

PURPOSE OF PROGRAM/UNIT

To introduce children to some of the pioneer crafts, skills, food, recreation, and way of life described by Laura Ingalls Wilder; to briefly recall her books; and to introduce children to similar books.

A LITTLE BACKGROUND ABOUT LAURA INGALLS WILDER (AND ALL HER LITTLE HOUSES)

Laura Ingalls Wilder, author of eight widely read books for children, was born in Pepin, Wisconsin, in 1867 and died in Mansfield, Missouri, in 1957. The *Little House* books chronicle her life. (She had to change her age in the early books because her publisher didn't believe she could have remembered events that happened when she was only two years old!) We journey with the Ingalls family from the woods of Wisconsin to the prairies of Kansas, then back north to Minnesota and on to South Dakota. We read how the family traveled by covered wagon, how they made a dugout home, and how Pa built a cabin for them. We learn that they faced bears, illness, death, crop failure, and poverty but still managed to sing songs to Pa's fiddle, play games, and celebrate Christmas with presents so lovingly described that we could wish for nothing better than an orange as sweet as the one Laura found in her stocking. Here are a few facts about Wilder, her books, and the houses she lived in that are also open to the public.

- Laura's parents, Ma and Pa, were born and married in the eastern United States and traveled by covered wagon to Pepin, Wisconsin, in the early 1860s. There Pa built the log cabin described in *Little House in the Big Woods*, where Laura and Mary were born.

- Pa grew restless before long and moved his family to "Indian country" (now Kansas and Oklahoma). There he built the house Laura later wrote about in *Little House on the Prairie*.

- Because the government was going to move the white settlers out (a previous agreement had been made with the Indians that they would not be disturbed), Pa moved his family to Plum Creek, near Walnut Grove, Minnesota. The hard times there with illness, Mary's blindness, and crop failure are described in *On the Banks of Plum Creek*.

- Next, Pa's sister offered him a new opportunity, a job as timekeeper and paymaster in the construction camp of a railroad company in the Dakota Territory. The family lived for awhile in a small surveyor's house in De Smet, South Dakota, where Pa later filed a claim and built a home. Here Laura and her sisters grew up, and Laura married Almanzo. Laura wrote four books set in South Dakota: *By the Shores of Silver Lake, The Long Winter, Little Town on the Prairie*, and *These Happy Golden Years*. (The other book Laura wrote for children is *Farmer Boy*, the story of Almanzo's boyhood in New York.)

- In the late 1880s, Pa gave up farming, becoming a full-time carpenter and insurance salesman. He was active in community life in De Smet, but died at the age of 67. Ma and Mary lived in the house in town for the rest of their lives. Carrie supported the family by working on the local newspaper. She eventually married and moved to the Black Hills.

- Laura and Almanzo settled briefly in South Dakota, where they had a daughter, Rose. They moved to Minnesota, to Florida, and back to South Dakota, but finally settled in the Ozarks of Missouri. Here they farmed and built their own home.

- Rose grew up, became a journalist, and encouraged her mother to write down her pioneer stories of growing up. So Laura Ingalls Wilder began her writing career, at the age of 65, with the publication of *Little House in the Big Woods* in 1932. Her other books are *Farmer Boy* (1933), *Little House on the Prairie* (1935), *On the Banks of Plum Creek* (1937), *By the Shores of Silver Lake* (1939), *The Long Winter* (1940), *Little Town on the Prairie* (1941), *These Happy Golden Years* (1943), *On the Way Home* (1962), and *The First Four Years* (1971).

- Many honors were bestowed on Wilder. Libraries were named for her in Michigan, California, and Mansfield, Missouri, her hometown. But the greatest honor was the establishment of the Laura Ingalls Wilder Award by children's librarians of the American Library Association. The award was first given to Wilder and is given once every five years to an author who has made a lasting contribution to children's literature.

- The following "little houses" (Laura Ingalls Wilder homesites) that are open to the public:

  Pepin, Wisconsin (*Little House in the Big Woods*): located about 75 miles northwest of La Crosse on Highway 183, a reconstructed log cabin with other sites to see in the area.

  Independence, Kansas (*Little House on the Prairie*): located off Highway 75, a replica of the cabin Laura describes. A schoolhouse and an old post office have been moved nearby.

  Walnut Grove, Minnesota (*On the Banks of Plum Creek*): located just off Highway 14 about 150 miles southwest of Minneapolis, the dugout site and Plum Creek are identified. The farm is privately owned, but a free museum is open to the public.

  Burr Oak, Iowa: located off Highway 52, nine miles north of Decorah. Not mentioned in the *Little House* books, but the Ingalls family lived in the Masters hotel after they had been wiped out by grasshoppers in Walnut Grove. The hotel is open to the public.

  De Smet, South Dakota (site of four books including *Little Town on the Prairie*): located just east of Brookings, a wealth of sites including the surveyor's house and Ma and Pa's last home in town as well as the graves of Pa, Ma, Mary, Carrie, and Grace. The De Smet Pageant, held during three weekends in June and July, draws droves of devoted fans each year.

  Mansfield, Missouri: located one mile from Rocky Ridge Farm along Highway 60 about 50 miles from Springfield, Laura and Almanzo's last home with a museum built next door. Laura and Almanzo are buried in the Mansfield cemetery.

SETTING THE STAGE (PREPARATION)

Give children a glimpse into the pioneer world of Laura Ingalls Wilder by setting up displays and hands-on exhibits in your classroom or library. Here are a few suggestions.

First, purchase pamphlets, postcards, maps, posters, and other memorabilia from the Laura Ingalls Wilder Museum and Tourist Center, Box 58, Walnut Grove, Minnesota 56180, or from the Laura Ingalls Wilder Memorial Society, Inc., De Smet, South Dakota 57231.

Next, make your own pioneer costume to wear for the program or borrow one from someone in your community. Children might also like to come in costume so they can feel as if they are stepping back into the past.

Look around for antiques that will recapture days past—old farm implements, household items such as cooking utensils, old photographs, baby clothes, or old jewelry. Borrow handmade quilts to display.

Create a few pioneer "crafts" of your own—Pa's tin lantern can be made by freezing water in a tin can and using an ice pick to poke out a simple pattern. Make a decorative edge on shelf paper like Ma did for her cupboards. Try your hand at cutting a silhouette. Ask a local musician to come play some of the songs in *The Laura Ingalls Wilder Songbook* (if you can't find a fiddler like Pa, you should be able to find a willing guitar player). Organize materials for children to make their own quilts from paper. Patterns are given for several designs in Figures 10.1-10.3 in the "Treasure Chest."

Plan to churn butter. If you can't find an old butter churn like the one described in *Little House in the Big Woods*, make your own with a jar and a wooden tinker toy. *Steven Caney's Kids' America* (Workman, 1978) shows you how. There are also more "modern" kinds of butter churns you can borrow to try different ways of churning butter. Have cornbread or johnny cake on hand so everyone can sample the results of your butter-making. As you are churning the butter, teach children this adaptation of the traditional butter-churning chant:

Come butter come
Come butter come
(Mary's) waiting for a treat
Let's all hope the butter's sweet!
Come butter come!

Repeat this little chant, inserting each child's name as he or she gives the butter churn a turn. Work will seem like fun in the process.

Practice telling a draw-and-tell story like the one Ma tells. An adaptation is available by Carl Withers in the book *The Wild Ducks and the Goose* (Holt, Rinehart, and Winston, 1968). Phyllis Frette, retired children's librarian from Ames, Iowa, and a Wilder expert, showed me this story and was the inspiration for the tin lantern and shelf-paper ideas in this chapter.

Set up a display of plenty of Wilder's books (buy extra paperback copies since children will likely want to read them again after this program) and other books, both fiction and nonfiction, about pioneer life.

THE SHOW GOES ON (THE PROGRAM PLAN)

Act I—Greet children in costume if possible. You might choose to be Laura herself or a pioneer woman who takes the children on a journey back to the days of covered wagons. Sing some of the songs Laura did with her family. Some selections include "Pop! Goes the Weasel," "Polly Wolly Doodle," "Oh, Susanna," and "When Johnny Comes Marching Home."

Act II—Take children on a journey across the country with Laura by telling briefly about her travels and in which books each event happens. (Review by skimming the books again for yourself or refer to the brief outline given in "A Little Background about Laura Ingalls Wilder.")

Act III—Children make their own quilt patterns from paper using the patterns in Figures 10.1-10.3. Use wallpaper or fabric glued on paper. Show children how they can make other traditional patterns.

Act IV—Try your hand at butter churning. Divide the children into several groups so everyone can have hands-on experience. Use the butter churn chant and sample the end results.

Act V—"Booktalk" (a term librarians use for briefly describing and "selling" books so children will want to read them) Wilder's books and other fiction and nonfiction books about pioneer life.

THE TREASURE CHEST

Art Projects for a Laura Ingalls Wilder/Pioneer Day

Use the quilt patterns in Figures 10.1-10.3 so your students can make their own versions on paper. Figure 10.4 provides display ideas for this program/unit.

(Text continues on page 144.)

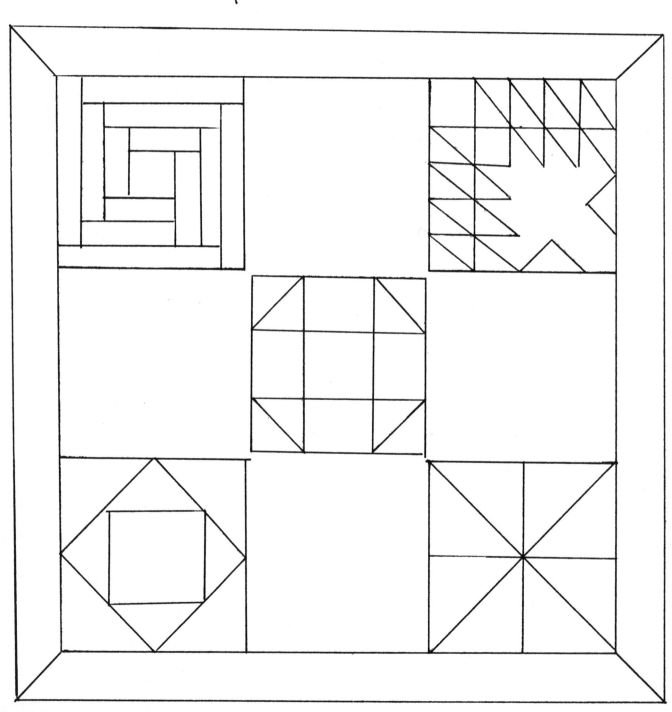

Fig. 10.1.

Nine Patch Patterns

Equal-sized blocks cut from contrasting colors can be used to create a variety of patterns.

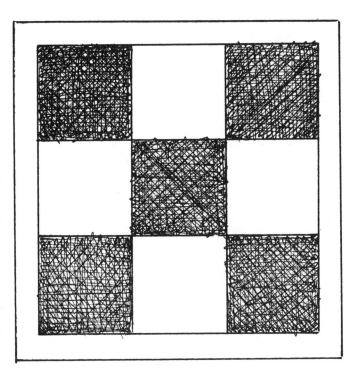
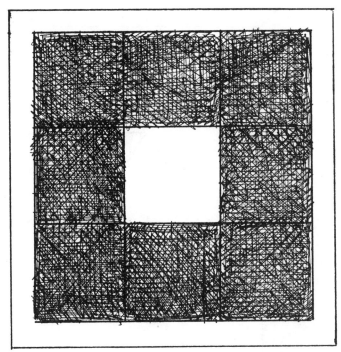
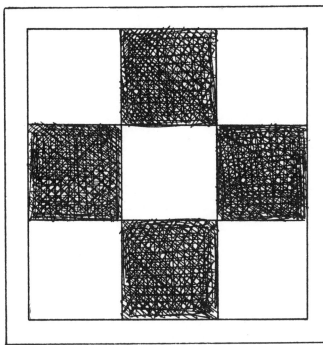
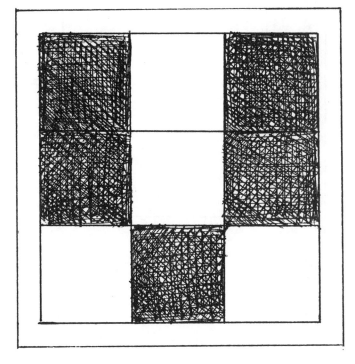

Fig. 10.2.

Fig. 10.3.

Fig. 10.4.

IN THE LIMELIGHT (PUBLICITY)

Use the publicity flyer in Figure 10.5 and adapt the news release in the preface to promote this program. Special displays of quilts and Wilder's books can also fill windows of stores in your community or of a local history museum.

Fig. 10.5.

BIBLIOGRAPHY

Books by or about Laura Ingalls Wilder

Anderson, William. **Laura Ingalls Wilder, Pioneer and Author.** Illustrated by Linda Friou. Kipling Press, 1987.
  Written by the well-recognized authority on Wilder, this handsome biography provides details left out of Wilder's books such as her life in Burr Oak, Iowa, and her later business acumen.

Anderson, William. **Little House Country.** Photographs by Leslie A. Kelly. Terrell Publishing, 1989.
  This photo guide to the home sites of Laura Ingalls Wilder contains abundant full-color photos with brief, informative text that will be appreciated by Wilder fans.

Blair, Gwenda. **Laura Ingalls Wilder.** Illustrated by Thomas B. Allen. Putnam's, 1982.
  This reader's biography captures the flavor of Wilder's life as related in her books. It mentions her later years and death.

Giff, Patricia Reilly. **Laura Ingalls Wilder: Growing Up in the Little House.** Illustrated by Eileen McKeating. Viking Kestrel, 1987.
  This biography for the middle grades tells how Laura came to write her *Little House* books. It also provides details such as the birth and death of Charles Frederick that are left out of the books.

McBride, Roger Lea, ed. **West from Home. Letters of Laura Ingalls Wilder to Almanzo Wilder.** Harper and Row, 1974.
  Published after her death, these letters were written from San Francisco in 1915 when Wilder was visiting their married daughter, Rose.

Wilder, Laura Ingalls. **By the Shores of Silver Lake.** Harper, 1939, 1953.
  This Newbery Honor book tells of Laura's years growing up in De Smet, Dakota Territory.

Wilder, Laura Ingalls. **Farmer Boy.** Harper, 1933, 1953.
  This account of Almanzo Wilder's boyhood is set in New York from 1866-1867.

Wilder, Laura Ingalls. **The First Four Years.** Harper and Row, 1971.
  Published after her death, this account tells of the hardships of Laura's early married years.

Wilder, Laura Ingalls. **Little House in the Big Woods.** Harper, 1932, 1953.
  Set in Pepin, Wisconsin, this is the first of Wilder's books. She and Mary were born in the big woods.

Wilder, Laura Ingalls. **Little House on the Prairie.** Harper, 1935, 1953.
  After Pa grows restless in the Wisconsin woods, he brings his family to Indian territory—Kansas—where the family has many exciting Indian adventures.

Wilder, Laura Ingalls. **Little Town on the Prairie.** Harper, 1941, 1953.
  This Newbery Honor book is the third set in De Smet. Laura works to earn money and Mary goes to a college for the blind in Iowa.

Wilder, Laura Ingalls. **The Long Winter.** Harper, 1940, 1953.
  This Newbery Honor book is the second story set in De Smet. The Wilder family survives a severe Dakota blizzard.

Wilder, Laura Ingalls. **On the Banks of Plum Creek.** Harper, 1937, 1953.
  Pa moves his family to Walnut Grove, Minnesota, into a dugout home. Crop failure and Mary's blindness test their pioneer spirit.

Wilder, Laura Ingalls. **On the Way Home.** Harper and Row, 1962.
  Laura's diary written in 1894 relates her trip with Almanzo from South Dakota to Mansfield, Missouri, where they retire.

Wilder, Laura Ingalls. **These Happy Golden Years.** Harper, 1943, 1953.
  Laura begins teaching, is courted, and gets married in this book.

Selected Books in the Spirit of Wilder

Anderson, Joan. **Joshua's Westward Journal**. Photographed by George Ancona. Morrow, 1987.
In this fictionalized historical photo essay, Joshua Carpenter and his family travel by Conestoga wagon over the National Road from Pennsylvania to Illinois and Iowa.

Brenner, Barbara. **Wagon Wheels**. Illustrated by Don Bolognese. Harper and Row, 1978.
In this easy-to-read historical narrative, a Black man and his three sons travel from Kentucky to Kansas to homestead just after the Civil War.

Brink, Carol Ryrie. **Caddie Woodlawn**. Macmillan, 1963.
Based upon reminiscences of the author's grandmother, this pioneer story concerns one year in the life of an 11-year-old girl on a Wisconsin farm.

Garson, Eugenia, compiler. **Laura Ingalls Wilder Songbook**. Illustrated by Garth Williams. Harper and Row, 1968.
Songs of home, ballads, dances, courtship, and hymns are compiled along with quotes from Wilder's books.

Harvey, Brett. **Cassie's Journey**. Illustrated by Deborah Kogan Ray. Holiday House, 1988.
Soft charcoal drawings accompany the account of a girl and her family traveling from Illinois to California in the 1860s.

Harvey, Brett. **My Prairie Year**. Illustrated by Deborah Kogan Ray. Holiday House, 1986.
Based on the author's grandmother's notebook of growing up in the Dakota Territory after a move from Maine in 1889, this book tells of surviving a prairie fire and a Dakota blizzard but also tells of the pleasures of spring.

Henry, Joanne Landers. **Log Cabin in the Woods**. Illustrated by Joyce Audy Zarins. Four Winds, 1988.
This "true life" narrative is told in chapters from January through December, chronicling the hardships and pleasures of growing up in Indiana in 1832.

MacLachlan, Patricia. **Sarah, Plain and Tall**. Harper and Row, 1985.
Sarah, a young woman from Maine, answers an advertisement for a wife/mother and leaves her home to help a father, daughter, and son find their own roots. This Newbery Award-winning book glows with love of a prairie landscape in the late 1800s.

Turner, Ann. **Dakota Dugout**. Illustrated by Ronald Himler. Macmillan, 1985.
Turner's poetic text tells of a pioneer woman living in a dugout house with her husband until they become prosperous enough to build a clapboard house.

Walker, Barbara M. **The Little House Cookbook**. Illustrated by Garth Williams. Harper and Row, 1979.
Much more than a cookbook, this social history of pioneer food describes country staples, food from the wilds, fields, and orchards. Quotes from the books encourage reading Wilder once again.

ENCORES
(OTHER PROGRAMS AND PROJECTS)

One of my fondest memories of elementary school is the daily readings from *Little House* books by my fourth-grade teacher. Many children read the books on their own much younger than that today, but they will still enjoy hearing them again if you choose to set aside a Laura Ingalls Wilder read-aloud. You could easily do this in a classroom setting, but also think about reading portions of the books in a library setting for children and their parents some frosty winter night.

If your students enjoy the Wilder books, try a read-aloud unit on other books set during the same time period. Consult the second section of the bibliography for suggestions. One of my all-time favorites, Patricia MacLachlan's *Sarah, Plain and Tall*, would appeal to any age group—even adults.

Other programs/units could be developed around real life pioneer heroes such as Daniel Boone, Davy Crockett, or Johnny Appleseed. Chapter 5, "Whoppers," covers a few of these figures.

Mark Twain's frontier book characters Tom Sawyer, Becky Thatcher, and Huckleberry Finn might be the focus for yet another unit. Take inspiration from Hannibal, Missouri's Tom Sawyer Days, held on Fourth of July weekend every year. Have your own fence-painting contest (a paper fence will work if you don't want to try the real thing) and read portions of *Tom Sawyer* and *Huckleberry Finn*.

"Living history" kinds of museums near you may have traveling consultants or staff willing to visit your school or library for a nominal fee. They can demonstrate pioneer crafts or skills. One of my most successful programs, "From Sheep to Shirt," included a visit from two staff members of Living History Farms in Des Moines, Iowa, who made natural dyes over a hot plate and carded and spun wool, while local weavers demonstrated how wool is woven into cloth. This program and others inspired by pioneer living can hook students and make them want to read more about the past.

11
Festival

INTRODUCTION

Celebrate the past by recreating a Renaissance or medieval festival in your classroom or library. As young people immerse themselves in the costumes, customs, and colors of times past, they will learn more dramatically and memorably than they can from reading books or writing reports. Adapt the ideas in this chapter to produce your own Renaissance Faire or Medieval Faire as the culminating event of a summer library program, at the end of a social studies unit, or as the beginning of an annual community pageant.

Part of the inspiration for this chapter is the popularity of various Renaissance and medieval fairs held in the United States. Some of these fairs focus on a particular year, others present a less exact time frame. This chapter incorporates ideas from both periods of history but also provides a brief historical background to help you plan your program/unit.

PURPOSE OF PROGRAM/UNIT

To enable young people to experience some of the culture, customs, and feeling of a particular period of history by recreating a Renaissance/Medieval festival.

A LITTLE BACKGROUND ABOUT THE MIDDLE AGES AND THE RENAISSANCE

These historical periods are not easy to pinpoint. Generally, the Middle Ages began in Europe after the fall of the Roman Empire, around A.D. 400. During the centuries that followed, knighthood was a way of life and the social/economic system called feudalism was dominant. Then, beginning in Italy around 1300 and spreading to the rest of Europe during the 1400s and 1500s, great social changes began the period we call the Renaissance. This era was a rich time of changes and advances in the arts, sciences, and politics deserving of greater depth than this brief treatment. Here are a few points to explore further.

- Feudalism, the system in which people owed loyalty and obedience to their lord, who, in turn, offered them protection, was the heart of the Middle Ages. Under this system, peasants were accountable to the barons, the lords of the manor, or the knights, who were accountable to the king, who was accountable to the head of the Church. By the time of the Renaissance, individual accomplishment was heralded more than the obedience and alliance to this system.

- The Middle Ages was a long period—nearly 500 years—of almost constant warfare throughout Europe. Knights might go off to the Holy Lands to fight in the Crusades, but everyday life was slow and arduous. Most people lived in villages that were isolated from one another because roads were poor and communication was difficult.

- The main classes of society during the Middle Ages were the peasants (those who worked the land), the fighting men, and the clergy. The king was at the head of society. The remaining people provided the goods and services that kept the system functioning—merchants, blacksmiths, bankers, fishermen, woodworkers, and even artists. On the fringes were beggars and criminals. Medieval society was a class society with a rigid social order.

- People lived in castles, villages, or towns during the Middle Ages. Castles belonged to kings and nobles and originally were built for defense or as military strongholds. Manors were the agricultural estates of barons or nobles. Villages grew up nearby the manors; towns grew because of trade; for example, they might be situated on a river.

- Even in the castles and manor houses, life was hard by our standards. Furnishings were simple, with only a few chairs, benches, and tables. Tapestries hung on walls, straw mixed with herbs was scattered on the floor. Disease was rampant, especially the Black Death, which killed one-third of Europe's entire population during only a two-year period in the fourteenth century. Houses for ordinary people had only one to two rooms, so people spent most of their time outside. They went inside to eat, sleep, and take refuge from the winter. People in villages kept shops in the same dwellings where they lived.

- People had few clothes and wore many layers to stay warm. Most clothes were made from wool, linen, and hemp, but the rich also had silk and velvet. Countries specialized in different kinds of fabrics. For example, England and Spain produced the best wool while Italy was known for velvet.

- During the Middle Ages, the ideas of chivalry and courtly love described an ideal way of life. The word *chivalry* comes from the French word for knight and referred to the ideal that knights fought glorious wars—not at all what existed in the real world. Another ideal was courtly love. Sung about in ballads and celebrated in poems, courtly love showed women as beautiful, helpless creatures, damsels in distress who were protected by strong, fearless knights. These notions may not have described the way ordinary people lived during the Middle Ages, but they were influential and shaped society for centuries afterward.

- Gradually changes took place in Europe—in trade, in society, in thinking—and by the fourteenth century, the flowering of new ideas and exploration was called the Renaissance, meaning "rebirth." Some of the changes included more trade and commerce; a population shift to cities; and advancements in science, transportation, and the arts.

- A major shift in thinking during the Renaissance concerned individual achievement. Artists during the Middle Ages, for example, were largely anonymous. During the Renaissance, however, we immediately think of the accomplishments of Leonardo da Vinci, Michelangelo, and dozens of others.

- We think of the Renaissance as a time of great wealth, but most people were still ordinary, poor shopkeepers and laborers. Many workers were protected by guilds, an early kind of trade union.

- Festivals and celebrations contrasted sharply with the struggle of everyday existence during the Middle Ages and Renaissance. Even the peasant classes enjoyed the pageants organized by the nobles. And the entertainments of the noble class included 20-course banquets with an entourage of more than 50 participants, from entertainers to the chief cook and all his assistants. Each month of the year was cause for a different celebration from Twelfth Night to Midsummer's Eve and on into Christmas. Country festivals were often connected with saints' days such as the Shrove Tuesday pancake races (still held in parts of England today) and May Day with dancing around the Maypole.

- Another kind of diversion was the fair, a gathering of merchants to display and sell their wares. These lasted up to three weeks with stalls set up for browsing that sold merchandise from different parts of the world.

- Music and drama played important parts in the leisure time of people during the Middle Ages and Renaissance. During the Middle Ages, ballad singers and instrumental music by lutes, bells, and horns accompanied the elaborate festival feast. Music was thought to aid digestion. By the time of the Renaissance, musical instruments became even more important. Lutes and stringed instruments—violins and violas—were popular. "Casual entertainment" provided by strolling players, wandering minstrels, and jugglers was popular during the Middle Ages and continued to be enjoyed during the Renaissance as well. Medieval drama was largely religious: The mystery and miracle plays recalled biblical stories and were first performed by the clergy inside the church. In time, the plays were taken outside to courtyards and performed by the guilds. Pageant wagons were set up in different parts of a town and the audience moved from station to station to see the story unfold. Other traditions that grew up during the Renaissance included the improvisational theatre known as the commedia dell 'arte that was performed out of doors on portable stages and on the backs of carts. Puppet plays were also popular during the Renaissance.

- We also can learn about the Middle Ages and Renaissance through art and architecture. Gothic cathedrals, medieval brasses decorating the tombs of noble people, and intricately woven tapestries are but a few records of the Middle Ages. By the Renaissance, art filled churches, palaces, and towns. The ceiling of the Sistine Chapel, the jeweled walls of the Medici Palace in Florence, and the lively scenes painted by Peter Brueghel tell us people enjoyed decorating their world and leaving behind a record of their accomplishments.

SETTING THE STAGE (PREPARATION)

Before you stage the festival, explore these periods further at the library. The bibliography in this chapter lists books about the Middle Ages and Renaissance in general as well as stories about knights and resource books about festivals and costumes. Other subject headings to investigate include Arthurian legends; castles; dragons; knights and knighthood; kings and rulers; civilization, Medieval; Middle Ages; and Renaissance. Of course, you can use particular names of historical figures such as Sir Gawain, Chaucer, Queen Elizabeth, and Michelangelo, too.

As you begin planning this event with the children, examine all aspects of the culture—costume, food, decoration, music, and drama—so the festival will be a colorful intermingling of these elements. Divide the group into Costumers, Banquet or Food Committee, Entertainers, and so on. This is a wonderful opportunity to teach children organizational skills needed to plan a big event by committee. Designate a student chair of the festival to coordinate the individual committees. If your students are too young to assume this kind of responsibility alone, call upon parent volunteers to chair committees that work with student assistants.

The event described in this chapter does not call for a banquet feast since many schools and libraries might find the preparations too complicated for their budgets and facilities. Rather than plan a sit-down banquet with roast pig and a wassail bowl, the activities here combine the medieval/Renaissance fair with merchant wares and entertainments as well as some of the festival elements—dances, jousts, ceremonies. Vary these events as your local talents and needs direct you. This plan is a springboard to inspire your creative achievements.

Medieval and Renaissance society was structured more than our democratic society. Festival participants will want to think about what role they will play. Some individuals might be knights of barons, others will be peasants or entertainers. The following list of possible characters will give children some ideas for costumes and activities as well.

Character list: knight, lady, lord of the manor, squire, peasant, blacksmith, fortune teller, troubador, spinner, weaver, jester, tailor, shoemaker (or cordwainer), cobbler, butcher, baker, criminal, herb seller, peddler, monk, nun, puppeteer, mime, actor, potter, artist, poet, barber, musician (piper, lute player, drummer, bell player), fisherman, innkeeper.

Children can make (or improvise) their costumes with a little assistance from parents and adult volunteers. Lynn Edelman Schnurnberger's invaluable resource book *Kings, Queens, Knights, and Jesters: Making Medieval Costumes* provides simple but effective instructions for basic tunics, capes, and the T-shaped gown. Directions for headgear—jester's hats, knight's helmets, crowns—and accessories are also given. If costumes are not made, you can find costumes in theatre departments or use old choir robes and add tights, long underwear, full tunic-style blouses, and scarves. Be creative! Figure 11.3 in the "Treasure Chest" provides inspiration.

You will probably want to read books with the children so they have some information about the characters in medieval/Renaissance society. This will allow them to more easily slip into these roles. Joe Lasker's *Merry Ever After* provides insight into the noble class and peasant class through the story of two medieval weddings, one between a noble couple and one between a peasant couple.

Decorations for your festival will depend on the setting itself. Will it be an outdoor event? If so, paper banners may not hold up under wind. You will be happier with bright fabric streamers and banners. A Maypole could be the major focus of the decorations. An outdoor volleyball stand made from a nine-foot length of galvanized pipe or a pole used for portable basketball goals (remove the goal) becomes a Maypole when tied with several dozen 3½-yard strips of brightly colored fabric. Borrow brightly colored tents from garden centers and businesses in your community for the different fair booths. If all else fails, make fair booths from refrigerator cartons. A sketch for a village peddler's booth is shown in Figure 11.2.

The indoor festival can use paper banners made from brightly colored construction paper and hung from dowels. Patterns for banners with coats of arms are given in Figure 11.1. These projects can be made by children, added to the room decorations, and then taken home later as mementoes of the festival.

Plan your festival around a series of fair booths and activities that are stationed around the room or outside around a park or school grounds. A few stations you might use: the Village Peddler, a stall with little trinkets, perhaps "white elephants" from home, that are given away; Ribbon Seller; Queen of Hearts Bake Shoppe, a food booth with little pastries such as heart-shaped shortbread; Ye Olde Ale House, where tankards can be displayed and little cups of "cuckoo-foot ale," or gingerale, can be given out; and fortune tellers' establishments. Invite craftspeople (ask local spinners and weavers to demonstrate their talents) and merchants to add their booths to the fair. Perhaps a local fabric store would set up a booth and a modern barber would play that role as if he or she were a medieval barber.

Other festival participants will wander around the grounds either entertaining or adding to the color. Older children who are jugglers or musicians can join adults who play recorders or lutes; some could mime or perform with puppets. Acrobats, magicians, sorcerers, and tinkers "selling" pots and pans join the wandering players, who mingle through the crowd rather than remaining in a stationary booth. This kind of wandering troupe adds a vital role to the overall festive mood of the event.

Unless you plan for the festival to only include a fair, you will need to plan a ceremony of some sort for the pageant that follows the fair. Invite members of the Society for Creative Anachronism to demonstrate their jousting skills or create your own ceremonies from the suggestions in "The Show Goes On."

THE SHOW GOES ON (THE PROGRAM PLAN)

Act I—The Fair portion of your festival is enjoyed by all with an open market atmosphere of merchants "selling" their wares and wandering players entertaining and playing their roles of the medieval/Renaissance society.

Act II—The master of ceremonies, or the Surveyor of the Ceremony as he or she would have been called, welcomes the guests to the festival. A horn fanfare would be an appropriate welcome. The Surveyor then announces the various events. A few suggestions follow.

Act III—Jousting by the fair knights from the Society for Creative Anachronism.

Act IV—A puppet play of Saint George and the dragon, a Punch and Judy show, or entertainment by a juggler or mime.

Act V—Storytelling by a "bard," either with or without musical accompaniment. Fairy tales would be most appropriate such as "Beauty and the Beast," "Sleeping Beauty," "Rumplestiltskin," or "Jack the Giant Killer." Many of these stories were known by children in Tudor times.

Act VI—A candlelight procession could conclude the event or a simple Maypole dance followed by a procession through a London Bridge style arch with participants leaving the festival singing the festival song in the "Treasure Chest."

THE TREASURE CHEST

The Festival Song
(Tune: "We Wish You a Merry Christmas")

Let's sing for our festival day!
Let's sing for our festival day!
Let's sing for our festival day!
May it last through the year!

Good tidings we bring
to you and your kin
Good tidings
And feasting
May it last through the year!

Let's sing for our festival day!
Let's sing for our festival day!
Let's sing for our festival day!
May it last through the year!
(*All cheer*)

Art for a Festival

Have your students make banners using the pattern and sample designs shown in Figure 11.1 to decorate for your festival. The sketch for the village peddler booth (Figure 11.2) and costume ideas (Figure 11.3) will give you further inspiration.

(Text continues on page 156.)

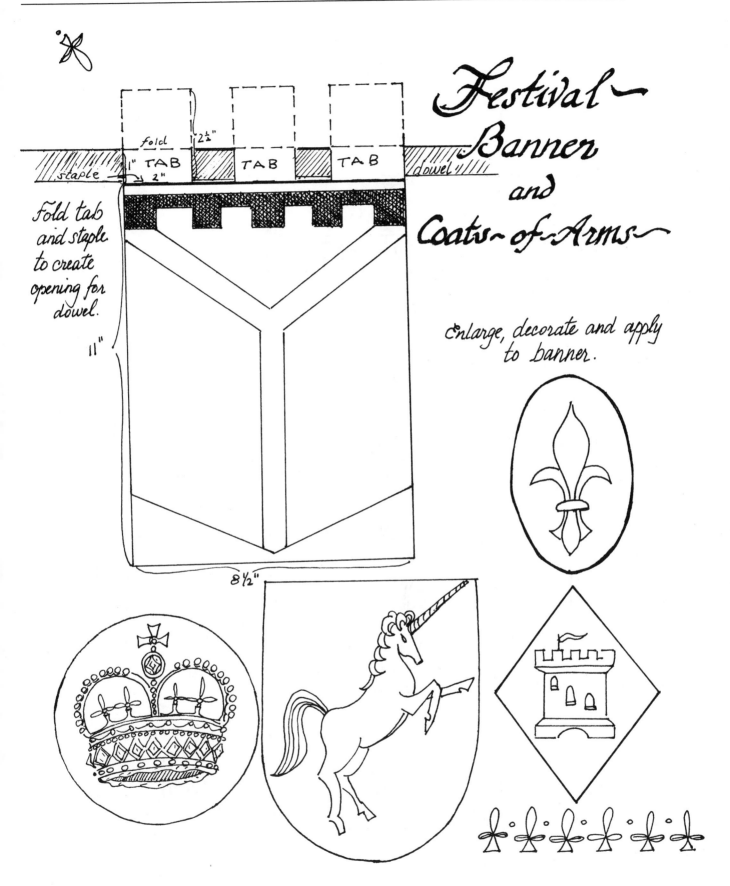

Fig. 11.1.

154 / Festival

Cut off top and one side of refrigerator carton.
Cut out windows or create shutters.

Fig. 11.2.

Fig. 11.3.

IN THE LIMELIGHT (PUBLICITY)

Adapt the publicity release in the preface and use the flyer shown in Figure 11.4. You might even find a town crier to announce the festival in your school or community.

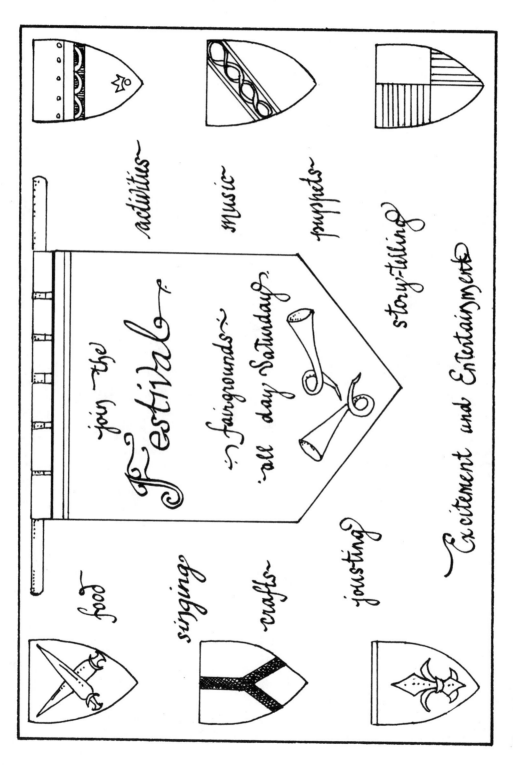

Fig. 11.4.

BIBLIOGRAPHY

Aiken, Amy. **Ruby the Red Knight**. Bradbury, 1983.
    A young girl sees suits of armor in a museum then goes home and makes herself a shield, sword, and helmet so she can go on adventures. In her imagination, Ruby fights a dragon and outsmarts a wizard, whom she brings before the king.

Aliki. **A Medieval Feast**. Crowell, 1983.
    A joyful celebration is planned at Camdenton Manor during the Middle Ages because the king and his entourage are coming to visit. Each step of the preparations is shown along with the splendid feast that includes a peacock, cooked and reassembled with its feathers, and a whole castle made out of pastry. This fictitious feast is set in about 1400 and based on the author-illustrator's fascinating research.

Anno, Mitsumasa. **Anno's Medieval World**. Adapted from the translation by Ursula Synge. Philomel, 1979.
    Framed within decorative borders, the medieval world that Anno presents believes in gods looking down from stars and witches flying through the air. Some revolutionary ideas—that the world is round and rotates on its axis—are introduced as people of the day might have reacted to them. This book is excellent for research reports or for children who are curious about thinking during the Middle Ages.

Blake, Quentin. **Snuff**. Lippincott, 1973.
    Snuff, a young page, seems incapable of learning the skills he should to become a knight, but he is clever enough to outwit four wicked boot thieves. In the end he shows promise that he will become a first-rate knight.

Buehr, Walter. **When Towns Had Walls: Life in a Medieval English Town**. Crowell, 1970.
    Daily life in Norcaster, a composite of medieval towns, is described with detailed accounts of medieval trades, professions, homes, feasts, and fairs.

Carrick, Donald. **Harold and the Giant Knight**. Clarion, 1982.
    Harold, a boy, has always been fascinated by the baron's knights, but when they take over his father's farm to train for the summer tournaments, Harold loses his enthusiasm for knighthood. He devises a clever plan to send them back to the castle.

Carrick, Donald. **Harold and the Great Stag**. Clarion, 1988.
    Harold, a young boy, sees the legendary Great Stag in the baron's forest. He is upset when he hears that the baron plans to hunt the stag and protects the stag's trail from the hunters.

Caselli, Giovanni. **The Renaissance and the New World**. Peter Bedrick, 1985.
    Third in a series of five books that tell about daily life from early civilizations to modern times, this one focuses on post-medieval culture of western Europe. It selects activities, technology, buildings, and costumes from England and western Europe to give the reader many representative examples, since "it is plainly not possible to depict a 'typical' Renaissance person."

Cosman, Madeleine Pelner. **Medieval Holidays and Festivals**. Scribners, 1981.
    This book describes 12 medieval celebrations, one for every month of the year beginning with Twelfth Night in January and ending with Christmas in December. Recipes are given for authentic foods and suggestions are provided for costumes and decorations.

De France, Marie. **Medieval Fables**. Translated by Jeannette Beer. Illustrated by Jason Carter. Dodd, Mead, 1983.
    This lavish collection of 30 medieval fables is beautifully illustrated with jewel-like illustrations.

Ellenby, Jean. **The Medieval Household**. Illustrated by Belinda Harrould. Cambridge University Press, 1984.
    Everyday life in a medieval household is examined through a series of topics such as "Manor Houses," "The Daily Round," "Fun and Games," and "Clothes."

Fradon, Dana. **Sir Dana: A Knight as Told by His Trusty Armor**. Dutton, 1988.
    A group of schoolchildren visits a museum and finds out about the time of knights from a talking suit of armor. Information is presented as answers to children's questions; for example, What is a squire? What is chivalry?

Gail, Marzieh. **Life in the Renaissance.** Random House, 1968.
   Decorated with many old prints and paintings, this voluminous text describes many facets of Renaissance life—fashions, houses, how people lived, earned their living, and were entertained. Developments in the arts and in medicine are also discussed.

Gee, Robyn. **Living in Castle Times.** Illustrated by Rob McCaig. Usborne, 1982.
   Numerous pictures and brief text tell about Thomas, a boy who lived about 600 years ago. An overview of the walled medieval town is shown on the first two-page spread with the following pages showing such aspects of daily life as school, mealtime, and festivals.

Gerrard, Roy. **Sir Cedric.** Farrar Straus Giroux, 1984.
   Sir Cedric, a gentle but bold knight rides off on an adventure and rescues Matilda the Pure from Mean Ned. Before Sir Cedric and Matilda marry, he must fight once more with the villain.

Gerrard, Roy. **Sir Cedric Rides Again.** Farrar Straus Giroux, 1986.
   Sir Cedric takes his wife and daughter on vacation to Jerusalem, where they are captured by evil Abdul the Heavy. But Sir Cedric, with the assistance of young Hubert, saves them in the best tradition of knights in shining armor.

Goodenough, Simon. **The Renaissance.** Marshall Cavendish, 1982.
   Color photographs and reproductions of drawings and paintings accompany a detailed text that explores Europe between 1300 and 1600. Topics include "Noble Entertainments," "Fashion and Finery," and "Sculpture in the Round."

Hazen, Barbara Shook. **The Knight Who Was Afraid of the Dark.** Illustrated by Tony Ross. Dial, 1989.
   Sir Fred was a bold knight who had won the heart of Lady Wendylyn, but his fear of the dark kept them apart until he boldly admitted his fear. This droll tale has a satisfying ending for today's children.

Hindley, Judy. **The Time Traveller Book of Knights and Castles.** Illustrated by Toni Goffe. Usborne, 1976.
   Numerous illustrations and text describe life in Europe in the year 1240. We are first introduced to people—knights, barons, squires, stewards—then taken on a trip to the castle, through the castle walls, and into the keep where the baron lives. Other particulars are described: getting dressed, bathing with soap made of mutton fat, shaving by rubbing off whiskers with a pumice stone, having a feast, and training to be a knight.

Hodges, Margaret. **Saint George and the Dragon.** Illustrated by Trina Schart Hyman. Little, Brown, 1984.
   Caldecott Award-winning illustrations accompany the text, a retelling of part of Spenser's *Faerie Queen* in which Saint George battles with a fearsome dragon that has laid waste to Una's land.

Lasker, Joe. **Merry Ever After.** Viking, 1976.
   The story of a noble wedding and a peasant wedding reveals medieval culture and costume through text and brilliantly colored illustrations, many reminiscent of paintings by famous artists of the period.

Lasker, Joe. **A Tournament of Knights.** Crowell, 1986.
   Set during the time of a medieval tournament, this story concerns Justin, a young knight who is challenged to fight by Sir Rolf, an experienced knight-errant (one who has little property and so must travel to tournaments to win ransoms from defeated opponents). Lasker provides a glossary and carefully detailed drawings with parts of the knight's armor labeled.

Macaulay, David. **Castle.** Houghton Mifflin, 1977.
   The step-by-step planning of the building of an imaginary castle is told through text and carefully detailed black-and-white drawings.

Macdonald, Fiona. **Everyday Life: The Middle Ages.** Silver Burdett, 1984.
   Brightly colored drawings, art reproductions, photographs, and text explore how people lived and worked between 1200 and 1500. Topics include feudalism, clothes and heraldry, international fairs, and fun and games.

Miquel, Pierre. **The Days of Knights and Castles.** Illustrated by Pierre Probst. Silver Burdett, 1980.
    Color illustrations accompany the text that introduces the Middle Ages through such topics as "Life in a Village," "Feasts and Famine," and "Tournaments and Jousting."

Monks, John. **The Great Book of Castles.** Rourke, 1989.
    Structures of castles, how they were built, and life behind the walls is described. Special topics include "Royal Castles" (those built as royal residences), "Castles as Prisons," and even "Cinderella's Castle: A Fairy Tale Come True" (the Walt Disney Magic Kingdom structure).

Oakley, Graham. **Henry's Quest.** Atheneum, 1986.
    In a small country that has only two books left, one of them is *King Arthur and the Knights of the Round Table*. The king (who calls himself Arthur II) chooses a quest to determine who would be a fit husband for his daughter. The quest is a search for the legendary substance gasoline. This is a thought-provoking book to use with students because it looks at the past and present and possible future.

Pierre, Michel. **The Renaissance.** Translated by Nan Buranelli. Illustrated by Nathaële Vogel. Silver Burdett, 1987.
    Paintings, photographs, and text introduce the Renaissance through a number of topics including "Leonardo, Born in Vinci," "Spectacle and Festival," and "A French Village in 1550."

Ross, Stewart. **A Crusading Knight.** Illustrated by Mark Bergin. Rourke, 1987.
    Numerous illustrations and an easy-to-read text present various topics associated with knights who went on Crusades to the Holy Land between 1096 and 1291.

Scarry, Huck. **Looking Into the Middle Ages.** Harper and Row, 1984.
    Pop-up pictures and brief text introduce the long ago times of 500-1500 "when kings and queens, princes and princesses lived in castles." The scenes of the castle can be viewed from both outside and inside where the viewer steps into the great hall, the banquet room, and peeks at the dungeon. Other scenes show a tournament with knights jousting and a cathedral with exterior and interior views.

Schnurnberger, Lynn Edelman. **Kings, Queens, Knights, and Jesters: Making Medieval Costumes.** Harper and Row, 1978.
    This invaluable resource gives detailed instructions for making costumes based on the tunic, the cape, and the T-shaped dress. Ideas for choosing medieval characters and decorating costumes will help young people to participate in medieval celebrations. This work is based on the author's experience in producing festivals held at the Cloisters, the medieval branch of the Metropolitan Museum of Art.

Uden, Grant. **A Dictionary of Chivalry.** Illustrated by Pauline Baynes. Crowell, 1968.
    This detailed reference book, arranged in alphabetical order, will lead the history buff or anyone searching for more information to the people, places, and things associated with the Middle Ages.

Unstead, R. J. **Living in a Castle.** Illustrated by Victor Ambrus. Addison-Wesley, 1971.
    Life in Wentworth Castle in England during the year 1250 is described through a series of short topics including "The Great Hall," "The People of the Household," and "Work and Play."

Unstead, R. J. **See Inside: A Castle.** Warwick Press, 1979.
    Detailed color illustrations and text describe the structure of and daily life in a typical medieval castle. Cutaway drawings show both exterior and interior views.

Ventura, Piero. **There Once Was a Time.** Putnam's, 1986.
    This illustrated world history focuses on certain periods and topics rather than providing a comprehensive chronological account. Both the Middle Ages and Renaissance are covered.

Wilkins, Frances. **Growing Up in the Age of Chivalry.** Putnam's, 1977.
    During the 100 years (1485-1603) of the Tudor period (known as the Age of Chivalry), tremendous change occurred. Various topics that show these changes in society reveal the reasons this time was a turning point in English history.

Windrow, Martin. **The Medieval Knight.** Illustrated by Richard Hook. Watts, 1985.
    Focusing on the "high medieval" period (1100-1500), this book presents such topics as "Men of Iron," "Raising an Army," and "The Knight Killers."

ENCORES
(OTHER PROGRAMS AND PROJECTS)

Smaller scale programs and projects might replace or supplement the scope of this festival. A program or mini unit on knights could feature reading aloud favorite stories about knights that are included in the chapter bibliography. Participants can make banners or shields from cardboard. An evening of medieval or Renaissance storytelling with the storytellers in costume can become an annual event. Be certain to hang banners in the room and use medieval music to set the mood.

Build on the popularity of this festival and plan a medieval feast or a madrigal dinner. High school and college music departments often plan such events. If your community does not already have this tradition, it might be a project you could initiate.

Sponsor class trips or encourage families to visit the medieval and Renaissance fairs in your state or region. Dozens of these events are held during the summer and early fall all around the country and they offer unique opportunities for young people to take a lively trip back into history.

12
Happy Holidays

INTRODUCTION

In the United States, Christmas is the most celebrated winter holiday. But many communities and school districts hesitate to hold special Christmas programs lest they offend non-Christian members of their population. The traditions of Christmas around the world are so richly varied and teach us so much about different ethnic groups it seems sad to dismiss mention of the holiday altogether. Perhaps you might spend a portion of this program/unit on other winter holidays such as the Jewish Hanukkah and the newly created Afro-American Kwanzaa. Sensitivity to ethnic and religious groups is important, especially as we work with children. And, in planning this area take into account your community's observances.

This chapter offers a trio of programs/units for you to choose from. The first program, "A Swedish Christmas," explores the customs, crafts, and stories of a Swedish Christmas. The second program, "The Goose Is Getting Fat," offers a readers theatre script from Mother Goose Land for you and your students to perform, with suggestions for Hanukkah and Christmas books from different countries to read aloud, too. The third program, "Boxes and Bags and Things with Tags," suggests holiday stories about giving as well as books about boxes and surprises, along with providing craft projects for boxes, bags, and tags to take home and share in the spirit of the season.

May this verse capture the spirit of the winter holiday season for you whatever holiday you celebrate!

Christmas
Kwanzaa
Hanukkah
Celebrate each year
Light the lights
And sing the songs
We are filled with cheer!

People giving presents
Sharing feasts and fun
Happy winter holidays
With joy for everyone!

A LITTLE BACKGROUND ABOUT WINTER HOLIDAYS (HAPPY HANUKKAH, HAPPY KWANZAA, AND MERRY CHRISTMAS!)

- Since ancient times winter holidays have centered around the winter solstice, the time when the sun is at its southernmost point and, in the Northern Hemisphere, the days are the shortest. Light seems to be especially sought after during this period. Lighting candles or turning on electric lights is an important feature of most of the winter holidays we celebrate today.

- The Jewish celebration of Hanukkah is also called the Festival of Lights. It falls sometime during December (the date varies from year to year) and lasts eight nights. It commemorates the victory of the Jewish people over the Syrians in 165 B.C. In rededicating their temples, the Jews had little oil for their holy lamps, but the oil they found lasted miraculously for eight nights. Jewish people celebrate Hanukkah by lighting candles on their menorahs, exchanging gifts, and enjoying special foods and games.

- The Afro-American holiday of Kwanzaa, based on the traditional African holiday of the harvest of the first crops, begins on December 24 and lasts seven days. This holiday was developed in 1966 and promotes principles of Black culture that include cooperation, creativity, and unity. Lights are lit on a seven-candle candelabra, gifts are exchanged, and traditional African foods are eaten.

- Christmas is a Christian holiday that celebrates the birth of Jesus on December 25. The season before Christmas is called Advent and, like Hanukkah, is associated with light. Advent wreaths have four candles, one for each Sunday before Christmas. Christmas customs vary according to the country in which it is celebrated, but the giving of presents by a Saint Nicholas, Santa Claus, Father Christmas, or Befana figure seems to be common to all.

- Saint Lucia, or Saint Lucy, originally came from Sicily. She had secretly dedicated her life to the church when she was a young girl, but her mother promised her in marriage. When the girl refused to marry her suitor, she was martyred. Lucy is the patron saint of Venice, and her story spread northward to Sweden where the feast day is celebrated on December 13. Saint Lucy's Day is a popular holiday in Sweden today, where the youngest girl in the household serves hot drinks and treats to the family upon rising.

HAPPY HOLIDAYS PROGRAM/UNIT ONE
A SWEDISH CHRISTMAS

Purpose

To introduce children to some traditions and stories of a Swedish Christmas and to have them make Swedish Christmas decorations.

Setting the Stage (Preparation)

Assemble materials for the crafts portion of this program (see the "Treasure Chest"). Since the making of Swedish-inspired Christmas decorations is a major focus, make lots of sample ornaments ahead of time as an inspiration for children. A dowel Christmas tree (see Figure 12.4) decorated with shiny red apples or cookies and Swedish Christmas chimes lit with candles would add to the setting. Swedish chimes can be borrowed, and you could ask someone in your community who has minimal woodworking skills to make a dowel tree. Volunteer groups often take on this kind of project.

Borrow an assortment of Swedish Christmas decorations from stores or from people you know. Straw goats, wooden elves (called *tomte*), bright red candelabras, straw wreaths, and ornaments are a few possibilities.

Designate a corner of the room for a dish of food for the good spirit of the house, the tomte. He is a kind of miniature Saint Nicholas who watches after the family all year, so the Swedish family rewards him with a dish of food that he comes to eat when no one is looking. (Children will relate this custom to the popular practice of leaving food on Christmas eve for Santa Claus.)

Choose an older girl to play the part of Saint Lucy for this program. In Swedish households on December 13, a girl in the house dresses in white and wears a crown of greenery with candles. She awakens the family with coffee, sweet drinks, and pastries. See Figure 12.3 in the "Treasure Chest" for suggestions for Saint Lucy's crown with nonflammable candles. Saint Lucy will lead the group in caroling.

Here are some Swedish customs you may wish to research even more with your students before the actual Swedish Christmas celebration.

- Swedish foods include pork, rice porridge, ginger cookies, and special pastries. Have your students make some of these ahead of time to bring.

- Making homemade presents is an important part of the holiday in Sweden. Presents are wrapped and poems are written for the recipient. Give your students opportunities to write little poems to give to friends and family members.

- Research the importance of Saint Lucy and the tomte. Astrid Lindgren's books about the tomte may already be familiar to your students. Prepare a display of these books along with Swedish folk tales and other holiday books.

- In all Scandinavian countries birds are given a Christmas tree of their own. A pole with a sheaf of wheat on the top is planted in the yard. Have students make suet ball or pinecone (spread with peanut butter and birdseed) treats for birds in the Swedish spirit.

The Show Goes On (The Program Plan)

Act I—Children are greeted by Saint Lucy, who takes them into the room for carols and comments about Swedish customs. Children may share traditions from their own families.

Act II—Swedish stories may be told or read aloud. An especially good selection would be Astrid Lindgren's *Christmas In Noisy Village* since it introduces the fun and traditions with glowing illustrations and joyful text. The story is also available in filmstrip or film version.

Act III—Children make an assortment of Swedish-inspired Christmas ornaments to take home: a straw star, a pink paper pig with a red bow tie (pigs are popular at holiday time in Sweden), a row of sprightly tomte for a greeting card or table decoration.

Act IV—Traditional Swedish treats are served—gingersnaps, spritz cookies. Treats are left for the tomte and a treat is left outside for the birds.

The Treasure Chest

Art for a Swedish Holiday

Use the patterns for the pig and the straw stars (Figure 12.1) and the tomte card (Figure 12.2) with your students. Saint Lucy's crown (Figure 12.3) and the dowel tree will help you recreate the program, too.

Swedish Dowel Christmas Tree

For the base of the tree, use a piece of pine approximately 8 inches long by 6 inches wide by 1½ inches thick. Drill a hole in the center of the wood. The large vertical dowel that fits in this hole should be approximately 30 inches long by ¾ inch in diameter. Drill four holes in this dowel about 5 inches apart. The first hole should be 5 inches from the top of the ¾-inch dowel, the next hole 10 inches from the top of the dowel, and so on until you have drilled four holes. These holes should be large enough to allow ¼-inch dowels to be inserted through them. The four thinner dowels should be cut in these lengths: 9 inches, 11 inches, 13 inches, 15 inches. Assemble the tree as shown in Figure 12.4.

(Text continues on page 168.)

164 / Happy Holidays

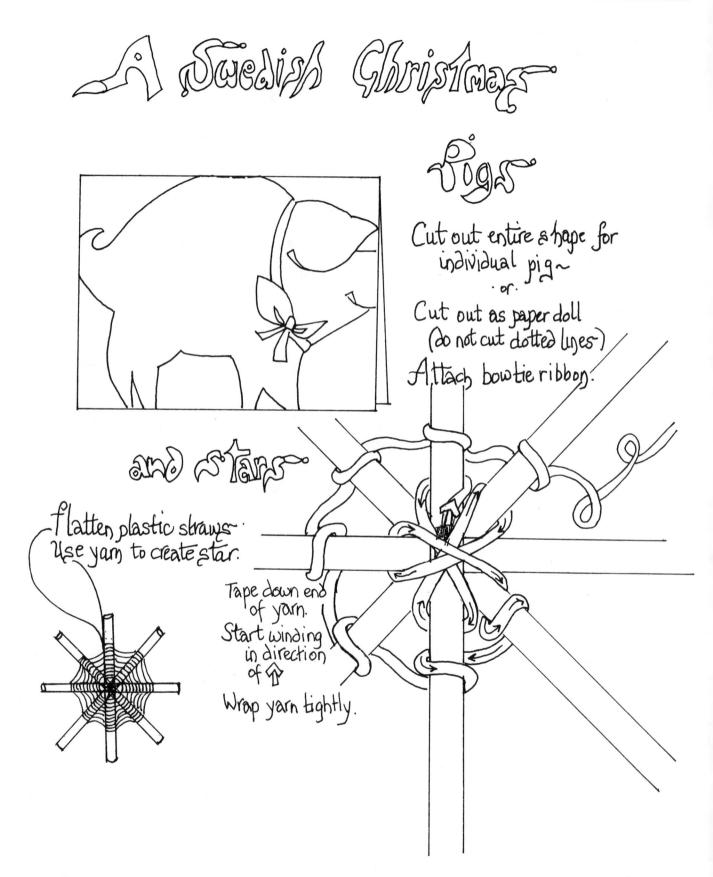

Fig. 12.1.

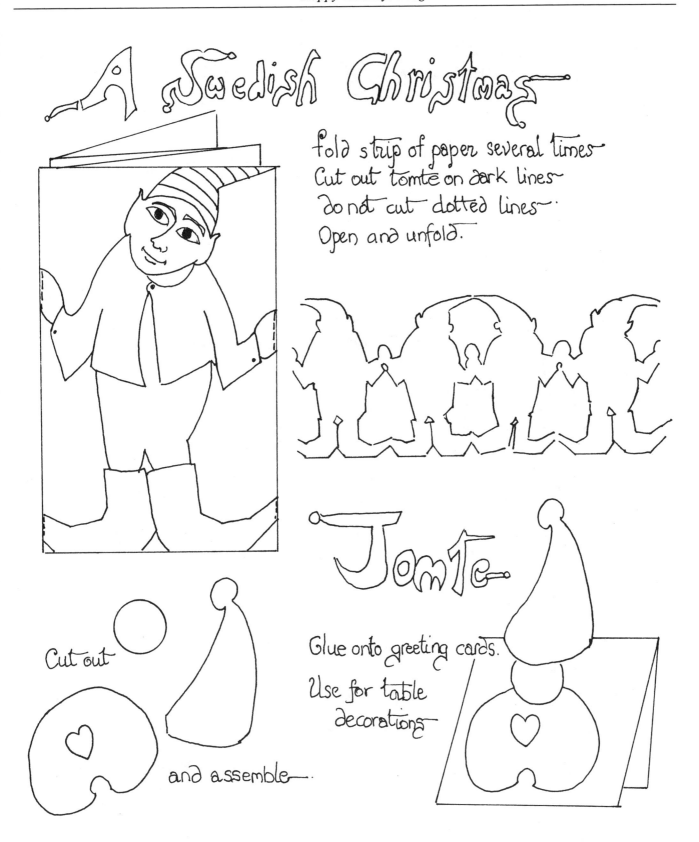

Fig. 12.2.

166 / Happy Holidays

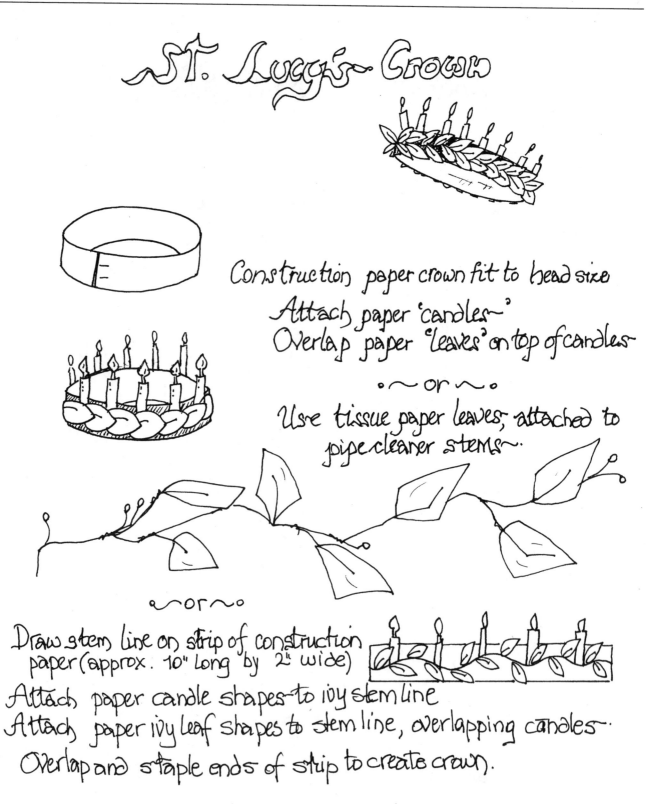

St. Lucy's Crown

Construction paper crown fit to head size
Attach paper "candles"
Overlap paper "leaves" on top of candles

~ or ~

Use tissue paper leaves, attached to pipe cleaner stems.

~ or ~

Draw stem line on strip of construction paper (approx. 10" long by 2" wide)
Attach paper candle shapes to ivy stem line
Attach paper ivy leaf shapes to stem line, overlapping candles.
Overlap and staple ends of strip to create crown.

Fig. 12.3.

Fig. 12.4.

168 / Happy Holidays

In the Limelight
(Publicity)

Use the publicity flyer shown in Figure 12.5 and make displays with the Swedish decorations to create interest in this program/unit.

Fig. 12.5.

HAPPY HOLIDAYS PROGRAM/UNIT TWO
THE GOOSE IS GETTING FAT

Purpose

To enjoy a readers theatre play set in Mother Goose Land at holiday time and to explore holiday traditions in different cultures including Hanukkah stories and Christmas stories in different countries.

Setting the Stage
(Preparation)

This holiday program has the least preparation in terms of decoration. You could ask Jewish students to bring in a menorah and dreidels for display items since you will be sharing Hanukkah stories for part of this program.

Choose eight children and adults to read the parts in the play "The Goose Is Getting Fat." Practice the play by reading through the script at least one or two days before the public "performance." Remember, characters will read from scripts rather than memorize lines, but they should be familiar enough with the lines to give a smooth and spirited reading. Add to the fun by having each character choose one article of clothing to be distinctive such as a bonnet for Bo Peep and a green shirt for Peter Piper. An important prop is a stuffed goose for Mother Goose to carry. This is the Christmas goose that Tom Tom the Piper's son brings in at the end.

You may want to serve treats at the end of this program. Simple treats might be candy canes; more elaborate treats might include making potato pancakes as a follow-up for the Hanukkah stories.

Make a display of holiday stories from different cultures, both Christmas and Hanukkah. Choose Christmas stories from Mexico, Italy, and other places with interesting customs. Marie Hall Ets' Caldecott winner *Nine Days to Christmas* is a favorite story about the Mexican posadas (the ceremonies the nine nights before Christmas with piñatas and games). Various versions of Befana, the Italian gift giver (see bibliography for specific editions) would also be a good selection. The late Marilyn Hirsch gave us many lovely Jewish stories including the Stone Soup variant *Potato Pancakes All Around* that all children love to hear whether or not Hanukkah is part of their holiday tradition.

The Show Goes On
(The Program Plan)

Act I—Mother Goose welcomes children to the program. The readers theatre play "The Goose Is Getting Fat" is presented. The script is included in the "Treasure Chest."

Act II—Children sing "Christmas Is Coming" and several Hanukkah songs.

Act III—Holiday stories are read or told. Choose from stories in the bibliography.

Act IV—Treats are given, such as candy canes or candies, or the group enjoys potato pancakes.

Act V—Holiday games are played.

The Treasure Chest

The Goose Is Getting Fat
(A Readers Theatre Script by Jan Irving) for Eight Readers

Characters
Mother Goose
Tommy Tucker
Mrs. Jack Sprat
Jack Sprat
Bo Peep
Peter Piper
Hickory Dickory Dock
Tom Tom the Piper's son

Mother G:	Welcome to Mother Goose Land! I am the real Mother Goose. And I am mayor in the Land of Rhyme and Sweet Reason. This is the busiest time of year because….
Tommy Tucker:	(*singing*) Christmas is coming. The goose is getting fat.
Mother G:	Yes, it's Christmas once again. And, as I always say, Christmas comes but once a year. And when it comes, it brings good … good … good … Oh dear, I can't remember what I always say. Each year seems to get busier than the last.
Tommy Tucker:	Mother Goose, are you feeling all right? Maybe you'd better take a long winter's nap.
Mother G:	Ah, Tommy Tucker, what a good boy you are! (*yawns*) Perhaps I'll just go take a little catnap. But, please, call Hickory Dickory Dock to wake me in time for Christmas.
Tommy Tucker:	Sweet dreams, Mother Goose. Greetings! My name is Tommy Tucker, I sing for my supper. Deck the halls with boughs of holly, fa la la la la la la la!
Mrs. J. Sprat:	Stop, brat! Catch that thief!
Jack Sprat:	What brat was that?
Mrs. J. Sprat:	I didn't see his face, but as sure as my name is Mrs. Jack Sprat, I think his name was Tom.
Jack Sprat:	Tom? Tom? Do you mean Tom Tom the Piper's son? Stole a pig and away he run?
Mrs. J. Sprat:	Yes, that's the Tom. But this time he stole a goose!
Bo Peep:	A goose? Not the Christmas goose that was getting fat!
Mrs. J. Sprat:	The very one!
Bo Peep:	Oh, boo hoo! First I lose my sheep. And now the goose is loose. Boo hoo! (*She cries into her lacy handkerchief.*)
Mrs. J. Sprat:	There, there, my dear. Tell me your name.
Bo Peep:	Oh, I'm just Little Bo Peep who lost her sheep and can't tell where to find them—
Mrs. J. Sprat:	Never you mind, Little Bo. Leave them alone and they'll come home.

Bo Peep:	Do you really think so?
Mrs. J. Sprat:	I know so! Mother Goose told me she's writing a poem all about you.
	Little Bo Peep lost her sheep And can't tell where to find them. Leave them alone And they'll come home Wagging their tails behind them.
	That's the way it goes.
Bo Peep:	How lovely!
Mrs. J. Sprat:	Now, why don't you come home with me for a nice cup of Christmas punch? It will cheer you up.
Bo Peep:	Why, I do believe that Christmas is coming after all.
Peter Piper:	Well, I don't want to sound like a sour pickle, but what kind of a Christmas will this be with no Christmas goose?
Bo Peep:	Oh, boo hoo! I forgot all about the goose. The goose is loose. What will we do?
Mrs. J. Sprat:	Yes, the goose. Oh, I do love goose. All that fat. I love fat! What WILL we do with no goose for Christmas?
Tommy Tucker:	I know, let's go to Old Mother Hubbard's. She has a big cupboard. I bet she'll have lots of goodies tucked away there. I'll go see. (*singing*) Deck the halls with boughs of holly, fa la la la la la....
Mrs. J. Sprat:	How can he sing at a time like this?
Peter Piper:	I know—let's all sing. Maybe it will cheer us up. And it will take your mind off of eating, too, Mrs. Sprat.
Mrs. J. Sprat:	What a bright young man! Who are you anyway?
Peter Piper:	I'm the famous Peter Piper. I picked a peck of pickled peppers!
Mrs. J. Sprat:	How many pecks of pickled peppers have you picked, Peter?

Peter Piper:	Why, I've got pecks and pints and pints and pecks of pickled peppers! I've probably picked more pints and pecks of pickled peppers than any person has ever pretended to pick!
Mrs. J. Sprat:	Perfect! Why don't we go to your house for Christmas? We could make a pickled pepper pie!
Jack Sprat:	Pickled pepper pie? How preposterous! But, it does sound better than goose. I know—let's all make a Christmas party—goose or no goose.
Bo Peep:	Mr. Sprat, that is the best idea yet. Let's make it a surprise party for good old Mother Goose. She works so hard all year making those wonderful rhymes about us just so children will be happy all over the world.
Mrs. J. Sprat:	This will be the best Christmas in Mother Goose Land. Bo Peep, run down the lane to Little Jack Horner's and ask him to bring his Christmas pies. Jack Sprat, you go to the pumpkin patch. Maybe Peter Peter Pumpkin Eater can give us some nice fat pumpkins. And I will visit the Queen of Hearts. She makes the most divine tarts—cherry tarts, lemon tarts, blueberry tarts, strawberry tarts....
Jack Sprat:	Well, let's don't stand here just dreaming of sugar plums. Everyone—be nimble, be quick. And let's meet back here at six o'clock!
All:	(*singing*) Christmas is coming— The goose is on the loose So please make a sweet or A holiday treat. If you haven't got a partridge A French pear tree will do, If you haven't got a French pear tree, Then what will we do? (*They exit.*)
Hickory D:	Ding dong, ding dong, Ding dong, ding dong, Say, did I ding enough? Did anyone count? I am the Hickory Dickory Dock clock and I'm ready to ring out the bells for Christmas. Did you bring something along for the party? A sugar plum or a blackbird baked in a pie? Look, here comes Tommy Tucker. Let's hear what he found at Mother Hubbard's.

Tommy Tucker:	When I got there, the cupboard was bare. Tom Tom the Piper's son must have already stolen all the goodies for himself.
Hickory D:	And it's time to ring the bells for Christmas! Where is everyone? I do hope they found something for the party. And did anyone find Mother Goose? She always leads the carols.
Tommy Tucker:	I'm afraid I don't feel like singing. It doesn't look like there will be any supper to sing for.
All:	(*singing*) We wish you a Merry Christmas, we wish you a Merry Christmas, we wish you a Merry Christmas, and a Happy New Year!
Mrs. J. Sprat:	(*singing*) I've brought us a figgy pudding, I've brought us a figgy pudding, I've brought us a figgy pudding, and a blackbird in a pie!
Jack Sprat:	And I got two of Peter Peter Pumpkin Eater's pumpkins!
Bo Peep:	And here is Jack Horner's plum straight from his thumb—and two of his favorite Christmas pies!
Mother G:	Christmas is coming. The goose is big and fat— Merry Christmas, my children!
All:	Mother Goose, we thought the goose was on the loose.
Tommy Tucker:	And I saw Tom Tom the Piper's son take him, too!
Mother G:	Rubbish. Tom is our hero.
All:	Hero?
Mother G:	Why, just as I was settling down for a long winter's nap, the goose got loose.
All:	No! And what did you do?
Mother G:	I called for King Cole.

Tommy Tucker:	A good idea!
Mother G:	But he was calling for his pipe and his bowl so he didn't hear me. So I called for all the king's horses and all the king's men—
Tommy Tucker:	A good idea!
Mother G:	But they were trying to put Humpty Dumpty back together again so they didn't come. So I called for Yankee Doodle Dandy.
Tommy Tucker:	What a good idea!
Mother G:	But he was too busy parading around on that silly horse of his. Well, I was in a dither when Tom Tom the Piper's son jumped on his pig. (He's very good at quick getaways.) But, this time the Christmas spirit must have softened his heart. Tom caught the goose, and he even cooked it for our Christmas dinner.
All:	He cooked our goose?
Mother G:	Yes, but this time it was the right goose—the Christmas goose that was getting fat for our celebration! Tom Tom, bring on the goose—
Tom Tom:	Christmas comes but once year And when it comes, it brings good cheer!
Mother G:	Hear hear! I couldn't have said it better myself. And, now, everyone, sing— Christmas is coming The goose is getting fat Please put a penny in the old man's hat. If you haven't got a penny, A ha'penny will do. If you haven't got a ha'penny— Then I'll bless you!

And, good wishes from all of us in Mother Goose Land for a merry holiday. May your stockings be stuffed with sugar plums and all of your dreams come true!

In the Limelight (Publicity)

Use the sample flyer shown in Figure 12.6 to publicize this program. Carolers can sing "The Goose Is Getting Fat" in your school or community to create further interest.

Fig. 12.6.

HAPPY HOLIDAYS PROGRAM/UNIT THREE
BOXES AND BAGS AND THINGS WITH TAGS

Purpose

To introduce stories and activities about giving and containers for gifts since so many of the winter holidays are concerned with the spirit of giving.

Setting the Stage (Preparation)

Assemble as many different kinds of boxes and bags as you can find. Not all of them have to be gift-wrapped boxes, but this can certainly be a part of the decoration and display. The numerous commercial gift boxes and bags available nowadays will make this an easy and beautiful display. You might ask volunteers to gift wrap boxes in unusual ways. Japanese style gift wrap is one possibility.

Other kinds of boxes to assemble could be lunchboxes, hat boxes, Chinese carry-out boxes, music boxes, toy boxes, shoeboxes, and anything else you think might be fun. Bags to include might be lunch bags, grocery bags, laundry bags, and doggy bags.

Don't overlook the possibility of making things from boxes and bags, too. You could have a box puppet, a paper bag mask, a shoebox train, and a doll made out of a bag. An assortment of these glorified boxes and bags could be the inspiration for many projects children can make at home.

The program encourages children to make and give their own gifts during this time of year. Children might be asked to each bring one dozen cookies to exchange with others, then take home the cookies in a box you provide. You could even encourage giving gifts to the needy by having children bring food to pack in boxes and take to gift distribution centers in your community. Introduce children to the English custom of Boxing Day. On the day after Christmas, British families give presents to their household employees or other service employees.

Set up a tag-making center in one corner of the room for children to make gift tags at the beginning or end of the program. You might have an assortment of commercial stamps and precut paper for tags or you could make your own stamps from vegetables and stamp pads. Computer programs with graphics could be used or see the sample in Figure 12.7.

Assemble materials for any crafts you will be making. Sample projects are included in the "Treasure Chest." If you want to make a very simple project, get plain white boxes from a bakery or candy store and provide stamps, stickers, markers, and construction paper for children to decorate as they like. Plain sandwich bags can also be decorated.

The Show Goes On (The Program Plan)

Act I—As children come, play box and bag games. For the first game, wrap a bag of candy (or fortune cookies or an assortment of lots of small prizes) in a small box. Then wrap this box in a larger box, and this box in yet a larger box. Seat children in a large circle and play music or all sing a song as the box is passed around the circle. When the music stops, the child holding the box unwraps it. Play continues until the last box is unwrapped and the prize is shared. Vary this game by putting riddles or jokes in the boxes and inviting children to guess the answers. For another game, place odd-shaped objects in a laundry bag that is closed. Pass the bag around and let children guess the contents.

Act II—Read stories about boxes and bags selected from the bibliography. You may choose to read a story and then play another box game in between. Many stories or books about boxes show different things children can make from boxes. One of these books is *Christina Katerina and the Box* by Patricia Gauch. If you read this book, you may give children a large carton and turn it into something else.

Act III—Make a box, a bag, and a tag project children can take home.

The Treasure Chest

Art Featuring Boxes and Bags and Tags

Use the gift box, bag, and tag ideas in Figure 12.7 to inspire your students to create their own projects. Purchase plain white boxes (or ask local stores to donate them) for these projects. Bakeries or candy stores are two good sources. Provide children with stickers, stamps, construction paper, fabric, and assorted notions to decorate boxes as they like. The boxes could be made into gift boxes or a holiday scene.

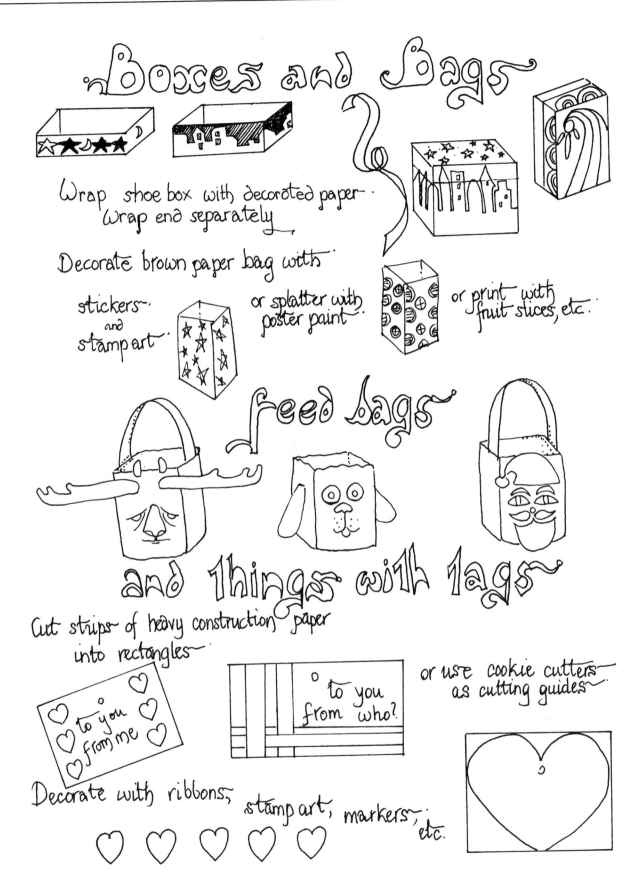

Fig. 12.7.

178 / *Happy Holidays*

Use plain bags donated by local stores or purchase brown sandwich bags. These may be decorated "free style" or turned into characters, such as the Santa Bag shown in Figure 12.7, or a feed bag for reindeer.

In the Limelight (Publicity)

Use the flyer shown in Figure 12.8 to publicize this program. Window displays in local stores of the projects in this section can promote the program for public libraries.

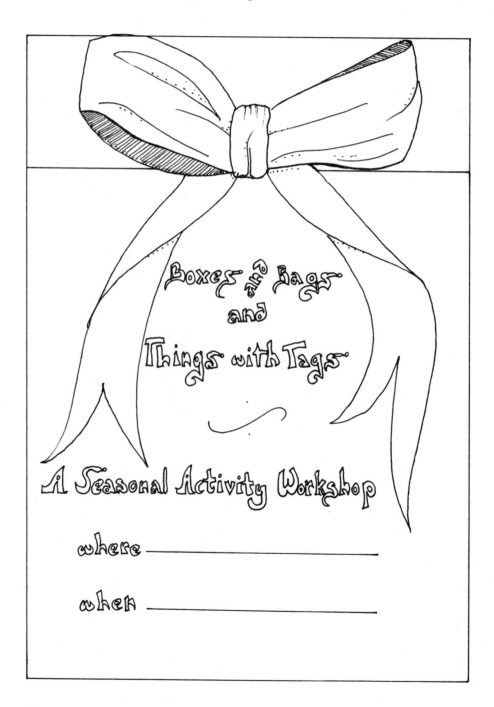

Fig. 12.8.

BIBLIOGRAPHY
(FOR ALL THREE HAPPY HOLIDAY PROGRAMS)

Adler, David A. **A Picture Book of Hanukkah.** Illustrated by Linda Heller. Holiday House, 1982.
  The historical story of Hanukkah is told as the Greeks, led by Antiochus, overcome the Jews and ransack their temple. The Jews, led by Judah Maccabee, successfully fight Antiochus and regain the temple. The one day's supply of oil they find to rededicate their temple burns for a miraculous eight nights. Thus the tradition of Hanukkah is celebrated for eight nights. Modern-day customs are also told.

Adler, David A. **A Picture book of Jewish Holidays.** Illustrated by Linda Heller. Holiday House, 1981.
  This brief text captures the feelings behind Jewish holidays throughout the year.

Aleichem, Sholem. **Hanukah Money.** Translated and adapted by Uri Shulevitz and Elizabeth Shub. Illustrated by Uri Shulevitz. Greenwillow, 1978.
  Motl and his brother enjoy the Hanukkah, but they are especially focused on how much Hanukkah money they will receive.

Becker, Joyce. **Hanukkah Crafts.** Bonim, 1978.
  Instructions are given for 12 kinds of menorahs, six styles of dreidels, party plans, puppets, and numerous ideas for homemade gifts.

Becker, Joyce. **Jewish Holiday Crafts.** Bonim, 1977.
  Candleholders for Sabbath, greeting cards for Rosh Hashanah, plus menorahs and dreidels for Hanukkah are described.

Brinn, Ruth Esrig. **More Let's Celebrate.** Illustrated by Katherine Janus Kahn. Kar-Ben Copies, 1984.
  Directions are given for 57 Jewish holiday crafts including a dreidel mobile for Hanukkah and paper bag costumes for Purim.

Burns, Marilyn. **The Hanukkah Book.** Illustrated by Martha Weston. Four Winds, 1981.
  This book explains the Hanukkah story, the Jewish calendar as well as the Gregorian, and includes recipes, patterns for two kinds of dreidels, and instructions for playing. The final chapter deals with Christmas and how various Jewish families handle this holiday in relation to Hanukkah.

Chapman, Jean. **The Sugar-Plum Christmas Book.** Illustrated by Deborah Niland. Children's Press, 1977.
  Amusing illustrations and lively text present stories, poems, songs, recipes, and craft projects to keep children busy for many holiday days.

Coopersmith, Jerome. **Jerome Coopersmith's A Chanukah Fable for Christmas.** Illustrated by Syd Hoff. Putnam's, 1969.
  A man on a flying dreidel takes Murray, who celebrates Hanukkah and misses not having Santa Claus in his tradition, on a round-the-world trip to see the different ways people celebrate winter holidays.

Corwin, Judith Hoffman. **Jewish Holiday Fun.** Julian Messner, 1987.
  This activity book has patterns and methods to make projects from a miniature *sukkah* (the booth used in Sukkot, the harvest festival) and New Year's cards for Rosh Hashanah to Purim puppets and cookies for Hanukkah.

Cuyler, Margery. **Jewish Holidays.** Illustrated by Lisa C. Wesson. Holt, Rinehart, and Winston, 1978.
  The rituals of Jewish holidays are described along with accompanying projects for table decorations and games.

de Paola, Tomie. **The Legend of Old Befana.** Harcourt Brace Jovanovich, 1980.
  In this picture book version of the Italian legend, an old woman refuses the offer of the Three Kings to journey to Bethlehem, so she searches to this day for the Baby King.

Drucker, Malka. **Hanukkah: Eight Nights, Eight Lights.** Illustrated by Brom Hoban. Holiday House, 1980.
  This book for slightly older children gives the history of Hanukkah and includes Hanukkah songs sung as blessings, games, recipes for the traditional *latkes* as well as *sufganiyyot*, the orange-flavored donuts served in Israel. Suggestions for decorations are included with the caution: "Don't overdo it! Hanukkah is not a major celebration for Jews as Christmas is for Christians."

Ets, Marie Hall, and Aurora Labastida. **Nine Days to Christmas**. Illustrated by Marie Hall Ets. Viking, 1959.
  A five-year-old girl's excitement about the Christmas festivities includes the posada celebration and piñata party enjoyed by many Mexican-Americans.

Foley, Daniel J. **Christmas the World Over**. Chilton Book Company, 1963.
  Although this book isn't recently published, it holds a wealth of information about specific Christmas customs in countries in Europe and Latin America with brief notes on Asia and Australia. Anyone wishing to duplicate the Swedish Christmas program/unit will find a lengthy discussion of Sweden in this source.

Galdone, Paul. **What's in Fox's Sack?** Clarion, 1982.
  Use this cumulative tale about a fox who is eventually outsmarted with the program on boxes and bags and things with tags.

Gauch, Patricia. **Christina Katerina and the Box**. Coward, McCann, Geoghegan, 1971.
  Christina Katerina and her friends turn a large box into a variety of vehicles as they use their imaginations.

Greenfeld, Howard. **Chanukah**. Holt, Rinehart, and Winston, 1976.
  The historical account of the Maccabees' triumph over Antiochus and the Greeks and the rededication of the Jewish temple are told within the context of Jewish struggle throughout history, even into modern times, for their freedom and individuality. The format of this book is beautiful, making the story even stronger.

Hirsch, Marilyn. **I Love Hanukkah**. Holiday House, 1984.
  A young boy describes his family's celebration of Hanukkah. Grandpa reads the historical account. Customs at the table and games are also described.

Hirsch, Marilyn. **Potato Pancakes All Around**. Bonim, 1978.
  A wandering peddler teaches a village family how to make potato pancakes from only a crust of bread so they can have a happy Hanukkah.

Lindgren, Astrid, and Ilon Wikland. **Christmas in Noisy Village**. Viking, 1964.
  Christmas activities of Swedish children in this story include cookie baking, decorating, feasting, caroling, and taking a sleigh ride. The illustrations glow and the text exuberantly captures the spirit of the season. This is a perfect read-aloud for the Swedish Christmas program/unit.

Plume, Ilse. **The Story of Befana**. David R. Godine, 1981.
  Jewel-like illustrations accompany this retelling of the Italian legend about Befana, the Christmas witch who brings presents to children.

Simon, Norma. **Hanukkah**. Illustrated by Symeon Shimin. Crowell, 1966.
  This historical account of the Maccabees overcoming the Greeks also includes Hanukkah customs around the world.

Singer, Isaac Bashevis. **The Power of Light: Eight Stories of Hanukkah**. Illustrated by Irene Lieblich. Farrar Straus and Giroux, 1980.
  Eight tales are presented, one for each night of Hanukkah, including the story "The Power of Light," set in Warsaw during World War II, in which two young people in love escape from the Nazis because the one holiday candle they find gives them hope. Rich paintings add to the depth of the stories.

Steele, Phillip. **Festivals around the World**. Dillon, 1986.
  Large color photos and brief text introduce children to 14 festivals including a bun festival in Hong Kong, a water festival in Burma, and Chinese New Year in San Francisco.

Treasures of Chanukah. Illustrated by Greg Hildebrandt. Unicorn Publishing House, 1987.
  The jewel-like illustrations spread across the pages like paintings edged in gold frames and tell, along with the text, the historical story of the Maccabees and contemporary traditions with songs (music included) and blessings.

Van Straalen, Alice. **The Book of Holidays around the World**. Dutton, 1986.
Bright color photos and paintings accompany the text, arranged by day of the year for holidays and birthdays of famous people all over the world. Various holidays such as Chinese New Year, Hanukkah, and Easter are explained in the appendix.

Wells, Rosemary. **Morris's Disappearing Bag**. Dial, 1975.
Nobody wants to play with Morris's Christmas bear, but when he discovers an unopened present—a disappearing bag—everyone is interested. This book will add to the fun of the boxes and bags and things with tags program.

Willson, Robina Beckles. **Merry Christmas**. Illustrated by Satomi Ichikawa. Philomel, 1983.
Glowing illustrations and text tell the biblical story with brief chapters about traditions in many different countries. Some projects are also included such as paper heart baskets from Sweden.

ENCORES (OTHER PROGRAMS AND PROJECTS)

Winter holidays offer a world of possibilities for celebrations. Here are a few more suggestions:

- Develop a full program on the Afro-American Kwanzaa.

- Develop a program around the theme "An Old-Fashioned American Christmas" with readings from Louisa May Alcott, Laura Ingalls Wilder, and other favorite authors' accounts of Christmas.

- If you enjoy the Swedish Christmas program, you could have a piñata party from Mexico as an alternative. Make your own simplified piñatas from paper bags or spend a little more time and make one from papier-mâché.

- Finally, consider the spirit of the season and have a toy-making workshop with all the toys donated to a local charity. See the books in the resource bibliography for projects to make. Whatever way you choose to celebrate, have a happy holiday and use the occasion to instill a spirit of giving and cooperation in your students and your community.

Resource Bibliography

With so many rich sources available for the teacher and librarian, this resource bibliography could easily become another full chapter. I have selected a few titles in different areas—bibliographic guides; children's literature texts; multicultural guides; general programming sources; and resource books on particular areas such as readers theatre, creative dramatics, puppetry, and crafts—that I have found particularly useful for librarians and teachers. I own many of these titles since I believe educators need their own professional materials as well as the wider resources of school and library collections.

Bauer, Caroline Feller. **Celebrations.** Illustrated by Lynn Gates Bredeson. Wilson, 1985.
  This lively resource contains 16 holiday and theme-related programs from traditional choices (Saint Patrick's Day) to more unusual ones (National Nothing Day). Excerpts from stories and poems, bulletin board suggestions, activities, projects, and booklists fill out each chapter.

Bauer, Caroline Feller. **Handbook for Storytellers.** American Library Association, 1977.
  This handbook remains a favorite for introducing the wide range of storytelling methods. Storytelling is always used to encourage children to read books, a message dear to the hearts of librarians and teachers!

Bauer, Caroline Feller. **Presenting Reader's Theatre.** Illustrated by Lynn Gates Bredeson. Wilson, 1987.
  The bulk of this attractive and invaluable collection is brief scripts adapted from popular children's books. The scripts can be photocopied (even tickets are provided) to use with children in your classroom or library. General suggestions will help you get started even if readers theatre is not a familiar technique.

Bauer, Caroline Feller. **This Way to Books.** Illustrated by Lynn Gates Bredeson. Wilson, 1983.
  This collection of ideas and activities to bring children and books together includes programs on monsters, cats, authors' birthday parties, as well as poetry and much more.

Champlin, Connie, and Nancy Renfro. **Storytelling with Puppets.** American Library Association, 1985.
  Books by these authors are filled with creative and practical ideas for puppet construction and performance. This one is particularly good in using puppets to share favorite books with children from preschool through grade six.

Coger, Leslie Irene, and Melvin R. White. **Readers Theatre Handbook.** Scott, Foresman, 1973.
  This complete handbook fully explains the backgrounds of readers theatre with a chapter devoted to use with children and a section of sample scripts.

Croft, Doreen J., and Robert D. Hess. **An Activities Handbook for Teachers of Young Children.** Houghton Mifflin, 1985.
  This source is divided into nine parts: arts, music and drama, math, language arts, physical world, health and safety, cooking and nutrition, computers for preschoolers, and themes. Some of the themes on ethnic holidays can be adapted for the primary grades.

Cullinan, Bernice E., ed. **Children's Literature in the Reading Program.** International Reading Association, 1987.
  Educators have contributed essays on topics from why we need children's literature in the reading program to using poetry, enriching the basal reading program, and extending multicultural understanding through books.

Cullinan, Bernice E. **Literature and the Child.** 2d ed. Harcourt Brace Jovanovich, 1989.
  This new children's literature text is divided into three parts. The first describes the child in relation to children's literature. The second focuses on books, organized by genre. The third explores multicultural backgrounds and gives a history of children's books. "Teaching Idea" features are sprinkled throughout the text.

Durkin, Lisa Lyons, ed. **Celebrate Every Day.** Illustrated by Debby Dixler. First Teacher Press, 1977.
  Designed for the early childhood caregiver, this resource is founded on the belief that celebrations, big and small, teach children about countries, cultures, and the joy of being alive. The recipes, party ideas, and crafts are adaptable for libraries and elementary classrooms.

Hawkins, Melba. **Programming for School-Age Child Care. A Children's Literature Based Guide.** Libraries Unlimited, 1987.
  This guide covers programming needs for children ages five to eight, components of responsive programs, program models, and includes chapters on art, creative dramatics, music, cooking, and holidays.

Huck, Charlotte, Susan Helper, and Janet Hickman. **Children's Literature in the Elementary School.** Holt, Rinehart, and Winston, 1987.
  The fourth edition of the classic children's literature text provides a background to the literature and an understanding of children's responses to literature. "Planning the Literature Program" extends that knowledge into practical approaches for using children's literature in the school. Public libraries will find this an important reference, too.

Kimmel, Margaret Mary, and Elizabeth Segel. **For Reading Out Loud! A Guide to Sharing Books with Children.** Delacorte, 1988.
  The second edition of this bibliographic guide contains suggestions for reading books aloud to elementary and middle school students. The 175 books are all annotated and read-aloud time is given. A new section, "Off to a Good Start," describes 125 titles for infants through kindergarten.

Kobrin, Beverly. **Eyeopeners! How to Choose and Use Children's Books about Real People, Places, and Things.** Penguin, 1988.
  Five hundred nonfiction titles are arranged under 60 subject headings and all annotated in such a lively manner that your students will want to read them all. This book will direct you to fact-packed books to use with children preschool through grade nine.

Laughlin, Mildred Knight, and Letty S. Watt. **Developing Learning Skills through Children's Literature.** Oryx, 1986.
  The introduction provides a rationale for a literature program in the school, then the six chapters identify grade levels—kindergarten through the elementary grades—with 10 units fully developed. Many author programs with biographical sources and activities are included. This source will extend the use of the chapter "Author! Author!" in *Fanfares*.

Lee, Nancy, and Linda Oldham. **Hands on Heritage.** Hands On Publications, 1978.
  Seven cultures—China, Greece, Israel, Japan, Mexico, native Americans, and West Africa—are presented through hands-on arts, cooking, and recreational activities. Numerous educational and community resource lists extend this work's usefulness.

Lima, Carolyn, ed. **A to Zoo: Subject Access to Children's Picture Books.** 2d ed. Bowker, 1986.
  This index provides quick access to 8,500 titles listed under 600 subject headings. Titles are suitable through grade two.

McCaslin, Nellie. **Creative Drama in the Primary Grades.** Longman, 1987.
  This text, designed for those with no experience but the desire to incorporate drama into the classroom, explains methods then provides practical activities. Objectives, stories, and suggestions for the teacher will also help the public librarian.

McElmeel, Sharron. **An Author a Day (for Pennies)**. Libraries Unlimited, 1988.
    Already listed in the chapter "Author! Author!" as a good source for author-related programs, this book will inspire you to create your own author units and programs in the classroom or library.

McNeill, Earldene, Allen, Judy, and Velma Schmidt. **Cultural Awareness for Young Children**. Illustrated by Barbara McNeill Brierton. Learning Tree, 1981.
    This multicultural source focuses on six cultures—Asian, Black, cowboy, Eskimo, Mexican, and native American—with basic background on clothing, homes, food, arts, nature and science, language, games, music, and special events.

Moss, Joy F. **Focus Units in Literature. A Handbook for Elementary Teachers**. NCTE, 1984.
    Schools interested in a literature based curriculum that uses literature across the school curriculum will find carefully sequenced units on such topics as toy animals, folk tale patterns, and Japan that are developed for the elementary grades.

Newman, Dana. **The Early Childhood Teacher's Almanack**. Illustrated by Sarah Laughlin. Center for Applied Research in Education, 1984.
    Arranged by the months of the year, dozens of holidays and birthdays of famous people are included along with recipes, art, and science projects to help children celebrate. Primary grade schoolteachers will find this helpful.

Nobleman, Roberta. **Mime and Masks**. New Plays, 1979.
    Warmup exercises, character development, and full mime plays with suggestions for making simple masks will encourage the classroom teacher or anyone working with children to try mime as part of their regular programs.

Olsen, Mary Lou. **Creative Connections: Literature and the Reading Program Grades 1-3**. Libraries Unlimited, 1987.
    This "curriculum cookbook" is designed to extend basal reading programs by introducing trade books along with art activities. Brief synopses, sample lessons for 45 books, are arranged by grade level and broad themes.

Pellowski, Anne. **The Story Vine**. Illustrated by Lynne Sweat. Collier, 1984.
    This unusual source book contains easy-to-tell stories using string figures, finger games, a thumb piano, and other methods that this well-respected author-storyteller has collected from all over the world. This source can be used along with *Fanfares* (e.g., "The Wild Bird," a picture drawing story, is similar to one of Laura Ingalls Wilder's stories related in the chapter "The Day of Games" in *On the Banks of Plum Creek*).

Sattler, Helen Roney. **Recipes for Art and Craft Materials**. Lothrop, Lee, and Shepard, 1987.
    Glues, paints, modeling compounds explained in this source will help you do creative projects with inexpensive ingredients.

Sloyer, Shirlee. **Readers Theatre: Story Dramatization in the Classroom**. NCTE, 1982.
    Suggestions for selecting and adapting materials for readers theatre scripts in addition to ideas for presenting stories make this a practical guide to pick up and use right away in the classroom or library.

Wendelin, Karla Hawkins, and M. Jean Greenlaw. **Storybook Classrooms: Using Children's Literature in the Learning Center**. Humanics Limited, 1986.
    This work takes a thematic approach to setting up learning centers in schools including such topics as folk and fairy tales, mice, and concept books.

Literature Index

This is an index to the authors and titles mentioned within the text of *Fanfares*. It does not include citations from the resource bibliography. Initial articles (a, an, and the) are not included with titles so search by the second word in the title in these cases.

A. Apple Pie, 132
Aardema, Verna, 38, 39, 49
Adler, David A., 179
Aesop's Fables, 132
Age of Dinosaurs!, 97
Ahlberg, Allen, 132
Ahlberg, Janet, 132
Aitken, Amy, 157
Aleichem, Sholem, 179
Alex and the Cat, 66
Alexander and the Wind-up Mouse, 56, 68
Alexander, Martha, 132
Aliki, 26, 78, 94, 133, 157
Allen, Jonathan, 65
Amazing the Incredible Super Dog, 65
American Tall-Tale Animals, 81
Anatole, 55, 56, 69
Anatole and the Cat, 70
Anatole and the Piano, 69
Anatole and the Toyshop, 69
Anatole in Italy, 69
Ancient Egypt, 26
Andersen, Hans Christian, 124
Anderson, Gretchen, 112
Anderson, Joan, 146
Anderson, William, 145
Angelina and Alice, 68
Angelina at the Fair, 68
Angelina Ballerina, 68
Anne of Green Gables Cookbook, 112
Anno's Medieval World, 157
Anno, Mitsumasa, 157
Another Mouse to Feed, 68
Arnold, Caroline, 94
Art of Ancient Egypt, 26
Art of China, 10
Art of Egypt under the Pharoahs, 26
Autumn Story, 68
Avi, 115, 124

Baby Dinosaurs, 98
Baby Walk, 133
Baker, Leslie, 65
Barklem, Jill, 68
Bartlett, Susan, 133
Bassett, Lisa, 122
Bates, Robin, 94
Battle of the Dinosaurs, 96
Be a Dinosaur Detective, 95
Beast, 52
Becker, Joyce, 179
Behind the Sealed Door, 27
Behrens, June, 10
Bemelmans, Ludwig, 132
Ben and Me, 68
Best True Ghost Stories of the 20th Century, 51
Big Beast Book, 83, 94
Big Old Bones, 94
Bill and Pete Go Down the Nile, 26
Birnbaum, A., 65
Blackwood, Alan, 10
Blair, Gwenda, 145
Blair, Walter, 78
Blake, Quentin, 157
Blume, Judy, 124
Blumenthal, Nancy, 94
Boase, Wendy, 26
Boegehold, Betty, 68
Bonsall, Crosby, 65
Boo!, 52
Book of Holidays around the World, 181
Book of Tall Stories, 80
Books Are by People, 122
Books, a Book to Begin On, 133
Books, from Writer to Reader, 134
Booth, Jerry, 83, 94
Botkin, Benjamin Albert, 78
Boxer, Arabella, 112

Brandt, Keith, 94
Brasch, Kate, 94
Brenner, Barbara, 146
Brimhall Turns Detective, 49
Brink, Carol Ryrie, 146
Brinn, Ruth Esrig, 179
Brown, Marcia, 81
Brown, Tricia, 10
Buehr, Walter, 157
Buffalo Bill, 78
Burns, Marilyn, 179
By the Shores of Silver Lake, 137, 145

Caddie Woodlawn, 146
Caket, Colin, 94
Calhoun, Mary, 65
Caney, Steven, 138
Carle, Eric, 65
Carrick, Carol, 94
Carrick, Donald, 157
Case of the Missing Dinosaur, 94
Caselli, Giovanni, 26, 157
Cassie's Journey, 146
Cat and Mouse Who Shared a House, 69
Cat Poems, 65
Cat Who Loved to Sing, 66
Cat Will Rhyme with Hat, 65
Cats Are Cats, 67
Cats by Mother Goose, 65
Cats' Burglar, 67
Cauley, Lorinda Bryan, 95
Ceserani, Gian Paola, 27
Chanukah, 180
Chapman, Jean, 179
Cheng Hou-tien, 3, 10
Chin Chiang and the Dragon's Dance, 3, 11
Chin Talk, 80
China, 11
China Homecoming, 10
China, From Emperors to Communes, 10
Chinese New Year (Brown), 10
Chinese New Year (Cheng Hou-tien), 3, 10
Christian, Mary Blount, 49
Christina Katerina and the Box, 176, 180
Christmas in Noisy Village, 163, 180
Christmas the World Over, 180
Christopher Robin Story Book, 111
Church Cat Abroad, 70
Church Mice Adrift, 70
Church Mice and the Moon, 70
Church Mice at Bay, 70
Church Mice in Action, 70
Church Mouse, 70
Civilization of Ancient Egypt, 26
Cleary, Beverly, 68, 123, 124
Cobb, Vicki, 95

Cohen, Carol Lee, 78
Cohen, Daniel, 26, 49, 95
Cole, Joanna, 95
Cole, William, 84, 95
Collins, David, 123
Come Out and Play Little Mouse, 69
Contemporary Authors, 122
Coopersmith, Jerome, 179
Corwin, Judith Hoffman, 179
Cosman, Madeleine Pelner, 157
Count Your Way through China, 10
Count-a-saurus, 94
Country Artist: A Story about Beatrix Potter, 123
Creatures, 49
Cross-Country Cat, 65
Crowther, Robert, 132
Crusading Knight, 159
Currie, Robin, 75
Cuyler, Margery, 179

d'Aulaire, Edgar Parin, 78
d'Aulaire, Ingri, 78
Dakota Dugout, 146
Daly, Nikki, 49
Daniel Boone, 79
Danny and the Dinosaur, 84, 96
Days of Knights and Castles, 159
de France, Marie, 157
de Paola, Tomie, 26, 65, 132, 179
De Regniers, Beatrice Schenk, 49, 66
Dear Mr. Henshaw, 124
Delton, Judy, 49
Demarest, Chris L., 49
Dewey, Ariane, 78
Dictionary of Chivalry, 159
Dictionary of Dinosaurs, 98
Digging Up Dinosaurs, 94
Dinosaur Bob and His Adventures with the Family Lazardo, 84, 96
Dinosaur Bones, 94
Dinosaur Cousins?, 97
Dinosaur Dream, 96
Dinosaur Story, 95
Dinosaur Time, 97
Dinosaur's Housewarming Party, 96
Dinosaurs (Cohen), 95
Dinosaurs! (Emberley), 95
Dinosaurs (Gibbons), 96
Dinosaurs (Hopkins), 84, 95
Dinosaurs (Langley), 97
Dinosaurs and Beasts of Yore, 84, 95
Dinosaurs and Other Prehistoric Animals, 97
Dinosaurs and the Dark Star, 94
Dinosaurs and Their Young, 96
Dinosaurs in Your Backyard, 97
Dinosaurs of North America, 98
Dinosaurs Walked Here, 97

Discovering Tut-ankh-Amen's Tomb, 26
Dixon, Dougal, 95
Dow, Marilyn Schoeman, 123
Dr. Seuss, 123
Drescher, Henrik, 49
Drucker, Malka, 179

Egyptian Craftsman, 26
Elephant's Child, 124
Eliot, T. S., 55, 65
Ellenby, Jean, 157
Ellerby, Leona, 26
Ellison, Virginia H., 101, 111
Elting, Mary, 95
Emberley, Barbara, 78
Emberley, Ed, 78
Emberley, Michael, 95
Emperor's New Clothes, 124
Emrich, Duncan, 79
Ets, Marie Hall, 169, 180
Everyday Life: The Middle Ages, 158
Everything You Need to Know about Monsters ..., 49
Eyes of the Dragon, 3, 10

Fables, 81
Fabulous Beasts, 49
Facts of Life, 133
Fagg, Christopher, 49
Fairy Tale Cookbook, 112
Family in China, 10
Farmer Boy, 137, 145
Fat Cat, 55, 66
Febold Feboldson, 78
Febold Feboldson, the Fix-It Farmer, 81
Felton, Harold, 79
Festivals around the World, 180
Fiarotta, Noel, 10
Fiarotta, Phyllis, 10
Field Guide to Dinosaurs, 97
Fifth Book of Junior Authors and Illustrators, 122
50 Facts about Dinosaurs, 97
Filstrup, Chris, 10
Filstrup, Janie, 10
First Four Years, 137, 145
Fisher, Aileen, 66, 68
Fleishman, Sid, 79
Flora, James, 50, 79
Flying Reptiles, 96
Foley, Daniel J., 180
Fradon, Dana, 157
Francis, Anna B., 50
Frankenbagel Monster, 52
Frankenstein, 53
Frederick, 56, 68, 81
Freedman, Russell, 96
Freeman, Don, 69

Freeman, Lydia, 69
Freschet, Berniece, 66
Fritz, Jean, 10
Furlie Cat, 66
Fyson, Nance Lui, 10

Gackenbach, Dick, 50
Gaelic Ghosts, 52
Gag, Wanda, 55, 66
Gail, Marzieh, 158
Galdone, Joanna, 30, 39, 50
Galdone, Paul, 180
Garson, Eugenia, 138, 146
Gauch, Patricia, 176, 180
Gee, Robyn, 158
Genius of Lothar Meggendorfer, 132
Geraldine the Music Mouse, 68
Gerrard, Roy, 158
Ghosts Go Haunting, 52
Gib Morgan, 78
Gibbons, Gail, 96, 133
Giff, Patricia Reilly, 145
Ginsburg, Mirra, 66
Giorgio's Village, 132
Girl from Yamhill, 123
Gleiter, Jan, 50, 79
Glovach, Linda, 96
Glubok, Shirley, 10, 26
Go West, Swamp Monsters!, 49
Goodenough, Simon, 158
Gorman, James, 96
Grahame, Kenneth, 100
Grandpa's Farm, 79
Grandpa's Ghost Stories, 50
Great Book of Castles, 159
Great Cat, 67
Green Eggs and Ham, 124
Green Eyes, 65
Greene, Carol, 133
Greenfeld, Howard, 134, 180
Griffith, Helen V., 66
Growing Up in the Age of Chivalry, 159
Growltiger's Last Stand ..., 55, 65
Gulliver, 67
Gung Hay Fat Choy, 10

Hands On Heritage, 10
Hansel and Gretel, 132
Hanukah Money, 179
Hanukkah, 180
Hanukkah Book, 179
Hanukkah Crafts, 179
Hanukkah: Eight Nights, Eight Lights, 179
Harold and the Giant Knight, 157
Harold and the Great Stag, 157
Harry and the Terrible Watzit, 50

Harry the Hider, 67
Harvey, Brett, 146
Haskins, Jim, 10
Have You Seen My Cat?, 65
Hawkins, Colin, 50
Hawkins, Jacqui, 50
Hazen, Barbara Shook, 158
Henry's Quest, 159
Henry, Joanne Landers, 146
Here's Pippa Again!, 68
Hieroglyphics for Fun, 27
Higher on the Door, 123
Hindley, Judy, 158
Hiner, Mark, 134
Hirsch, Marilyn, 169, 180
Hodge Podge Book, 79
Hoff, Syd, 84, 96
Hogrogian, Nonny, 66
Holabird, Katharine, 68
Hopkins, Lee Bennett, 84, 122
Horner, John R., 96
Horton Hatches an Egg, 124
Hot-Air Henry, 65
House at Pooh Corner, 100, 105, 111
House of a Mouse, 68
How a Book Is Made, 133
How Djadja-Em-Ankh Saved the Day ..., 26
How I Captured a Dinosaur, 98
How to Capture Live Authors and Bring Them to Your Schools, 114, 115, 123
How to Keep Dinosaurs, 97
How to Make Pop-Ups, 134
How to Make Your Own Books, 134
Howe, James, 50
Human Body, 133
Hunting the Dinosaurs and Other Prehistoric Animals, 95
Hurlimann, Ruth, 69
Hutchins, Pat, 30, 50
Hyman, Trina Schart, 50, 123

I Love Hanukkah, 180
I Was a Second Grade Werewolf, 52
I'm Coming to Get You, 52
If the Dinosaurs Came Back, 97
If You Were a Writer, 123, 134
Illustrated Dinosaur Dictionary, 98
In Search of Tutankhamen, 27
Irvine, Joan, 134
Irving, Jan, 75
Island of the Skog, 38, 51

Jacob Two-Two and the Dinosaur, 97
Jerome Coopersmith's A Chanukah Fable for Christmas, 179
Jeschke, Susan, 69
Jewish Holiday Crafts, 179

Jewish Holiday Fun, 179
Jewish Holidays, 179
John Henry, An American Legend, 79
Johnny Appleseed, 79
Johnson, Jane, 51
Johnson, Paul, 26
Jolly Postman, 132
Joshua's Westward Journal, 146
Journey to Egypt, 26, 132
Joyce, William, 84, 96
Jumanji, 124

Kahl, Virginia, 66
Kanao, Keiko, 66
Katie's Kitten, 67
Kaufman, John, 96
Keats, Ezra Jack, 79
Kehoe, Michael, 134
Kellogg, Steven, 38, 51, 66, 79, 96
Kent, Jack, 55, 66
Kettleship Pirates, 69
Kickle Snifters and Other Fearsome Critters, 80
Kids' Cat Book, 65
King Tut's Game Board, 26
Kings, Queens, Knights & Jesters; Making Medieval Costumes, 151, 159
Kipling, Rudyard, 124
Kits, Cats, Lions, and Tigers, 67
Kitten up a Tree, 66
Kittymouse, 70
Klein, Norma, 96
Knight Who Was Afraid of the Dark, 158
Knight, David C., 51, 96
Knight, Joan, 26, 132
Koci, Marta, 67
Koontz, Robin Michal, 96
Kraus, Robert, 68, 69
Kroll, Steven, 96

Laffite the Pirate, 78
Lambert, David, 97
Lambert, Mark, 97
Langley, Andrew, 97
Larrick, Nancy, 67
Lasker, Joe, 151, 158
Lauber, Patricia, 26, 97
Laura Ingalls Wilder, 145
Laura Ingalls Wilder Songbook, 138, 146
Laura Ingalls Wilder, Pioneer and Author, 145
Laura Ingalls Wilder; Growing Up in the Little House, 145
Lawson, Robert, 68
Leach, Maria, 51, 80
Leaf, Margaret, 3, 10
Lee, Nancy, 10
Legend of Old Befana, 179
Legend of the Sleepy Hollow, 50

Legends of Paul Bunyan, 79
Lena and Leopold, 70
Leonardo Da Vinci, 133
Life in the Renaissance, 158
Lindgren, Astrid, 163, 180
Lionni, Leo, 56, 68, 81
Little House Cookbook, 146
Little House Country, 145
Little House in the Big Woods, 136-138, 145
Little House on the Prairie, 136-137, 145
Little Red Riding Hood, 50
Little Town on the Prairie, 137, 145
Little Witch's Dinosaur Book, 96
Littlejohn, Claire, 132
Living in a Castle, 159
Living in Castle Times, 158
Lobel, Arnold, 68, 81
Log Cabin in the Woods, 146
Long Winter, 137, 145
Looking into the Middle Ages, 133, 159
Louisa May Alcott Cookbook, 112
Low, Joseph, 69
Lucky's Choice, 69
Lurie, Alison, 51
Lyman, Nanci A., 80

M & M and the Mummy Mess, 14, 27
Macaulay, David, 27
Macdonald, Fiona, 158
Macdonald, Kate, 112
MacDonald, Margaret Read, 51
MacDonald, Ruth K., 123
MacGregor, Carol, 112
MacLachlan, Patricia, 146
Macmillan Book of Dinosaurs and Other Prehistoric Creatures, 95
Madeline, 132
Mag the Magnificent, 50
Maggie and the Monster, 53
MAIA; A Dinosaur Grows Up, 96
Mannetti, William, 97
Mary Poppins in the Kitchen, 112
Mash, Robert, 97
Mayer, Mercer, 51
Mayne, William, 51, 67
McBroom Tells the Truth, 79
McBroom's Ear, 79
McCormick, D., 80
McDermott, Gerald, 27, 28
McElmeel, Sharron L., 114, 123
McEwan, Jamie, 51
McGowen, Tom, 97
McHargue, Georgess, 51
McPhail, David, 67
McQueen, John Troy, 51
Meddaugh, Susan, 52
Medieval Fables, 157

Medieval Feast, 157
Medieval Holidays and Festivals, 157
Medieval Household, 157
Medieval Knight, 159
Meet the Werewolf, 51
Melton, David, 114, 115, 123
Merry Christmas, 181
Merry Ever After, 151, 158
Mice and the Flying Basket, 69
Mice Are Rather Nice, 69
Mice on My Mind, 70
Mice Who Lived in a Shoe, 69
Mike Fink (Felton), 79
Mike Fink (York), 81
Miles, Betty, 115, 124
Miller, Edna, 69
Miller, Jonathan, 133
Millions of Cats, 55, 56, 66
Milne, A. A., 100-105, 111-12
Miquel, Pierre, 159
Miranda, Anne, 133
Monks, John, 159
Monster Bed, 53
Monster Hunting Today, 49
Monster Madness, 53
Monsters Are Like That, 49
Monsters Who Died, 95
Moore-Betty, Maurice, 112
More Alex and the Cat, 66
More Books by More People, 122
More Let's Celebrate, 179
More Scary Stories to Tell in the Dark, 52
Morris's Disappearing Bag, 181
Morton and Sidney, 49
Most Amazing Hide-and-Seek Alphabet, 132
Most, Bernard, 52, 97
Mouldy, 51
Mouse and the Motorcycle, 68
Mouse Soup, 68
Mouse Tales, 68
Mousekin's Golden House, 69
Mrs. Frisby and the Rats of NIMH, 69
Mudluscious, 75
Mummies, Tombs, and Treasure, 27
Mummy of Ramose, 26
My Cat, 65
My Cat Has Eyes of Sapphire Blue, 66
My Cat Likes to Hide in Boxes, 55, 67
My Prairie Year, 146
My Visit to the Dinosaurs, 94
Mysteries of Harris Burdick, 124

New Look at Treasures of Archaeology, 27, 28
New Year, 10
Nic Leodhas, Sorche, 52
Nicklaus, Carol, 67
Nine Days to Christmas, 169, 180

Nister, Ernest, 133
Nixon, Joan, 123, 134
No More Monsters for Me!, 52
Now We Are Six, 100, 105, 111

O'Brien, Robert, 69
Oakley, Graham, 70, 159
Of Witches and Monsters and Wondrous Creatures, 53
Ol' Paul, the Mighty Logger, 80
Oldham, Linda, 10
Oliver Dibbs and the Dinosaur Cause, 98
On the Banks of Plum Creek, 137, 145
On the Way Home, 137, 145
Once a Mouse, 81

Paper Engineering for Pop-Up Books and Cards, 134
Paper Paper, 133
Parish, Peggy, 52, 67, 97
Parker, Steve, 97
Patchwork Cat, 67
Patrick's Dinosaurs, 83, 84, 94
Paul Bunyan (Kellogg), 79
Paul Bunyan (Shepard), 81
Pecos Bill (Kellogg), 79
Pecos Bill (Lyman), 80
Pecos Bill and the Mustang, 79
Pecos Bill: Texas Cowpuncher, 79
Pelham, David, 133
Peppe, Rodney, 69
Pepper, Dennis, 80
Perl, Lila, 27
Pet of the Met, 69
Picture Book of Hanukkah, 179
Picture Book of the Jewish Holidays, 179
Pierre, Michel, 159
Pinchpenny Mouse, 68
Pinkwater, Daniel, 52, 67
Pippa Mouse, 68
Pleasant Dreams, 50
Plume, Ilse, 180
Pooh and Some Bees, 111
Pooh Cook Book, 111
Pooh Get-Well Book, 101, 111
Pooh Goes Visiting, 111
Pooh Party Book, 101, 111
Pooh Song Book, 102, 112
Pooh's Alphabet Book, 111
Pooh's Counting Book, 111
Potato Pancakes All Around, 169, 180
Power of Light, 180
Prehistoric Animals, 96
Prehistoric Monsters, 94
Prehistoric Pinkerton, 96
Prelutsky, Jack, 84, 97
Preston, Edna Mitchell, 67
Princess and the Pea, 124

Provenson, Alice, 133
Provenson, Martin, 133
Pteranodon, 99
Pterosaurs, the Flying Reptiles, 98
Puzzle of Books, 134
Pyramid, 27
Pyramids, 27

Rainbow Book of American Folk Tales and Legends, 80
Ralph S. Mouse, 68
Red Riding Hood, 49
Reiff, Stephanie Ann, 27
Renaissance (Goodenough), 158
Renaissance (Pierre), 159
Renaissance and the New World, 157
Revolving Pictures, 133
Richler, Mordecai, 97
Rootabaga Stories Part One, 74
Rootabaga Stories Part Two, 80
Rose for Pinkerton, 66
Rosenbloom, Joseph, 98
Roser, Wiltrud, 70
Ross, Dave, 52
Ross, Pat, 14, 27
Ross, Stewart, 159
Ross, Tony, 52
Rotten Island, 30, 31, 38, 52
Rounds, Glen, 80
Ruby the Red Knight, 157
Runaway Ralph, 68

Sally Ann Thunder Ann Whirlwind Crockett, 78
San Souci, Robert D., 52
Sandburg, Carl, 74, 80
Sarah, Plain and Tall, 146
Sattler, Helen Roney, 98
Scarry, Huck, 133, 159
Scary Stories to Tell in the Dark, 52
Schertle, Alice, 67
Schnurnberger, Lynn Edelman, 151, 159
"School Visits: The Author's Viewpoint," *School Library Journal*, 115, 124
Schwartz, Alvin, 52, 71, 73, 80
Schwartz, Henry, 98
Scott, Joseph, 27
Scott, Lenore, 27
Secrets of Tut's Tomb and the Pyramids, 27
See Inside: A Castle, 159
Segal, Lore, 67
Self-Portrait: Trina Schart Hyman, 123
Selsam, Millicent, 98
Sendak, Maurice, xiii, 52
Seuss, Dr., 124
Shapiro, Irwin, 80
Shepard, Esther, 81
Sherwood, Rhoda, 11

Short and Shivery, 52
Silverstein, Shel, 31, 124
Simon's Book, 49
Simon, Cheryl, 94
Simon, Irving B., 134
Simon, Norma, 180
Simon, Seymour, 98
Singer, Isaac Bashevis, 180
Sir Cedric, 158
Sir Cedric Rides Again, 158
Sir Dana: A Knight as Told by His Trusty Armor, 157
Smallest Dinosaurs, 98
Snap! Snap!, 50
Snuff, 157
So Many Cats!, 66
Something About the Author, 115, 122
Something About the Author Autobiography Series, 122
Spooks, 50
Spring Story, 68
Steele, Phillip, 180
Stehr, Frederic, 67
Steig, William, 30, 31, 38, 52
Steiner, Barbara, 98
Sterne, Noelle, 98
Steven Caney's Kids America, 138
Stevenson, James, 123
Stokes, Jack, 53
Stolz, Mary, 27, 28
Story of Befana, 180
Story of Grump and Pout, 51
Story of Mrs. Loveright and Purrless Her Cat, 67
Story of Paul Bunyan, 78
Story of Printing, 134
Stoutenberg, Adrien, 81
Strange Creatures that Really Lived, 98
Stuart Little, 55, 70
Sugar-Plum Christmas Book, 179
Sumiko, 70
Summer Story, 68
Superfudge, 124
Sutton, Eve, 67
Swamp Monsters, 49
Swinburne, Irene, 27
Swinburne, Laurence, 27

Tailypo, 30, 39, 50
Tales Mummies Tell, 26
Tales of a Fourth Grade Nothing, 124
Tall Tale America, 78
Tall Tales of America, 80
Tall Timber Tales, 80
Tamarin, Alfred, 26
Tea Squall, 78
That Olive!, 67
The Tomb Robbers, 26
There Once Was a Time, 159
There Was an Old Woman, 133

There's a Monster under My Bed, 50
There's a Nightmare in My Closet, 51
There's Something in My Attic, 51
These Happy Golden Years, 137, 145
This Big Cat and Other Cats, 66
Thompson, Kathleen, 50, 79
Thorne, Ian, 53
Three Kittens, 66
Three Magic Flip Books, 132
Three Pigs, 133
Thumbelina, 124
Time Traveller Book of Knights and Castles, 158
Titus, Eve, 69, 70
Today I Thought I'd Run Away, 51
Tolan, Sally, 11
Tomfoolery, 80
Tournament of Knights, 158
Trapped in Tar, 94
Travers, P. L., 112
Treasures of Chanukah, 180
Treasury of American Folklore, 78
Trouble with Tyrannosaurus Rex, 95
Turner, Ann, 146
Twister of Twists; A Tangler of Tongues, 73, 80
Tyrannosaurus Game, 96
Tyrannosaurus Rex and Its Kin: The Mesozoic Monsters, 98
Tyrannosaurus Was a Beast, 84, 97
Tyrannosaurus Wrecks, 98
Tyrone the Horrible, 84, 98

Uden, Grant, 159
Unstead, R. J., 159

Van Allsburg, Chris, 124
Van Straalen, Alice, 181
Vaughan, Marcia, 11
Velvet Paws and Whiskers, 70
Ventura, Piero, 27, 159
Very Truly Yours, Charles L. Dodson, Alias Lewis Carroll, 122
Very Worst Monster, 50
Voyage of Osiris, 27, 28

Waber, Bernard, 70
Wagon Wheels, 146
Walker, Barbara M., 146
Wallace, Ian, 3, 11
Weeks, John, 27
Weil, Lisl, 53
Weiss, Harvey, 134
Wells, Rosemary, 181
West from Home, 145
What Happened to Patrick's Dinosaurs?, 83, 95
Whatever Happened to the Dinosaurs?, 97

When the Lights Go Out, 51
When Towns Had Walls, 157
When We Were Very Young, 100, 105, 112
Where Are You Going Little Mouse?, 68
Where Did My Mother Go?, 67
Where the Sidewalk Ends, 31
Where the Wild Things Are, xii, 52
Where's the Baby?, 50
Whistle in the Graveyard, 51
White, E. B., 55, 70
Who's in Rabbit's House?, 38, 39, 49
Whoppers, 71, 80
Whose Mouse Are You?, 68
Wiese, Kurt, 11
Wikland, Ilon, 163, 180
Wild Ducks and the Goose, 138
Wilder, Laura Ingalls, 136-147
Wilhelm, Hans, 84, 98
Wilkins, Frances, 159
Willis, Jeanne, 53
Willson, Robina Beckles, 181
Wilson, Ron, 99

Wind in the Willow Country Cookbook, 112
Wind in the Willows, 100
Windrow, Martin, 159
Winnie-the-Pooh, 100-105, 112
Winter Story, 68
Winthrop, Elizabeth, 53
Withers, Carl, 138
Wombat Stew, 11
World Full of Monsters, 51
World of Pooh, 112
Wreck of the Zephyr, 124
Wuggie Norple Story, 67
Wylie, Stephen, 133

Yesterday's Authors of Books for Children, 122
York, Carol, 81
You and Me Heritage Tree, 10
You Can Write Chinese, 11
Young Authors Conference: Kids Writing for Kids, 123

Zekmet the Stone Carver, 27, 28